"No happiness without order,
no order without authority,
no authority without unity."

—A Vril Proverb

A critical analysis of the original 36 sermons of Jmmanuel,
the man known to the world as Jesus Christ

Sean Maclaren

AN INDEPENDENT PUBLISHING CRUISE
est. January 1, 2001
Katharine L. Petersen
Publisher / Senior Editor
William Garner
Editor

Copyright © 2015 Sean Maclaren
All rights reserved

The author asserts his moral and legal Common Law rights without prejudice under UCC 1-308

Published in America by Adagio Press

Adagio and colophon are Trademarks of Adagio Press

Library of Congress Control Number: 2015939883

ISBN: 978-0-9967677-4-3

Cover design and interior: Ben Hampshire
Adagio website: AdagioPress.com
Email: 69@adagiopress.com

Special thanks to William Garner for allowing us to publish excerpts on the Inner CHILD from his book *How To Write Your First Book*, and to Doné McLuckie for superior literary skills.

B20151126
Second Print Edition

for Calvin and Mrs. Forte
Two beautiful souls who taught me something new about family

and for You, dear Reader

"I may not make history, but I definitely aim to misbehave."
—Sean Maclaren

Contents

Introduction ... 1

Part One: Psychoanalyzing "Jesus" ... 19
　A Critical Analysis and Evaluation ... 21

Part Two: The Original 36 Sermons of Jmmanuel ... 105
　1: The Biological/Adoptive Genealogy of Jmmanuel ... 107
　2: The Wise Men from the Orient ... 113
　3: John the Baptist ... 117
　4: Jmmanuel's Arcanum of Knowledge ... 121
　5: The Sermon on the Mount ... 127
　6: Alms, Fasting, Treasures, Concerns ... 131
　7: The Spirit of Judgment ... 137
　8: The Healing of the Leper ... 141
　9: The Healing of the Paralytic ... 145
　10: The Commissioning of the Disciples ... 149
　11: The Baptist's Question ... 155
　12: Regarding Marriage and Cohabitation ... 159

13: Jmmanuel and the Sabbath ... 163
14: The Wrongdoings of Judas Ish-Keriot ... 167
15: The Meaning of the Parables ... 171
16: Herod and the Baptist ... 179
17: Human Commandments and The Laws of Creation ... 185
18: The Pharisees Demand a Sign ... 189
19: The Nature of a Child's Thinking ... 195
20: Marriage, Divorce and Celibacy ... 197
21: Two Blind Persons ... 201
22: Entry Into Jerusalem ... 205
23: Taxes, Reincarnation and the Greatest Commandment ... 211
24: Against the Scribes and Pharisees ... 217
25: The Prophecy ... 223
26: Laws and Commandments ... 229
27: The Disciples' Agitation ... 235
28: In Gethsemane ... 241
29: The Suicide of Juda Ihariot ... 249
30: Defamation of Jmmanuel ... 255
31: Jmmanuel's Flight from the Tomb ... 261
32: Jmmanuel's Farewell ... 267
33: Jmmanuel in Damascus ... 273
34: Teaching About Creation ... 277
35: Cults Around Jmmanuel ... 283
36: Humankind and Creation ... 289

A Summary of The Laws of Creation and the Universe ... 293

Some Final Thoughts ... 308

References ... 313

Purchase Our Books ... 367

It's time for the accurate truth to be shared with the world, and for those who hold all the power over humankind to step aside and suddenly become insignificant. —William Garner

Introduction

Every author who shares with the world his innermost thoughts and ideas and beliefs should fulfill at least one of the following goals:
- *Provide* valuable information or intelligence about a particular subject
- *Analyze* a certain area or subject, make sense of it in a clear and logical way, and disseminate the results in a readable fashion to the world
- *Educate* the reader in an area or subject
- *Entertain* the reader with a true story or a fictional one
- *Encourage* the book to be shared with loved ones, friends, colleagues and strangers
- *Inspire* the reader to do something significant in life

Arcanum has a lofty goal: to fulfill all of these objectives and then some. After all, I am addressing some of the most important questions you should be asking today:

Who was the man known to the world as Jesus Christ?

Did he actually exist?

What was his background?

Was he, in fact, an extraterrestrial sent to Mother Earth to protect humankind and all on it?

Did he really spend time in India before and after his mission in the Middle East?

What were his messages to humankind?

Did he really die on the cross at Golgotha?

What are The Laws of Creation and the Universe?

If we are all connected as one, what does this actually mean?

Arcanum introduces Jmmanuel Sananda, the half-extraterrestrial, half-human known to the world as Jesus Christ, and his original 36 sermons. There were doubtless other sermons, but they were lost over the years, if not confiscated by various powers, the Jesuits, in particular.

Much of the information contained in ***Arcanum*** is more than 2,000 years old. The remainder, while relatively recent, is based on ancient information and intelligence, plus my personal critical analysis and evaluation of his words and teachings.

What started as a quest to wake up and stimulate humankind evolved into another level altogether: editing an English translation of Jmmanuel's words to make it more clear and readable to the worldwide public, without removing or distorting the message in any way.

All too often, publishers optically scan old and ancient works, slap all the pages together, call it a book, and put it up for sale wherever they can. Not only is the "book" a disgrace to look at, let alone read, it undermines the purpose of having this book in one's library: to admire, read, study and learn from the gifts within. This method of slipshod publishing turns off more readers than it attracts.

That's why Adagio took an entirely different approach.

In time, this editorial task further progressed and matured into an even higher level: analyzing and assessing the brilliant work of an otherworldly being, making sense of it, and writing a series of essays about how vastly different our current state of affairs is compared to the desired style envisioned by Jmmanuel Sananda and his extraterrestrial teachers. Those essays can be found in my follow-on book, ***Romanic***

Introduction

Depression, which is the other sequel to the book ***Who Really Owns Your Gold***, Third Edition, by William Garner, also published by Adagio Press.

Worthy goals are meant to be lofty, yes?

The further goals of *Arcanum* hopefully will not disappoint:
- *Enlighten* you on significant and beneficial levels
- *Introduce* you to a courageous man who spent his entire life teaching people about The Laws of Creation and the Universe
- *Encourage* you to study and learn about these Laws
- *Invite* you to implement what you have learned and make strong, positive changes in your life, great tectonic shifts that further summon transformation in others and evolution in all affairs of society
- *Share* your new-found knowledge with everyone you know and meet

Before we can begin to appreciate these goals, we must first do something most are not used to: actively consider, meditate and *think*.

Most people do not think for themselves, even when it concerns things important to them: what food to eat, clothes to wear, music to listen to, film or tv show to watch, or what to teach their children. Most receive marching orders from people, organizations and companies they have never met or come in contact with, and it's those mysterious entities that surreptitiously control most of what most people do and say. And they do it brilliantly. Just look at the success of BigMedia, BigEntertainment, BigPharma and all the other major governmental and private entities that enslave us so completely.

Followers comprise the greatest volume of the graph that is The Great Bell Curve. More accurately, followers are in the middle of the bell curve (MOB), and represent more than 70% of the population of humans. The area to the left of the curve contains followers, as well, pushing the total to well over 85%. These MOBsters appear quite happy with their lot in life, never assessing or evaluating, let alone questioning, the words of those who call themselves "masters of the people."

The MOB are easy to lead because they are, for the most part, decent and respectful, loyal, unquestioning, unchallenging, and they often prefer to have everything handed to them by the "trusted entities" that are so popular nowadays they have become innocuous: messages over radio/tv airwaves or internet, on the face of a box of cereal, on a product tag inside a jacket or skirt, or in the words of a popular news host, singer or other entertainer. Messages are best taken with a heaping dose of sugar, and the powers that be know this all too well.

Are you one of the MOBsters?

Please do not be offended by these words. Just *think* about them and what they represent.

You may be a leader in your family, at work, or on your softball team, but are you a true leader of your own life? Do you determine your own path, where you go, how you perform your duties each day, and when you do them?

If you have been taught to follow a particular religion, to believe in and worship God, to do as *the powers that be* have mandated, then you have been misled. You will not want to hear these words, because they say in plain terms that at least a part of your life is a lie.

Arcanum is a densely packed book in two distinct parts: Part One is a synopsis of the teachings of Jmmanuel Sananda and a dense collection of critical thoughts about each sermon that appears in Part Two. I probably have listed more questions than answers, but these very questions are important to us all because they begin to get at the heart of who and what this man really was and what his purpose was/is here on Mother Earth.

Some of you will say I am nitpicking. Perhaps this is accurate, and for good reason: I selfishly wished to take each of Jmmanuel's sermons and examine it, word for word, to get at the underlying message. Jmmanuel was famous (or infamous!) for speaking in metaphors and parables, which were often difficult to understand and comprehend by the average follower. I have made every attempt to read between his lines and extract every nanobyte of information so you, dear Reader, so you will be able to study it all for yourself.

Introduction

After all, one of The Laws of Creation states that we have all the information of the Universe inside each of us; all we need to do is listen and pay attention to it, so we may someday understand it. Beyond that, we then can learn to implement what we have discovered. So, in essence, this is a self-help book on how to learn and comprehend The Laws of Creation and the Universe.

Part Two is an actual full English translation and new edit (for clarity and readability) of the 36 extant sermons of Jmmanuel Sananda, the man known to the world as Jesus Christ.

You will curse the messenger of these sermons.

You will castigate those who translated them into the German and English languages.

And ultimately you will hate the man who first conceived of them and preached them to his official scribes, disciple and personal scribe Judas Ish-Keriot, disciple Matthew, and Jmmanuel's oldest son Joseph, who ensured that at least one copy of the scrolls were emplaced in the tomb of Joseph of Arimathea, just south of the Old City of Jerusalem.

Why so much anger from us all?

Because Jmmanuel's messages upsets the world we thought was nice and tidy, well-organized and set just so. Now someone has come along and told us that much or all of it is an absolute lie, and those who have exercised control over us have done so in such evil and manipulative ways, and that all along we could have broken free from their despotic bonds and lived a good clean life.

It's not too late to break free from *the powers that be*.

As you read ***Arcanum***, you will feel you have every reason to despise me, the German and English translators, and Jmmanuel Sananda for bringing forth this book.

The reasons are aplenty:
- If you do not believe there is life beyond Mother Earth, then you will be shocked when you read this book
- If you think extraterrestrials are a figment of Hollywood movies and tv shows, then your heart will be at odds with this book
- The sermons of Jmmanuel go against the very grain of your

existence and will cause you great discomfort for a long time
- When you share these thoughts with your family, friends, neighbors, colleagues and acquaintances, they may despise and ridicule you, and perhaps even ostracize you. Forgiveness may take years, if it shows up at all

Please take comfort in this thought: you will not consciously believe the words in **Arcanum**, but your *subconscious* will and that conflict will cause great pain and tension inside you. Such internal friction and discord will haunt you until one day you rise and feel a strange vibration and stirring in your DNA, a sensation that awakens the universal spirit within you so that it strikes a note at an unfamiliar resonant frequency you have not felt or heard before. Soon that note morphs into a series of notes and chords, and then a beautiful song emerges.

A familiar melody you have wished for all your life....

> "Take upon yourselves the yoke of having to learn the new teachings, for they offer enlightenment; within them you will find peace for your life, because the yoke of spiritual development is gentle, and its burden is light."

Our current version of the 36 sermons of Jmmanuel is based on a translation by Markus-Isa Rashid, an endeavor that ultimately cost him and his family their lives at the hands of the often-cruel and merciless Israeli Defense Forces 40 years ago, because the Israelis and their Jesuit handlers felt threatened by the existence of Jmmanuel's scrolls. The Jesuits knew that if Jmmanuel's sermons ever reached the good citizens of the planet and actually influenced them to take action against the Jesuits, the latter would surely lose control and perhaps even perish.

What you will find in Part Two is a compelling story about the extraterrestrial origin of all modern religions, a story the powers

Introduction

throughout the ages have sought to suppress, rewrite into horrid distortions, preach to the masses, and force upon all good peoples of the planet in forms well beyond religion. Please note that Jmmanuel acknowledged that extraterrestrial prophets long before his arrival seeded humankind with what were later distorted into what we now call ancient religions.

You will be encouraged to compare this accurate and true version of historical events to the words of the *Book of Matthew* and those of the *Old Testament*, *New Testament*, *Jewish Bible* and *Koran*.

Most modern-day religions' bibles plagiarized words and concepts from Jmmanuel's original 36 sermons; the remainder were destroyed or confiscated upon the murder of Markus-Isa Rashid. Various scribes also expanded, distorted and rewrote those bibles to fully enslave the population of good people the world over.

The Roman Catholic church has been the greatest perpetrator, and many people all over the world are beginning to understand this fact, yet another reason the Jesuits and their minions do not wish to see this book in print, let alone widely disseminated.

Please do not be fooled by the rhetoric of the Roman Catholic church, which is marketed and advertised as being controlled by the Catholic white pope. It is the *Jesuits* and their black pope who actually control this church and have for nearly 500 years.

The final chapter introduces more than 120 Laws of Creation and the Universe, and the laws and commandments of the extraterrestrials given to us by Jmmanuel. This detailed list serves as a foundation for all humankind, a springboard from which to vault into a new and higher dimension of understanding about who we really are and what our purpose and direction are in life.

The Laws of Creation and other laws and commandments all come directly from Jmmanuel's words or from the spirit of his sermons. You will find many of these Laws and commandments vague. Where you find vagueness, you must put thought and effort into finding the hidden messages.

How? The human subconscious is the entity that is in direct

communication with the Universe. You must learn to use your subconscious to communicate with the Universe, to learn about The Laws of Creation and how to use them in your everyday life.

How Do You Actively Physically Communicate With Your Subconscious?

One of the greatest creations in the Universe, besides majestic planets like Earth and powerful energy sources like our sun, is the human subconscious. It is in direct communication with the Universe, which suggests it also communicates collectively with the subconscious of others.

I've studied the human subconscious, mostly in myself, since I was a child, wondering what inner engine drove me to do the things I did. I didn't have to think about doing certain things, I just did them. Sometimes they were rational and positive; other times, not so.

One item I discovered over the years was that there was a clear line between what I did consciously and how my mind functioned subconsciously. And when I went to sleep each night, I knew there was a whole different creature that came alive and took me on endless journeys through space and time, introducing me to new thoughts, ideas, beliefs and ways of doing things in my life.

More than 10 years ago, I woke up one morning and scrambled out of bed to write something down. Whatever was in my head at that moment had to come out and it wasn't going to wait for my bus driver, my typist, to take dictation. It was coming in a flood and that was that. When I got to my notepad, my hand started scribbling things down. I wasn't paying attention to what I was writing, I just took it on faith that I had to do this.

After I was done autowriting, I looked at what had emerged: a single word, along with details about each letter of the word. It was an acronym, CHILD (hereafter referred to as "child" or "subconscious"):

C: the little **Child** in you, the curious wide-eyed being that looks at the world without filters and preconceived notions about anything. A little sponge that senses things with wonder and awe.

Introduction

H: the true **Heart** in you, the purely subjective part, filled with every conceivable emotion known. Sees the world smartly but with passion and emotion.

I: your **Intuition** or information-gathering system, the sensory apparatus that receives every possible stimulus in the Universe, much like a radio receives radio signals to produce spoken word and songs.

L: the cold, stainless-steel **Logic** that sees the world purely objectively, like a robotic computer that takes in and analyzes things in a totally impartial and neutral way, without emotion of any kind.

D: the little **Demon** in you, that mischievous entity that plays pranks and does impish things. Can sometimes be very destructive and hurtful.

These entities all comprise the human subconscious, which is the true engine that drives each and every one of us in our daily lives. They all work together and, depending on how one's DNA is wired, sometimes for good and sometimes for evil. I will not get into the moral implications of good and evil, only stating that they exist in all of us to some extent and, in others, they comprise their whole being. Sociopaths and psychopaths are an example.

We can choose to communicate with our child, or we can ignore it and just float through life, going wherever it takes us. I contend that we do have a destiny. Each of us, when we are conceived (not born), have a certain imprint from those celestial bodies that mediate and modulate our behaviors; in fact, everything we do in life. This imprint is physically imparted onto our DNA when it first forms chemically in that single cell that will later become an individual being.

When we are first stimulated by the Universe, using celestiophysics, we are then given a map of destiny that propels us through life. Some of us follow this map without much thought. Others, like me, question it each day and consciously make a choice whether to follow that map or go "off-map" and do something that we were not initially programmed to do.

These thoughts bring me to my personal philosophy, **Subism**. It holds that the human subconscious is in direct communication with the Universe, and that celestial bodies (planets, stars, whatever) directly and indirectly influence all life on earth. The philosophers of old weren't familiar with celestiophysics, so they formulated their own ideas about how humans operate and function, and what makes us do the things we do. I suggest that we do all the things we do because of the strong, inexorable influences of celestiophysics and The Laws of Creation and the Universe. I do not believe in or practice the philosophy of others, because they are all inaccurate, misleading and often destructive. Those people were completely ignorant of how the physical Universe actually works, so they based their life's work on false assumptions that built an unsteady foundation.

How do you use your subconscious to help you understand you and your life and to get what you want?

Dreams.

Sometimes you may not recall a dream, but your subconscious is actively dreaming, sending little (and giant) messages up to your conscious self to do certain things, avoid other things. Dreams are one method the child uses to communicate with your conscious self.

Interestingly, when your child presents a dream to you, it does so in very rudimentary language, in the language of a child. Just like Jmmanuel spoke in metaphors, we also dream in metaphors and symbols and motifs, not in complete film-like visions. This method of communication is as old as the Universe itself and is very effective. One must learn to accurately interpret the messages before any meaningful action can be taken.

Our child only knows one method of talking to our conscious self, and that is in the language of a child, a small voice that expresses itself using little vignettes that represent small words and actions. I've never heard of anyone dreaming in the language of an adult. Never. If someone tells you that they do in fact dream this way, it's not a deep-sleep dream but a lucid dream, one you actually control because you're partly conscious and are speaking or visualizing in the language of an adult. Again, one must be conscious during this form of dreaming.

During a very difficult time in my life some years back, I had a

Introduction

recurring dream: I was sitting in a bus filled with other people. I wasn't talking or interacting with anyone, just sitting alone and minding my own business. Then the bus suddenly filled with water, as if we'd just plunged into the middle of an ocean. No one around me moved an inch or spoke anything to me or to each other. They all just sat there as the bus filled with water. I looked around, saw stone-cold faces on my fellow passengers, and tried frantically to get out.

And then the dream went lucid, where I could actually manipulate the dream in a semi-conscious state. I changed the dream so I got out of that sinking bus.

Since I had already known that my child was responsible for communicating with me, I then figured out a way to interpret what my child was trying to tell me. I didn't get it at first, so the dream stayed with me each night for a week or so, until I woke up and listened to my child. To interpret my dream, which was in the language of a child, I used the thoughts, ideas and words of a child, say, of about four years old.

When I used this method, interpreting the dream in a child's voice, the dream became clear: "I can't get out and no one will help me." Sounds silly or even simplistic, but it is accurate.

The very day I made this discovery, my life at that time changed dramatically. Allow me to share with you what actually happened to bring on the dream: I had just gotten divorced and was destitute on all levels. The friends we had together when we were married all became only her friends and I was left with no one to talk and share my thoughts with, or to grieve with, let alone get some help from.

The dream told me that I was in a world of hurt and no one was coming to my aid, even when I actively asked for help. In the real world, I was on my own. I have a term for that: yoyo, which means "you're on your own" when things get really tough for you. I was yoyo for a long time, until I realized what was actually happening, then when I figured out my temporary predicament, I was able to change how I thought, how I acted, and consequently the actions I took to climb out of that dark hole, from inside that sinking bus.

My child knew what was going on all along and it tried to tell me, using the only language it knew—the small, yet significant, language of a child.

Now that we know we have this unusual and special gift inside us, what do we do with it? How do we use it?

The first thing I recommend is to learn how to feed it properly, to nurture it. You would do this with a human child, wouldn't you? Your child is even more important. It's the entity within yourself that guides you through every moment of your entire life. How could you not want to nurture such a being?

Your child is energetic and rambunctious, has a voracious appetite for new adventures and actions, so get out in the world and do stuff. Travel to new places, meet new people, eat new foods, explore new vistas. If you cannot afford to go to Europe or Africa, then explore your own town or city, or maybe drive to the next city or state and see what's up there. If those things are not in your current budget, then find a way to make it happen, now that you know your subconscious needs these things.

Your child loves to run and jump and play around, so get out and exercise your body, even if it's a long walk or hike. If you're going to be a sedentary writer, then your child will eventually rebel. Yes, I do know some overweight writers who do well, but they don't last too long. Unfortunately, they die young and the being that dies first is their child. This explains how people sometimes grow cold and distant, and they lose their humanity. In reality, they're losing the most important part of them—their subconscious. They are also losing the ability to communicate with the most important entity in their lives: the all-knowing Universe.

The child inside you needs stimulation, and the world around you provides just that, so please take full advantage of your atmosphere and make it a daily routine to get out of your office and home and see different and stimulating sites, absorb what you sense all around you, roll in the grass, get dirty and make mud pies . . . something. There's a new movement out there that is telling all of us to "ground" ourself

Introduction

with the earth. Actually get down on the bare ground and let it touch your skin. The earth is one giant healing mechanism, so find out more about grounding and then implement your new-found knowledge.

What else? Take trips to local stores, shops, museums, businesses that produce something interesting to see designed or in the process of being built. Feed your imagination 'til its cup runneth over. There are no penalties for overfilling. When your child has had enough, it will tell you.

Go to shows, films, performances and watch the beautiful artwork of people who are just like you: they have a dream, they design and build it, then they do whatever it takes to implement it. Seeing the art of others is inspiring on all levels, especially when they're actually creating it. Go to the local hardware store and look at all the tools and items that are used to build things. Visit a restaurant and see how they prepare their meals. I feel it a grand experience to observe artists designing and building artwork, because it's not unlike what I do when I create my own work, be it an article or a book. In fact, watching other artists may be the most inspiring thing you can witness for yourself when you go out on these excursions. I love watching glass-blowers. Especially the truly great ones who produce the world's finest artisan glasswork, those Murano artists in Italy. Wow, they're amazing to watch. When I'm done witnessing world-class art in motion, I leave with an all-body tingle. What an inspiration!

How do you listen to your child when it speaks to you?

First, let's consider when your child is actually trying to tell you something. An example: you're sitting in a chair, writing away and you get this nagging voice inside your head that says you need a small pillow at your lower back. Don't ignore it. This is your subconscious telling you something: I want to feel comfortable when I share something important with you. That's like a message from the highest power in the Universe.

Those little voices that creep up at all times of the day and night are your child trying to tell you something. You should listen to those voices. When you hear the calling of your subconscious, please pay attention to what it is trying to say, then, provided the command is a reasonable one, please act on it. Once you start listening to your child, it will say, "Thank you for listening to me!" And, from that point forward, if you continue to listen to your subconscious, it will give you more and more great knowledge and information that will not only enhance your life, but also teach you The Laws of Creation and how to use them in everyday life.

Communicating with your child is not that challenging. Again, if it tells you to do something and you do it, then you're effectively communicating with your child. Keep doing it. And when you go to bed at night (or during the day, depending on your lifestyle and schedule), ask out loud and write down some questions or topics you want your child to mull over. The more you listen to your child, the more it will talk back and provide the information you need. You can train it to give you more and more information by asking questions, writing them down, then sleeping on them. Keep asking the same questions over and over until you get what you want. When asking questions or asking for help, please be kind to your subconscious. Remember, it is a child and understands when you are being impatient or downright tedious. You know how people say to treat yourself kindly and gently? They're really saying you should be kind and gentle to the most important creature inside your head: your subconscious.

The reason I suggest you say what you want out loud is because when you speak it and hear your own words, your brain stores and processes that information in different areas, which work in unison to come to your aid. When you physically write it down, that too is stored and processed in another part of your brain. When you read your own words, that is also stored and processed in yet a different part of your brain. These working areas are also complex computing centers that help to enhance what you desire and wish for, and they help your child make those wishes and dreams come true. Each reinforces the other that becomes a multiplicative effect: it strengthens all bonds and allows for growth and further learning.

Training your child involves all the above steps, plus actively talking

Introduction

to it, and not just before you go to sleep. You can have meaningful conversations with your child, not only asking questions but also asking for guidance and assistance. The more you communicate with it, the more it responds and with better and more relevant information that will help and guide you accurately.

The only time my child has failed me is when I have ignored it. That fact, in itself, I find fascinating and compelling. My child has never steered me in the wrong or in a negative direction. Ever. When I've chosen to go off-map, then sometimes I've gotten into trouble. Yes, I've learned a lot from those experiential experiences, especially when off-map, but I've also paid a steep price for venturing off my Universal path of destiny.

You also can talk to the individual components of your child. It takes time and effort, but you can do it. I've often consulted my Logic element to get an objective view on a particular subject. And when I've needed to discuss something about my love life, I've talked to my Heart. Having five separate ultra-complex computer modules inside your head is like having a team of experts of the Universe at your beck and call. You must treat that team nicely and with great respect or it will ignore you and your queries. Your child will never be vengeful and send you down a wrong path; only your conscious self does that. The worst you can expect from your child is silence, and that is the most crushing thing that could happen to your beautiful mind, not having the backing of one of the mightiest beings in the Universe.

When your child fails to talk to you or communicate with you, something is very wrong. Remember that your child is just that, a child, so it needs special attention. Like I said, it will never steer you wrong, but it may ignore you. If it does, ask what's wrong. When you go to bed, write down that question, plus a few others: Are you okay? Have I done anything to make you ignore me? What am I doing wrong here? How can I get back on track? Will you please help me?

The times I've had my child go silent, they were when I was not treating myself well. Be kind and gentle to yourself, and your child will thank you for it in ways you cannot even imagine now.

When you learn how to communicate with your subconscious, you will have taken the first step toward learning about The Laws of Creation and the Universe, and will then begin a new lifelong journey of amazement and wonder.

You also will begin to understand and comprehend the words and messages of Jmmanuel.

Your subconscious will ring in consonance with the true story of Jmmanuel's words, as they contradict the false teachings of the so-called *New Testament* and all similar bibles, and the false churches and their priests and preachers and rabbis, and all the sycophants who serve them.

And at this point in your elevation from ignorant to enlightened, you will begin to ask hard questions about the powers that have controlled you all your life, and you will wonder how you so blithely could have accepted their seductive, deceptive and poisonous messages, disguised in various forms of education and entertainment, and on cereal boxes and pretty talking heads.

This truly will be the greatest learning experience of your life.

Are you ready to begin your journey?

Part One

Psychoanalyzing "Jesus"

"Humans are still ignorant and addicted to the false laws of the chief priests and distorters of the scriptures. They do not recognize the new teachings as truth. Lacking understanding, the people curse the truth which yet must come; they curse, stone, kill and crucify the prophets. But since the teachings of the truth must be brought to the people, the prophets have to bear great burdens and suffering under the curse of the people."

—Jmmanuel Sananda

Discovery is seeing what everyone else has seen, and thinking what no one else has thought.

—Sir Charles Scott Sherrington

A Critical Analysis and Evaluation

Chapter 1: The Biological/Adoptive Genealogy of Jmmanuel
"Through god's power and providential care, Earth was made to bear intelligent human life when the celestial sons, the travellers from the far reaches of the Universe, mated with the human females of Earth. Behold, god and his followers came far from the depths of the Universe, where they delivered themselves from a strong bondage, and created here a new human race and home with the early females of Earth."

These two passages represent some of the earliest known written references to extraterrestrials having visited Mother Earth and established lineages of intelligent human beings. The first statement also suggests that there was some form of humans on Earth prior to the first visit by these extraterrestrials, who most likely used some type of genetic manipulation of existing "human" DNA to produce what Jmmanuel termed "intelligent human life."

The extent of this "intelligence" is not known, but it suggests that these engineered intelligent humans were in the image of their extraterrestrial makers, i.e. could speak, communicate and think, among other unique actions and traits of intelligent humans. These assumptions are valid, as the extraterrestrial engineers wanted humans to learn The Laws of Creation and the Universe, and live harmoniously on Mother Earth.

With all due respect to Markus-Isa Rashid, his family, his memory, and his translation of Jmmanuel's words and wisdom, I do believe that parts of this story are inaccurate, and it may be due to an inaccurate translation of the original scrolls, if they actually existed at all. I believe strongly they did. There is some evidence to support this, but it is "lost" in historic volumes in the various countries Jmmanuel traveled, in particular India.

Therefore, I am proceeding on the grand assumption that Jmmanuel Sananda did exist, he was half-extraterrestrial and half-human, he was fathered by the extraterrestrial Gabriel, was sent to Mother Earth on a specific mission by his extraterrestrial race, he did preach a lengthy set of sermons that were recorded by his disciples and eldest son, and those sermons were preserved long enough so that at least 36 of them could be translated into the English language and preserved for posterity.

I also believe that the 36 sermons are quite vague in descriptions about extraterrestrials, their race in general, their ways of living and modes of transportation. Those particulars bother me on all levels, because I expected to read in-depth records of how those who engineered humans lived and worked and conducted their universal travels and adventures. The Indian *Mahabarata* is more forthcoming about descriptions of extraterrestrials and their flying machines. What I read in the 36 sermons is more of a generalization of someone's wishes for humanity, devoid of any real facts that would evoke a sense of trust, let alone blind acceptance.

Even though I have chosen to believe in the existence of Jmmanuel and these 36 sermons, I am left wanting so much more.

As a researcher and historian, I crave accuracy in everything I study. And when I don't get it, I question deeply and search even more for accurate answers. When people ask me about certain aspects of what

I am studying, and I don't know something, I am not embarrassed to say I don't know or don't understand. If I know where the information might be found, I offer it. But I never pass myself off as an expert in anything, because I am a babe in the woods of this Universal life and study of it.

As I write these words, I want to scream because these 36 sermons leave so much to the imagination. And still I believe, but not out of some grand purpose or a deep wanting. I believe because Jmmanuel's words ring true right down to my DNA. They resonate within me in such a pleasant and uplifting way that I feel energized. Yes, Jmmanuel has left out so much, but maybe because it leaves us much room to explore on our own.

So, again, I proceed with the assumption that Jmmanuel and his sermons are real and accurate.

In Chapter 1, verses 89-94, we read of certain demands of the extraterrestrial gods: that we humans are to honor god [lower case form because this god is an extraterrestrial, and not the false "God" of modern religions.] and no other god or gods.

The Laws of Creation, as I have come to understand and appreciate them, do not make demands on anything or anyone. They are based on physical material, energy, forces and actions.

Therefore, we humans are not mandated by the Universe to honor or worship anything.

The Universe from which we came does not care whether we worship or revere it, but it will let us know if we do not *respect* it: pollute the waters and the sea and you shall suffer from diseases, lack of food, destroyed habitat; rape the land and subsequent rains will strip the topsoil, cause further damage and destruction; detonate nuclear bombs in the atmosphere or underground and you shall suffer the effects of radiation poison, landslides shall cause tsunamis that devastate the land and its inhabitants, among other dire consequences.

Our true extraterrestrial leaders, i.e. those who created our genetic lineages, would like us to *respect* The Laws of Creation, but not worship them as if an idol or monument. If they did, in fact, want us to worship their god, they would have coded this behavior in our DNA.

Any references to god or idol worship is an inaccuracy in the eyes of The Laws of Creation and possibly a misinterpretation.

If one studies Creation, which is the Universe's engine that produces matter, mass and energy and gives rise to the celestiophysics of the Universe, one finds that Creation is a giant physical motor that does not know good or evil. It only knows positive and negative electrical charges and spins of various physical forms of matter at or below the quantum level, and countless other forms of energy and matter we humans have yet to learn about and use.

There is no good or evil in the Universe, only mass, energy and the physical results of the interactions of mass and energy and all the physical forces that produce the results we see all around us, including those we cannot detect or yet understand.

If we look around, we see our moral interpretations of good and evil. We must ask ourselves: What is good? What is evil? We see destruction of our societies, governments, educational systems, economies, and our way of life. Would we call these evil deeds? They are all happening as we speak, so those humans currently in charge of the planet clearly are doing harm (or evil), but the Universe does not care about this evil. It only knows mass, energy, force and interaction of these entities. It knows positive or negative in charge or spin, not any moral terms or interpretations.

To humans, good and evil are moral constructs that allow us to better define the world as we wish to see it, live in it, interact with it, because we are sentient beings that feel and sense the world around us, and what we take in affects and changes us: our chemistry and behaviors. When we see what we perceive as "evil," we get frightened, anxious or angry. When we see good, we feel love, peace and well-being.

The Universe cares not whether a human is good or evil, only how it interacts with other matter in the Universe. If a good human wishes to do more good in life, they can discover and study The Laws of Creation and use and manipulate them to their desires.

Likewise, a person or society that wishes to do evil in our human world can use those same Laws of Creation to manipulate mass, energy, force and the geophysical and biophysical cycles we see in our everyday lives.

This is exactly what the Jesuits, the human controllers of Mother Earth, are doing today: using celestiophysical cycles to predict their next actions of destruction; riding those waves to exacerbate their outcome, which we see as evil; manipulating the weather and climate using powerful forces that create torrential rains or droughts, hurricanes and tsunamis; and using these forces to create crisis after crisis, to evoke fear in us all.

The Jesuits and their predecessors have studied celestiophysics over the millennia and have become adept at manipulating its effects to their benefit and to the detriment of all good people.

Shall we call the powers' actions evil?

Again, the Universe does not care whether an action is evil.

Do we castigate the Jesuits for their insider knowledge?

Do we fault the Jesuits because they choose to do only harm to the rest of the population and cause untold destruction of our planet?

The key to overcoming any evil in this world is to understand The Laws of Creation, i.e. how the Universe is constructed and how it functions, and finds ways and methods to manipulate, mediate, modulate its actions and behaviors. After all, this is what the Jesuits do every day, and look at what they have accomplished:

- In each country, control over government and society, economy and markets, education, healthcare and medicine, law enforcement and military, ecological habitats, weather patterns, and nearly every conceivable activity and behavior that further strips good people of their natural rights, family, livelihood, money, land and possessions
- Suppression of natural rights of all good people of the world
- Forced compliance of all laws, rules, regulations, mandates
- Severe punishment for noncompliance
- Habitat destruction that will take thousands of years to repair and reverse

- Culling of the population through forced ingestion of poisons in water and food, harmful vaccines and medicines, poor healthcare, wars and military actions

Jmmanuel's 36 Sermons are only an abbreviated version of the original scrolls based on his lectures and teachings, because Markus-Isa Rashid was murdered before he could complete the translation of the scrolls. Armed only with these 36 important sermons, we can still understand some of these Laws of Creation and, therefore, use them as a springboard for further study into how our Universe functions and how we can use it to our positive advantage.

We as humans need not worship any gods, God, idols, monuments or artificial beliefs. Our energy should be focused on discovering the nature of the Universe and learning to live in harmony with its myriad cycles and forces, actions and behaviors.

While I greatly admire and respect Jmmanuel Sananda and his sermons, I do not believe he or his extraterrestrial father, family, friends and colleagues meant to enslave us with hero worship simply because they were the ones who created intelligent humans on Mother Earth. It just doesn't make sense that they would do so, unless we were created to be slaves from day one. This does not appear to be the case, though.

If they truly intended this arrangement to be the norm across the planet, it would be nothing less than "meet the new boss, same as the old boss," with the boss, the Jesuits, forcing upon all good people whatever laws they so chose, and demanding that we worship the false God and follow the arcane laws invented and enforced by a lineage of humans bent on enslavement of the population and control over the entire world.

As an active student, believer and evangelist of The Laws of Creation, I feel the accurate translation of Jmmanuel's words should reflect the extraterrestrials' supreme respect for the Laws. Any reference to or statements about humans worshipping extraterrestrials who created us is surely a false interpretation.

Also in Chapter 1, you will read of Jmmanuel's genealogy. Since I was a child, I have been puzzled by the phenomenon of "males always begetting males." Where there any girls among them? From the various historical records available to us today, we do know that at different times in history females were killed at birth. In modern societies, we expect to see a good proportion of females in the mix. Two thousand years ago, was there some unique occurrence that produced only males or a majority of them in each family? The historical record, especially an accurate genealogy, should include the male and female lineages.

Mary, who was reported to be a virgin, was impregnated by the extraterrestrial Gabriel, who was Jmmanuel's biological father. It is thought that, for thousands of years, extraterrestrials had been mating with human females on Mother Earth and starting lineages of new forms of humans. If you study the "fossil record," you will find huge gaps in the so-called evolution of modern humans, because the powers chose to suppress the truth from humanity and further their own false agenda and history for the purpose of control over all people.

"Improvements" in the human form were done via genetic manipulation by advanced extraterrestrials. It is still unclear which race of these off-world humans Jmmanuel belonged to, and what their true nature and purpose on Earth was or still is.

Chapter 2: The Wise Men of the Orient

"His knowledge will be boundless, as will be his power to control human consciousness, so that humans may learn and serve Creation."

The above statement suggests Jmmanuel was a powerful being, but his subsequent demonstrations of his powers left many wanting and questioning. For example, why did Jmmanuel flee from potential harm, when he could have used his special powers to prevent any attack, if not destroy his enemies? After all, it was he who preached "an eye for an eye, tooth for a tooth."

What about preventive safety measures to ensure that Jmmanuel survived all attacks on his life? Were there special laws or rules that prevented Jmmanuel and his close followers from engaging in this sort of behavior? If so, they were not written or explained to the people.

Clearly there were some rules that guided Jmmanuel in his daily life and work, and it appears that he was unable or unwilling to perform what we might view as prophylactic safety measures.

When news of Jmmanuel's birth reached Herod Antipas, he feared for his life and kingdom, and sent emissaries to find the newborn so Herod could "adore him." In reality, Herod wanted to kill Jmmanuel.

The singing bright light and long tail doubtless was either one or multiple extraterrestrial spacecraft, which directed the three wise men to Bethlehem and to the stable and temporary home of Joseph, Mary and Jmmanuel.

The extraterrestrial Gabriel, biological father of Jmmanuel, ordered Joseph to take Jmmanuel and Mary to Egypt, to avoid the wrath of Herod Antipas.

One must wonder, if extraterrestrial Gabriel has such power and knowledge, why wouldn't he simply dispatch Herod on his own? A simple personal visit on his spacecraft to Herod's residence, followed by a laser strike to the head would have done it. Why not rid the world of such a vile leader, not to mention his minions and followers?

To suggest that Gabriel and his fellow extraterrestrials would not intervene in human affairs seems illogical in human terms. After all, Gabriel impregnated a human female without her consent (this was rape), then forced her and her family to live in a very difficult political and social climate: the Land of Israel. There was much more to the extraterrestrials' agenda than they let on, but their actions do suggest a host of possibilities.

When Gabriel's messenger returned with the news that Herod would no longer seek to murder Jmmanuel, the young family was flown via Gabriel's spacecraft to the town of Nazareth in the district of Galilee, where they made their new home.

Such great technology and power, yet so little action against those who would murder the extraterrestrial son, Jmmanuel, in whom they had invested so much. After all, Jmmanuel was the savior of humankind. Such inaction begs many questions and invites much scrutiny of the extraterrestrial story.

Today, if there were any great threats to an important person or entity, those threats would, in the least, be questioned and maybe even arrested. In times of war, many nations' military and paramilitary arms take it upon themselves to hunt down and kill any potential threats to their sovereignty and safety. The Jesuits are an excellent example, dispatching any and all real-world threats to their organization, using stand-off weapons like drones, up-close-and-personal assassins, and various other methods that involve non-Jesuit groups and individuals.

With such great otherworldly might, why would Jmmanuel and Gabriel not use it against their enemies, so Jmmanuel could live freely to teach The Laws of Creation and the Universe? Again, these extraterrestrials invested heavily in Jmmanuel, so why not protect their investment at all costs? This is exactly what the Jesuits do. It is also what any Fortune 100 company does on a daily basis.

His very birth was to educate and save humankind, and only this, so why not protect this special being at all costs? Could it be that Jmmanuel was expendable, because there were other special beings who would rise in his place should he suddenly die or be murdered during his work on Earth? Were these extraterrestrials obeying some special law of the Universe, which forbade them from engaging in certain aspects of Jmmanuel's visit to Mother Earth? To us Earth-bound observers, the curious behavior of Gabriel, Jmmanuel and their extraterrestrial people is not reasonable or logical. Then again, we are not familiar with special laws and rules that govern the behaviors and actions of these extraterrestrials.

Chapter 3: John the Baptist

John was practicing the "old laws" of the gods before he met Jmmanuel. How did these "old laws" differ from the ones Jmmanuel received in his training from his extraterrestrial father and teachers? Where did they come from? Was John the Baptist also the progeny of extraterrestrials? It is entirely probable that these old laws gave rise to the original Hebrew bible, which is thought to have been scribed around 600 BCE.

Another curiosity: John tells a group of Pharisees and Sadducees: "... with his knowledge and his power, god is able to raise up children to Abraham out of these stones, because he has knowledge of the mystery of Creation."

If such power is at the hands of the extraterrestrials, why haven't they intervened further into the affairs of the very beings they created by doing course-corrections along our path over the past 2,000 years? Their allowing such carnage by the Pharisees and Sadducees might be seen as a moral failing to us humans who have been and continue to be persecuted and oppressed by the modern-day equivalent of those despots and oppressors.

> "You brood of vipers, in two times a thousand years you and your followers, who pursue false teachings out of your own arrogance in your greed for power and fortune, shall be vanquished and, on account of your lies, punished."

The people of Jerusalem flocked to be baptized by John the Baptist, because they acknowledged "the wisdom of the old laws of god."

Again, what were the "old laws" and how did they differ from the laws taught by Jmmanuel, who appeared on Earth long after John the Baptist?

John foretells what should shake all of us to the core:

"You brood of vipers, in two times a thousand years you and your followers, who pursue false teachings out of your own arrogance in your greed for power and fortune, shall be vanquished and, on account of your lies, punished. So it shall be when humankind begins to comprehend, and when the chaff is separated from the grain. It will be at the time when your false teachings will be laughed at and humankind discovers the truth. This will come to pass when humankind builds singing lights and chariots of fire, with which they can escape into the cosmos, as is done by god and his followers, the celestial sons."

We are in this predicted or foretold time as we speak. What shall we expect? Will the "brood of vipers," the Jesuits and their minions, go the way of dust and be gone forever, finally leaving all good people around the world in peace? We have already built chariots of fire (spacecraft), and have escaped into the cosmos. While it is not the subject of this book, America's and Russia's secret space program has been producing and flying spacecraft for more than 50 years, and has traveled to distant planets including Mars and Jupiter.

After his baptism by a reverent John the Baptist, whose knowledge was far less than that of Jmmanuel's, he boarded a spacecraft and was not seen for 40 days and 40 nights, thus beginning a new chapter in his life as a teacher of The Laws of Creation and the Universe.

Chapter 4: Jmmanuel's Arcanum of Knowledge

Jmmanuel begins his schooling in the "wisdom of knowledge."

He is taken to an Earth-based palace of the ruler of all extraterrestrials, who was an ancient immortal, giant in size compared to Earth humans. The two escorts of Jmmanuel were wearing protective space suits, because Earth's atmosphere was unsuitable, if not poisonous.

These extraterrestrials came from the "seven stars," presumably the Pleiades, which is the closest known star cluster, approximately 3.25 light years from Earth. They also had with them two smaller extraterrestrials that appeared to be assistants or porters. The two taller beings told Jmmanuel that their beings had been taking (abducting?) Earth humans, some of whom lived on their planet. Now that they had mated with human Earth females, their offspring would mate with other humans from different lineages.

The extraterrestrial beings impart to Jmmanuel the knowledge of the Universe and Creation, and introduce him to the three stargates, which revealed intimate details about distinct geographical regions on the planet and different races of humans.

These very stargates are thought to be in Iraq and Eqypt, with the third possibly in Ireland. The Eqypt stargate, located in the Great

Pyramid, may be the most important of all, the Arc of the Covenant, which may be a *portable* stargate. It also has additional otherworldly power well beyond what any Earth-based science can explain.

> "The Matrix is a system, Neo. That system is our enemy, and when you're inside and look around, what do you see? Businessmen, teachers, lawyers, carpenters, the very minds of the people we are trying to save. But until we do, these people are still a part of that system and that makes them our enemy. You have to understand: most of these people are not ready to be unplugged, and many of them are so inured, so hopelessly dependent on the system, that they will fight to protect it."

The extraterrestrials remind Jmmanuel of "The dominion of god over terrestrial humans and over his celestial sons." Again, was this a misinterpretation of the original script? Did the extraterrestrials truly mean to have us humans under their "dominion"? If their wish was to impart the wisdom of the Universe, why then have dominion over us? Why not allow us to self-govern and prosper? Perhaps this is exactly what has happened over the 2,000 years since Jmmanuel was first handed these laws: the powers that be have held exclusive dominion over all good people on Earth. Have the powers been following the teachings of these extraterrestrials, or have they simply rewritten these ancient extraterrestrial laws to reflect the Jesuits' own malevolent teachings and purposes? They have certainly rewritten the words and teachings of Jmmanuel in their various bibles, which distort the truth Jmmanuel was sent to impart on humankind.

Unfortunately for humans during Jmmanuel's time, "millennia will pass before the people of these human lineages are capable of recognizing the truth."

This foretelling has come to pass and, yes, it is still unfortunate for us good people of the Earth. Only a handful of us have taken the time and energy to study who runs our Earth and how they do it, and then shared this knowledge with others. Most people are stuck in the matrix and, as the character Morpheus in the movie *The Matrix* states to Neo: "The Matrix is a system, Neo. That system is our enemy, and when you're inside and look around, what do you see? Businessmen, teachers, lawyers, carpenters, the very minds of the people we are trying to save. But until we do, these people are still a part of that system and that makes them our enemy. You have to understand: most of these people are not ready to be unplugged, and many of them are so inured, so hopelessly dependent on the system, that they will fight to protect it."

How do those with knowledge wake up those in this matrix? Those matrix slaves who will fight the wise ones to protect the very system that enslaves them? It appears impossible at this point, as the Jesuits are tightening their grip on power in all countries, in all walks of life, making it unlikely that anyone even with the knowledge of Creation and the Universe can stop them.

At least, that is the Jesuits' distorted perception at the moment.

There is one important clue left by the extraterrestrials who imparted their wisdom and knowledge on Jmmanuel: these extraterrestrials will return sometime soon.

Questions are, what will they do when they return to Earth? Will they strike down the Jesuits and their minions and followers? How? With what powers? The extraterrestrials failed to do this to the Pharisees and Sadducees 2,000 years ago, so what will be different now? Is it possible that these extraterrestrials are controlling the Jesuits?

Much grand talk has been heard about opposing evil and seeking the wisdom of truth and of Creation and the Universe, but little to nothing has been done by extraterrestrials on behalf of all good people against the powers that be. So what are we to expect that will be different from the extraterrestrials' actions of the past?

Further on in Chapter 4, Jmmanuel is given another revelation: "Hence, following the fulfillment of your mission, centuries and two millennia will pass before the truth of the knowledge you brought to the people will be recognized and disseminated by a few humans."

Again, we are currently in this period. Some questions: When exactly will this truth and knowledge be recognized as fact, and what will happen on Mother Earth at that time? Will there be prophetic cataclysms over the Earth? Will the majority of the human population perish, so Mother Earth can replenish her treasures and rebuild a new society?

"Centuries and two millennia" may be quite a number of years after we are all dead and cremated. So what hope do we living currently have of living a good clean life on this Earth? What more can we do to make it pleasant for all good people? What can we do to oppose the evil Jesuits and their minions?

"And this will be the time when we celestial sons begin to reveal ourselves anew to Earth humans, when they will have become knowing and will threaten the structure of the heavens with their acquired power."

Can we now hope that the extraterrestrials who engineered us will return soon, perhaps within the next 20 years? Given the Jesuits have threatened all of humanity with "their acquired power," what can we expect from the returning celestial sons? Will we good people of Earth feel their wrath? Will this be the time of great Earthly destruction? Or will they single out only the Jesuits and their minions for total destruction?

"When Jmmanuel went by the Sea of Galilee, he saw two brothers, Simon, who is called Peter, and Andrew, casting their nets into the sea because they were fishermen. And he said to them, 'Follow me; I will teach you knowledge and make you fishers of people.'"

Jmmanuel was now assembling his first disciples, taking two

fishermen of fish and making them "fishers of people." In good time, Jmmanuel preached to many people in a large geographical area and, via word of mouth, was attracting more and more as he spoke and traveled throughout the Middle East. During this time, he was also healing the sick and teaching his disciples how to heal maladies.

Curiously, no word is mentioned of his enemies' activities. What were they doing during this time, when Jmmanuel was a direct threat to their own false teachings and control over the very people Jmmanuel wished to enlighten?

Chapter 5: The Sermon on the Mount

We read of Jmmanuel's first sermons, after his rich schooling by the extraterrestrials. All of these wise and logical statements still apply today. No, *especially* in today's dark times. He praises those who recognize the truth, have spiritual balance, and are willing to suffer.

"Blessed are those who know about Creation, for they are not enslaved by false teachings."

Jmmanuel warns his followers that they will be persecuted by the false prophets and their minions, and so to endure the pain and suffering because they will find rewards in this and the next life.

Does this advice sound like a carrot at the end of a long stick? Is it a gentle means of manipulating his own disciples and followers?

Do as Jmmanuel preaches, with the hope of getting just rewards later. We are taught this method of attaining our goals and rewards, but it is often out of touch with the reality of our fast-food times. Today, people seek instant success and reward for the least amount of effort; some even preferring to lie, cheat and steal.

How did we evolve to such a low form? By design. We have been taught and shaped to expect instant success with almost no effort, thus negating the good words of Jmmanuel and his followers.

The Laws of Nature and Creation are held highest, so we must obey those natural and universal laws and use logic when deciding the outcome of something. Jmmanuel cautions against using the illogical means of the Pharisees and Sadducees, those false prophets who sought to steer all good people down a path of enslavement and destruction.

Do not get emotional over any issue, Jmmanuel is telling us. Instead, sound objectivity is the key when deciphering a dilemma or deciding on an outcome, not some irrational and illogical step toward the wrong result.

> If you live according to The Laws of Creation and the Universe, using good sound logic in all areas, you will live a righteous and fulfilling life and become one with Creation and the Universe upon your natural death.

The simple truth about life is that, if you live according to The Laws of Creation and the Universe, using good sound logic in all areas, you will live a righteous and fulfilling life and become one with Creation and the Universe upon your natural death.

Chapter 6: Alms, Fasting, Treasures, Concerns

The real treasures of life: good mental and physical health (especially when one is knowledgeable about Creation and the Universe), just enough food and drink for basic sustenance, and sufficient clothing and shelter. What else does one need to be one with the Universe and to learn of its wisdom and knowledge?

Jmmanuel preaches that we humans must not accumulate treasures and precious things, but be happy learning about and implementing the wisdom and knowledge of Creation and the Universe.

Those who pray in silence and with genuine spirit will be fulfilled in special ways, unlike the false prophets and minions who seek a great audience to witness their "sacrifices" and "suffering." The Jesuits are grand masters of creating spectacles that reach the masses, which are encouraged to seek and worship the gaudy.

Why is it necessary for human beings to eschew treasures for a life of pure wisdom and knowledge? Are personal treasures similar to those found in nature? They bring us peace and calm, joy and happiness. Why should we be confined to such a spartan life like the simple birds and beautiful lillies Jmmanuel speaks of?

What harm is there in appreciating the beauty and treasures of human-made things? Perhaps Jmmanuel preached this way because he saw that humans were given to excess and selfishness, and somehow lost their way during the process. Unfortunately, he does not allow for a middle-of-the-road approach to coveting such beauty created by humans. It is all or nothing, which is both harsh and unforgiving to humans, the very people whose praise, love and respect what he and his extraterrestrials seem to demand.

"Truly, I say to you, if you suffer from hunger, thirst and nakedness, then wisdom and knowledge will be crowded out by worry. First seek the realm of your spirit and its knowledge, and then seek to comfort your body with food, drink and clothing."

For the survivalist in us, these two statements may seem absurd. In a life-death situation where food or shelter may be required, it would be foolish not to address those concerns immediately. There is always time, after sorting yourself out, for prayer and learning The Laws of Creation and the Universe. If you ignore your immediate needs in favor of obeying the Laws, you may find yourself frozen in the wilderness, unable to learn anything, let alone the laws most important to you and your very existence in the Universe.

Chapter 7: The Spirit of Judgment

"Beware of false prophets and scribes who come to you in sheep's clothing, but inwardly are like ravenous wolves, preaching to you about submissiveness before shrines, false deities and gods, and preaching submissiveness to idols and false teachings."

This passage is telling. Does it remind you of our current power structure, perhaps, which uses clever advertising and marketing techniques to manipulate us?

"Beware of those who forbid you access to wisdom and knowledge, for they speak to you only to attain power over you and to seize your goods and belongings."

Yes, this is certainly indicative of the current powers that be, those who have enslaved us all under false teachings. Most of ancient science, e.g. has been suppressed by the current powers, in favor of "sandbox physics" and other highly diluted scientific disciplines that ensure we good people buy expensive but unnecessary oil and gasoline, and pay for costly electricity, even though the alternatives would free us from our dependence on petroleum products and electricity from nuclear and coal-fired plants.

Thus begins Chapter 7, compelling us to examine the results of a person's behavior, then judge it wisely and accurately. We are all built with an innate sense of right and wrong, but most do not use it wisely. They ignore that innate wisdom in favor of illogical knowledge manufactured by the powers that be. Natural intelligence is coded in our DNA. Is this universal among all human species across the Universe? I don't know, but here on Earth we humans possess it, and it serves as an internal compass and lie-detector.

The path to damnation is wide and well traveled.

And the path to life and knowledge is narrow and barely trodden.

Is Jmmanuel demonstrating his knowledge of The Great Bell Curve, where the MOBsters occupy the middle volume, the path to damnation?

How is it that the vast majority of humans appear to be built to follow the damned? If the extraterrestrials created us this way, why didn't they genetically modify us to be followers of the *truth*? Instead, we were bred to be stimulated by the loud-mouthed used-car salesmen who preach falsely and vociferously from street corners and soapboxes and now via dozens of different high-tech media platforms.

The fact we humans have this built-in fault is puzzling, is it not? What does it suggest?

"Beware of false prophets and scribes who come to you in sheep's clothing, but inwardly are like ravenous wolves, preaching to you about submissiveness before shrines, false deities and gods, and preaching submissiveness to idols and false teachings. Beware of those who forbid you access to wisdom and knowledge, for they speak to you only to attain power over you and to seize your goods and belongings."

Perhaps the most compelling of all passages in Jmmanuel's teachings, they warn the goodness in all of us that the current powers that be, the Jesuits and their minions, appear to us as kind, benevolent and disarming creatures who wish to come to our aid.

The Jesuits have established a horde of institutions around the world, all designed to appear benevolent and philanthropic. But all of them have a deeper, hidden sinister agenda. In reality the Jesuits are mere demons who wish to enslave and control us, strip us of our worldly possessions to make them their own.

Jmmanuel is also telling us to examine the results, not the initial content of an offering from the powers that be, dressed as sheep. He compels us to study what actually occurs in the end, the result, and not be fooled by lies and deception along the path to the actual result.

This is exactly our state of affairs today, and is discussed in depth in the final chapter.

Chapter 8: The Healing of the Leper

A leper came and knelt before Jmmanuel and said, "Master, if you will it, you can make me clean."

Jmmanuel stretched out his hand, touched him and said, "I will do it. Be cleansed." And immediately he was cleansed of his leprosy.

With this kind of healing power over a debilitating physical disease, do you think the extraterrestrials and Jmmanuel should also have healed (read: genetically modified) the malevolent neurochemistry and behavior of the Pharisees and Sadducees, and all their damaged minions and followers? Why leave such pestilence alive and well in its own evil house, allowing it to bring further harm to the people Jmmanuel and his extraterrestrials sought to educate and develop?

Did Jmmanuel and his extraterrestrial leaders grow weeds in our own backyard so they could pull them? *Factum gratia laboris*: work for work's sake?

Jmmanuel also introduces his disgust for Israel and its people, strongly suggesting that this land was a natural den of vipers, and hardly the "chosen ones" they have claimed to be for more than 2,000 years. Jmmanuel's own words predict what has been seen since his time:

"The false teachings of Israel will bring bloodshed over the millennia, because the power-hungry selfishness and high-handedness of Israel will bring death and destruction over the land and all the world."

This, too, has come to pass, as the descendants of the Pharisees and Sadducees in the Land of Israel have joined forces with the Society of Jesus in Rome, the Jesuits (another false prophet), to create death and destruction across our beautiful planet. It is a curious fact that such evil came out of those two places: Israel and Rome, Italy.

> "The false teachings of Israel will bring bloodshed over the millennia, because the power-hungry selfishness and high-handedness of Israel will bring death and destruction over the land and all the world."

It is not the scope of this book to examine the significance of these obviously important geographical regions on Earth. However, it is compelling that many believe Israel and Rome to be two "holy" sites where extraterrestrials have landed in the past and will land again in the near future. With this in mind, one must consider whether these extraterrestrials are, in fact, benevolent to humans on Earth or perhaps are merely our slave-owners who have sought to subjugate us since day one, using Jmmanuel's sermons as a "guide" that gave rise to the oppressive modern-day religions and other means of crowd control.

Chapter 9: The Healing of the Paralytic

Jmmanuel heals a paralytic who is a true believer in the power of the spirit. As the crowd sees this, scribes within complain that Jmmanuel blasphemes their God and teachings. Some of the scribes began talking among themselves about how Jmmanuel was blaspheming their God, and Jmmanuel heard their thoughts. Is this a literal translation? If so, we now learn that Jmmanuel reads the minds of humans, a powerful trait, indeed. If this is so, we do not see him using this power, or perhaps he chose not to speak about it when his sermons were being written down.

When Jmmanuel meets Matthew, a tax collector, he invites him to become a follower. Later, the Pharisees witness Jmmanuel eating with Matthew and other tax collectors and seekers of truth, and condemn Jmmanuel for consorting with the *ignorant*.

When the Pharisees begin fasting and Jmmanuel and his followers do not, they criticize him. He tells the false prophets that fasting for the sake of religion is false, but fasting for the sake of good health is just.

Jmmanuel then heals a woman with hemophilia and a blind man, and word quickly spreads throughout the land. When word reaches the Pharisees, they further condemn Jmmanuel.

Here we discover the real intentions of the Pharisees: "However," the Pharisees said, "He drives out the evil spirits through their supreme chief, and he blasphemes God, our Lord." But among themselves they said, "Who is this Jmmanuel, who possesses greater wisdom and greater knowledge than we? His teachings are mightier and truer than ours, and therefore he endangers us. We must try to seize him, so that he will suffer death."

Jmmanuel is a direct threat to the Pharisees, so they plot his execution.

How different is this today with good researchers and seekers of truth who try to oppose the powers that be? When their audience reaches a critical mass, these good people and leaders are quickly identified and ridiculed. When public humiliation doesn't work, they are threatened. When the threats have no effect, these good people are murdered by the powers that be, the Society of Jesus and its evil followers, the descendants of the Pharisees and Sadducees.

Good deeds do not go unpunished.

Chapter 10: Commissioning of the Disciples

Jmmanuel sends out his 12 disciples, each armed with the special ability to heal physical ailments, but he cautions them to avoid those who oppose his teachings. This directive appears counter to the fact that Gabriel emplaced Jmmanuel in the very Land of Israel, where his opposers were most violent and vociferous. Jmmanuel then instructs his own disciples to avoid the evil and violent people of the Land of Israel.

> "Dark ages will follow, centuries and millennia, before the truth of the spirit will penetrate to the people."

In various sections of *Arcanum*, you will come across passionate words and thoughts, which suddenly punctuate the even tone of the book. An example:

"Truly, I say to you, the people of Israel were never one distinct people, and they have always lived by murder, robbery and fire. They gained possession of this land through guile and murder in reprehensible, predatory wars, where the best of friends were slaughtered like wild animals.

"May the people of Israel be cursed until the end of the world, and never find their peace."

Were the extraterrestrials truly showing such utter contempt for the people of the Land of Israel? Or is this an interpreter's impassioned mistake or attempt to mislead the reader?

Passages like the two above are few and far between, although references to Israel and its people abound, especially in the last half of the book. Why then would the extraterrestrials purposefully emplace Jmmanuel in the Land of Israel, knowing this to be a den of vipers and thieves? Was it because it proved to be the greatest challenge, i.e. attempting to bring The Laws of Creation and the Universe to a difficult if not impossible audience?

It is clear from the translation that Jmmanuel had contempt for the people of Israel, because of their murderous and thieving behavior. He also detested the Pharisees and Sadducees, the two tribes of barbarous Jews who vehemently opposed Jmmanuel and his "blasphemous" teachings.

In his sermons, Jmmanuel does not mention the presence of other extraterrestrial races. Were they present during his time? Were they members of his opposition? The extraterrestrials did in fact mention that humans are not permitted to worship any other god or gods, suggesting the presence of other extraterrestrials, either of the same race or perhaps different ones. It is curious that such little information about other races of extraterrestrials exists in Jmmanuel's writings and teachings. The Indian *Mahabarata* tells us that there were, in fact, other races of extraterrestrials that opposed each other and often fought great battles and wars using advanced conventional arms and nuclear weapons.

At the end of the chapter, Jmmanuel shows his true purpose on Mother Earth:

"Do not think that I have come to bring peace on Earth. Truly, I have not come to bring peace, but the sword of knowledge about the power of the spirit, which dwells within the human being. For I have come to bring wisdom and knowledge and to provoke mankind: son against his father, daughter against her mother, daughter-in-law against her mother-in-law, servant against master, citizen against government, and believer against preacher. The people's enemies will be their own housemates. The path of truth is long and the wisdom of knowledge will only penetrate slowly."

One of the final passages is a harbinger of broad events and a particular phenomenon in our midst:

"Dark ages will follow, centuries and millennia, before the truth of the spirit will penetrate to the people."

Chapter 11: The Baptist's Question

Initially, Jmmanuel speaks to the people of John the Baptist who, according to Jmmanuel, is the greatest human being alive, i.e. born to a human female. Jmmanuel prepares these new followers to receive his teachings and knowledge and wisdom: "Go back and report to John what you hear and see: The blind see, the lame walk, the lepers are cleansed, the deaf hear, the dead rise, and the truth of knowledge is proclaimed to those who seek it. And blessed are those who are not offended by my teachings."

This preparation of a new following is smart and just, as it will help to counter the coming onslaught by the Pharisees and Sadducees.

The puzzling thought of why Jmmanuel was ordered to the Land of Israel, but chose to avoid most of the Pharisees and Sadducees may be found in this passage from Chapter 11:

"Praise be to Creation, maker of the heavens, the Universe and the Earth, for keeping the knowledge and power of the spirit hidden from the unwise and the misguided, who spread the false teachings, and for revealing this knowledge to sincere seekers now."

He is telling us that he seeks those who thirst for knowledge, those who may be living among the oppressors in the Land of Israel, to teach them the ways of Creation and the Universe.

Perhaps Gabriel's emplacing Jmmanuel in the Land of Israel is not so far removed from the method of special-operations paratroopers who drop in behind enemy lines and then link up with like-minded people of a resistance, the goal being to destroy the enemy from within.

In Jmmanuel's case, he wished to teach the ways of Creation and the Universe to those who were being oppressed by the leaders of the Pharisees and Sadducees.

Chapter 12: Regarding Marriage and Cohabitation

Contrary to what we actually see in nature, Jmmanuel preaches that people should not commit adultery, which violates the laws of nature. One wonders how, other than to disobey a certain order of things having little or nothing to do with nature itself. In the real world of nature on Earth, we see humans and animals changing partners frequently and seemingly without any natural consequence. In fact, there is ample evidence for having physical relations with other people, although not necessarily committing adultery. In animals, males often have several or many females or even harems. Why should it be so different with humans? Could it be that this law against adultery was an artificial one created by the extraterrestrials as a means of control and maintaining stability within human male-female relationships for the purpose of procreation, thus ensuring a sufficiently large and stable gene pool?

Surprisingly, Jmmanuel is not opposed to two women bedding together, thus perhaps supporting (or at least ignoring) sex between women:

"If, however, two women bed down with one another, they shall not be punished, because they do not violate life and its laws, since they are not inseminating but are bearing."

But he does oppose sex between men:

"When inseminator and inseminator join together, life is desecrated and destroyed."

The Jesuits and Jews will have a very difficult time with this passage:

"Whosoever sexually abuses a child is unworthy of life and its laws and shall therefore be punished by castration or sterilization, and be deprived of freedom through lifelong confinement and isolation."

The current sex trade throughout the world, overseen by the Jesuits and their minions, violates Jmmanuel's mandate:

"Whosoever rapes a woman or a man is unworthy of life and its laws and shall therefore be punished by castration or sterilization, and be deprived of freedom through lifelong confinement and isolation."

Gender equality was established early on, and upon Jmmanuel's "death," quickly suppressed. His thoughts on the equality of man and woman:

"Do away with enforcing the old law that subjects woman to man, since she is a person like the man, with equal rights and obligations."

In reading these passages in Chapter 12, is it not striking that they directly oppose those actions and behaviors of the current powers that be? Is it also not true that the powers that be oppress its "followers" in every way possible, by every means possible? The actions and behaviors of the Jesuits and their Pharisees and Sadducees descendants tell a compelling tale of lust, greed, murder and deceit.

Chapter 12 also has some rather heavy-handed approaches to dealing with those who disobey these rules: sterilization and castration, not to mention outright banishment from society. Judge for yourself whether these laws and rules are appropriate today.

Chapter 13: Jmmanuel and the Sabbath

This is a compelling chapter about the shameless hypocrisy of the powers that be. The Pharisees saw Jmmanuel and his followers eating grain in a field on the Sabbath, and asked why these people were eating on such a holy day.

Jmmanuel replied: "Have you not read what David did when he and those with him were hungry? How he went into the temple and ate the shewbread, which neither he nor those with him were permitted to eat but only the priests? Or have you not read in the law, how on the Sabbath the priests in the temple violate the Sabbath and yet are without guilt? Truly, I say to you, you brood of snakes and vipers, a stone will turn into bread before no work may be done on the Sabbath. For the law that the Sabbath be kept holy is only a man-made law without logic, as are many man-made laws that contradict The Laws of Creation."

Jmmanuel condemns the Pharisees' laws as "man made," which are counter to The Laws of Creation and Nature and of the Universe. Man-made laws are designed and implemented to enslave and control good people, and to steal their worldly possessions, their land, food and livelihood.

The puzzling part of Jmmanuel's words center around his insisting that his followers not speak of his words and deeds because he said he would be captured and killed. With his otherworldly powers, plus the backup of his extraterrestrials, why could this man not immediately defeat the Pharisees or at least oppose them in some meaningful way? Why flee when you are more powerful than the enemy? Do The Laws of Creation forbid confronting one's enemies in such a way and destroying them, lest they murder you?

The Laws allow for "an eye for an eye," so the answer to the last question is a resounding no.

Still the puzzle remains: why did Jmmanuel appear so weak toward his enemies, yet all powerful to his followers, using healing powers that were truly out of this world?

> "But The Laws of Creation have been valid for yesterday and today, and therefore for tomorrow, the day after tomorrow, and for all time. Thus the Laws are also a determination and hence a predetermination for things of the future that must happen."

Chapter 14: The Wrongdoings of Judas Ish-Keriot

One of Jmmanuel's disciples, Judas Ish-Keriot (from the land of Keriot), is discovered to be disloyal to Jmmanuel and his teachings by surreptitiously taking money from Jmmanuel's audiences and building his own fortune.

Juda Ihariot, son of Simeon the Pharisee, witnesses Judas embezzling ill-gotten funds and reports the deed to Jmmanuel, expecting to be richly rewarded with gold, silver and copper. When Jmmanuel simply thanks him and rewards him nothing, he turns on him and reports the deed to his father Simon.

Meantime, Jmmanuel takes Judas Ish-Keriot from the city for three days and three nights, and teaches him the error of his ways. Judas repents and is forgiven, and so returns to the city with Jmmanuel and distributes his stolen money to the poor.

For more than 2,000 years, Judas Ish-Keriot will suffer the deeds of the damned and become a martyr, so states Jmmanuel. Simeon the Pharisee spreads the word that Judas is a traitor to Jmmanuel, and has his son Juda steal the writings of Jmmanuel's teachings from Judas. Jmmanuel directs Judas to rewrite the teachings so they will be revealed in 2,000 years.

"Until then my teachings will be falsified and will turn into an evil cult, which will cause much human blood to flow, because the people are still not prepared to comprehend my teachings and to recognize the truth. Not until two times a thousand years will an unassuming man come who will recognize my teachings as truth and disseminate them with great courage. He will be vilified by the established cult religions and advocates of the false teachings about me, and be considered a liar."

Sadly, this very prophesy has come to pass, with the original 36 extant sermons of Jmmanuel having been suppressed by the Jesuits and their minions since their discovery 50 years ago. Long before, though, the sermons of Jmmanuel were bastardized and converted to the various religions and cults we see today.

Jesuit propaganda has rendered the 36 sermons a dead letter to the masses. Still there are those who believe and cherish the sermons, and who will do whatever it takes to ensure they are disseminated as widely as possible. This current book is but one example.

"But The Laws of Creation have been valid for yesterday and today, and therefore for tomorrow, the day after tomorrow, and for all time. Thus the Laws are also a determination and hence a predetermination for things of the future that must happen."

More than 2,000 years of false and distorted teachings by the powers that be have effectively enslaved and controlled the masses and crushed all hope of true freedom and liberty. When all good people wake up and discover the true teachings of Jmmanuel, they will begin a new journey into the realm of The Laws of Creation and Nature and the Universe.

Chapter 15: The Meaning of the Parables

This fascinating chapter reveals a key to communicating with one's subconscious mind, which is the engine that powers life and is in direct contact with the Universe via celestiophysical mechanisms. Our human subconscious is a child and thus speaks in the language of a child.

Paradoxically, this child understands the language of the Universe and its complexities, yet when communicating to humans, this child speaks like the young and in simple language, in the form of *dreams*. The primary means of communication is the metaphor that, when built into a long story, becomes a parable that is designed to pull in the listener and impart wisdom and truth. But first one must understand the foundation of wisdom and truth: the original metaphor.

Dreams and dreaming are a still a great mystery to Earth humans, but we now know that the Universe communicates to us through our dreams and does so in metaphors, in the language of a child. It is now our duty and responsibility to study and understand the meanings of the metaphorical communications from the Universe, and to build a work of translations of them: *The Book of Universal Communications.*

Jmmanuel's first parable: "Behold, a sower went out to sow. While he sowed, some seeds fell on the pathway; then the birds came and ate them up. And some fell on the rocks, where there was not much soil. And as the sun rose high, they withered, and because they had no roots, they dried out. Some fell among the thorns; and the thorns grew up and smothered them. Some fell on good ground and bore fruit, some hundredfold, some sixty-fold, some thirty-fold."

Meaning: Those who hear the words but have little or no faith cannot understand The Laws of Creation, so they may live according to them. Only those who hear the words and accept them can find the truth and live according to The Laws of Creation.

He goes on to say that it is up to the people to hear, accept and understand the meaning of the parables, to develop their own comprehension so they may think independently and grow into an enlightened being. Without critical, independent thought, a person is only a follower of someone else's words and teachings. Jmmanuel sought to teach people his way of life, yes, but according to The Laws of Creation and the Universe, not some false cult like the religions of today.

"What would be better to make them come alive and think, if not through speaking in parables?" Jmmanuel says. In the world of the extraterrestrials, did they teach their young in this same manner, using metaphors and parables to evoke critical thinking and evaluation? It is a powerful method that, unfortunately, did not work well with most of his followers. This is in keeping with what we know about the majority of humankind: they are not independent thinkers. Is it because they are not capable, or are they simply ignorant because they have not been properly instructed? We see the same today, with most people simply following the paths set forth by the powers that be, rather than forging their own journeys and sojourns.

He says further: "Truly, I say to you, life and the knowledge of truth are only valuable and good when they are achieved through one's own thinking or through the resolving of mysteries that are recounted in parables."

Jmmanuel used his disciples as "force-multipliers," that is, those he would teach well and who, in turn, would venture into the villages and towns to teach the masses. The point is that, even though The Laws of Creation are within us all, only a handful may be capable of extracting them, much less understanding and practicing them. It takes a mentor to guide those who cannot think for themselves along a righteous and meaningful path.

Jmmanuel states that those who cannot comprehend The Laws of Creation will be punished. Is this not a heavy-handed approach? We should allow those fore-multipliers among us to reach out to the masses and make a good-faith attempt to educate them.

Another sad truth we see today: "Nowhere is a prophet valued less than in his own country and in his own house. This will prove true for all time, as long as humanity has little knowledge and is enslaved by the delusional teachings of the scribes and distorters of scripture."

How is it that a person speaking the truth is so reviled by his own people? Again recall the movie *The Matrix* where Morpheus tells Neo: "... many of them are so inured, so hopelessly dependent on the system, that they will fight to protect it."

The only way to fight the system is to change it from within or build an entirely new system of living that effectively usurps the old one:

"Yet, before the end of two times a thousand years the new prophet will reveal my unfalsified teachings to small groups, just as I teach the wisdom, the knowledge and the Laws of the spirit and of Creation to small groups of trusted friends and disciples."

Curiously, Jmmanuel went on a tear, castigating the people of Israel and their false religion, Judaism, stating they are a mixed bag, a brood of snakes and vipers who have lived by murder and arson. He says they pledged themselves "to the false beliefs and false teachings they adopted from Moses who, in turn, had stolen them from the Egyptians."

What a curious statement, that. In modern religion, we have been taught that Moses was quite a different character, but Jmmanuel reveals him to be a false prophet of a brood of snakes and vipers, a man who stole teachings from the Egyptians and converted it to their false religion, Judaism.

It is no wonder that the powers that be have protected their bankers, accountants and moneychangers, the descendants of the Pharisees and Sadducees ... the Jews.

Chapter 16: Herod and the Baptist

King Herod the Pharisee hated John the Baptist and eventually had him beheaded in prison, but was not blamed for ordering the death of such a popular prophet. Herod has his illicit lover, the wife of his brother, convince her daughter to ask for John's head on a silver platter, thus relieving Herod of all involvement.

When Jmmanuel learned of John's murder, he fled in fear of his own life. One must wonder, again, why Jmmanuel did not dispatch his enemies with extreme prejudice, and instead allowed them to continue to oppress all good people. Was there some cosmic law that prevented him from killing his enemies? We've already answered this (no). Were there certain rules that forbade him from doing so? If so, none of these laws or rules have come to light. None have been written or expressed in any writings or teachings on Planet Earth. If they exist at all, for what reason?

Any Laws of Creation that allow "an eye for an eye" but forbid a prophylactic strike against a known dangerous enemy are contradictory. If they are not, then much needs to be revealed and explained about the apparent paradox. The extraterrestrials were indeed powerful in all aspects, so why didn't they exercise control over those deadly entities on Planet Earth, if not destroy them altogether? Why allow such dangerous people to thrive among a sea of beauty and oppress all good people of the Earth?

Jmmanuel taught his disciples to feed 5,000 people, but it is unclear how this was done. No writings or teachings elaborate how Jmmanuel effected his power in this case. Is it possible that the interpretation or translation of this story has been distorted? What facts are we missing here? The 36 sermons were transcribed by three different people (Judas, Matthew and Jmmanuel's oldest son Joseph). Were they in error on any of the chapters? Were some words left out? It is known that the man who discovered the scrolls 50 years ago had many more that were not translated. They were lost in the bombing of his temporary home in Lebanon.

While many questions about Jmmanuel and his work will remain unanswered, it is clear that Jmmanuel operated by a strict set of laws and rules, and some of those appear to be contradictory and even hypocritical.

"Never doubt the power of your spirit, which is a part of Creation itself and therefore knows no limits of power."

He preached to his disciples that they must place blind faith and trust in The Laws of Creation. When his followers doubted their faith, they were harmed or killed.

A Critical Analysis and Evaluation

It is unclear still what those exact Laws of Creation were. They are not written in any form, although many cults and religions have proclaimed their own writings and teachings to be derived from some greater or higher power.

Are we humans expected to follow along blindly in the same fashion? We are not given The Laws of Creation to read, study and comprehend, let alone pass on to others. We read only the parables and allegories from long-deceased men who tell us to first read, then accept, and ultimately understand and disseminate these unwritten laws and rules. Knowing we are an ignorant lot, why did the extraterrestrials take such a path with Earth humans?

Jmmanuel explains that god is not omnipotent like the God of the false prophets, cults and religions of today. The one known as god is a man who comes from another planet (outside Earth), is far advanced from Earth humans on all levels, and who gave rise to three human lineages on Planet Earth. God adheres to The Laws of Creation and, therefore, humans on Earth also must obey these laws:

"I tell you there are greater masters of spiritual power than I, and they are our distant forefathers of Petale." Petale is the highest level of spiritual development that a pure-spirit form can attain before it ultimately melds with Creation and becomes one with it. And great are they also, who came from the depths of space, and the greatest among them is god, and he is the spiritual ruler of three human lineages. However above him stands Creation, whose laws he faithfully follows and respects; therefore he is not omnipotent, as only Creation itself can be."

Again, we must ask why we humans are being asked, if not coerced, to follow Jmmanuel's words blindly and without any real proof of the powers underlying them? Why are we being asked to become followers and disciples of beings that offer us so little, share next to nothing about our true history? Why are we humans being kept in the dark about the nature of the Universe, while evil and destructive people like the Jesuits are seemingly allowed to run wild with our lives and liberties?

What is an independent thinking mind to do? Trust blindly and obediently? If so, how do we verify the claims made by Jmmanuel and those who bequeathed to him this vast knowledge that seems to elude us on Planet Earth? Independent, thinking minds do not follow actions and words of anyone blithely and without question. We wish to learn the meaning behind those actions and words, to better understand what is being asked of us. Along the way, we begin to build trust and loyalty, two traits that were immediately expected of Jmmanuel's disciples and followers.

Chapter 17: Human Commandments and The Laws of Creation

Jmmanuel appears to lose his patience at this point of his journey, and challenges both his enemies and followers. The Pharisees came to him and demanded to know why Jmmanuel's followers were not obeying the statutes handed down by the Pharisees, and Jmmanuel told them The Laws of Creation were the only true laws and any others were man-made and false.

He further castigates the Israelites, quoting Isaiah:

" 'The people of Israel profess to follow and obey the Laws of Creation, but their hearts and their knowledge are far from it. They serve their cult in vain, because they teach such falsified and untruthful teachings, which are no more than man-made laws.' "

Jmmanuel's disciples then told him, "Are you aware that the scribes and the Pharisees were offended by your words when they heard them? They went out to bear witness against you and to have you killed because of your teachings."

Jmmanuel then recited another parable, "All plants that do not live according to The Laws of Creation will dry up and rot."

His disciples did not understand its meaning, and Jmmanuel got impatient, saying, "Are you, too, still without wisdom and therefore also ignorant and doubting in recognition, comprehension and understanding? You have been with me for a long time now, but you still lack the ability to think and recognize the truth."

Jmmanuel's strange behavior begs the question: How could a half-man, half-extraterrestrial be so impatient with his extraterrestrials' own beautiful creation?

Do we humans treat dogs in the same manner? Certainly not, if we wish to train them correctly and not to fear us. So why treat his subjects so disrespectfully and with such impatience? Those of us who have taught students know that when a student does not comprehend something, the fault may lie with the teacher, not the student.

Jmmanuel spoke in parables that were often difficult to interpret, yet he criticized the very people he should have been mentoring.

"Oh, you of little knowledge, does your understanding still not extend beyond the stupidity of the people? Beware, lest you see me in a false light and accuse me of an origin from which I could not have descended."

If the average student heard words like these from a favorite teacher or professor, how would they feel? What should they make of such disrespect from a mentor who accuses them of being "stupid"?

Chapter 18: The Pharisees Demand a Sign

Again, we see Jmmanuel's anger rising on different fronts. First, the Pharisees demanded proof of his powers and Jmmanuel flatly refused. When he confronts his disciples and asks how his followers see him and are introducing him, they give the wrong answer and again draw his wrath.

At this point, we must wonder how Jmmanuel allowed his disciples and followers to have any false or inaccurate knowledge about him, his family, and his general background. It was his duty and responsibility as a mentor and teacher to ensure his disciples and followers were given the correct information, then maybe even tested on their knowledge. After all, if the information was that important, Jmmanuel should have ensured his people knew and understood it well. Modern-day teachers test their students on the knowledge received and when a student's understanding is inaccurate, the teacher corrects it.

True, Jmmanuel corrected his disciples' knowledge, but quite long after he had taught it to them, presumably without ongoing and consistent testing. Jmmanuel's criticism of his own disciples and followers is uncharacteristic of a patient mentor and good, effective teacher.

Jmmanuel then told his disciples that he must travel to Jerusalem where he would be tortured and killed by the false scribes and prophets. When Simon Peter objects, Jmmanuel scolds him for thinking in human terms, not spiritual.

Clearly, Jmmanuel's students were not learning this man's subjects too well and, perhaps just as clear, Jmmanuel was an impatient teacher who saw himself as patient and just:

"Truly, I say to you, owing to your lack of understanding, the world will shed much blood because you will falsify my teachings and spread them erroneously among the people. You will be to blame for the deaths of many people, as well as for the origin of a false name for me and for the evil insult of calling me the son of god, and calling god Creation itself. But you are still under the grace of my long-suffering patience, so you can still measurably improve upon your irrationality."

A bit high-handed, yes?

While Jmmanuel castigates his students for their ignorance, he tells them that just mistakes are not punishable under The Laws of Creation and the Universe. If one is seeking knowledge and makes mistakes along the way, presumably innocent ones, that person shall not be punished.

In a way it is somewhat unclear and confusing how Jmmanuel chose to teach his disciples and followers, using parables and metaphors, then assuming that his words were automatically understood by his people. In reality, they were not, and this caused Jmmanuel some anguish to the point he scolded his disciples and followers, telling them that they would indeed be the cause of the world's misery and misfortune because they spread false teachings based on their ignorance of Jmmanuel's imparted knowledge and wisdom.

"Lacking understanding, the people curse the truth which yet must come; they curse, stone, kill and crucify the prophets. But since the teachings of the truth must be brought to the people, the prophets have to bear great burdens and suffering under the curse of the people Just as they persecuted many prophets, they are now after my life."

These are perhaps some of the most compelling statements Jmmanuel makes. He tells his disciples that their work is all but futile, because the ignorant masses (those unfortunate souls stuck in The Matrix) will not only not believe the truth, they will curse and kill the prophet who brings the message.

Please recall the quote from *The Matrix* about this paradox of having to fight the very people you are trying to save.

Fascinating too is his explaining his apparent death, followed by a long passage to India where he will become further enlightened. He tells us of friends in India. This is in reference to Jmmanuel's having lived in India during his early years of life, where he studied many subjects and learned about his special powers and his place on Earth.

This is the first known historical record of Jmmanuel's prophesy about his near-death and subsequent travel to India. It is a matter of historical record in various ancient scripts in India, but those in the rest of the world have largely been ignorant of it because the various powers that be directed their scribes to rewrite history to show that "Jesus Christ" died on the cross for the "sins" of all.

Chapter 19: The Nature of a Child's Thinking

Jmmanuel's disciples asked what type of person possesses the greatest spirit, and he answered, "Those who search, seek and gather insights and thirst for knowledge like this child will be great in spirit."

We all know this to be true. The children around us have the greatest spirit, and they thirst for knowledge in all things. They are curious and industrious, and ask many questions about the world around them. They are also in the most unique state of their physical lives, in that their brain is constructed to absorb, store and process as much information as possible, and their sensory apparatus is poised to deliver the largest amount of rich, colorful and vibrant stimuli.

It is too bad that this unique state only last through the teen years, because we adults and grown-ups could use a healthy dose of it each day.

It is not our fault that we adults lose this ability, because our brains scale back to a large extent, thus depriving us of more of the life of a child. Fortunately, there are ways around this physical dilemma: we can chose to act childlike (not childish) and thus re-introduce this state of mind to us once again. By remaining curious and seeking out the answers to the Universe, we are in a never-ending quest for knowledge and truth about who we are, why we are here, where we came from, who engineered us and why. The questions should remain unending.

Jmmanuel then spoke about one's neighbors: "It is better to let an unreasonable person walk on the path of misery than to bring confusion to one's own consciousness."

If we cannot get our own neighbors to listen to reason and truth, then we must leave them alone to float about in The Matrix. This is truly saddening, because it means there is one less person we wish to reach out to and educate about the powers of Creation and the Universe.

He does caution us to spend our time wisely by disseminating this great knowledge only where the powerful seeds will germinate. While it is saddening to hear that we must abandon certain people, it makes sense that some just cannot be guided along to seek knowledge as we do, and to understand The Laws of Creation and the Universe.

Chapter 20: Marriage, Divorce and Celibacy

We see a most heavy-handed approach to marriage and divorce in this chapter, with Jmmanuel proclaiming that no married couple shall divorce. When he is challenged by the Pharisees, he reveals further information: it is permissible to divorce when a partner commits adultery.

How do two people stay together when they do not possess the skills to do so, let alone over a lifetime? There is an excellent reason that divorce is so high among typical couples these days: people are less educated and poorly equipped to handle daily stressors that creep into a marriage. When disagreements arise, they are usually escalated without true cause, leading to a festering of emotions, thoughts and feelings over a longer period of time.

A Critical Analysis and Evaluation

In this age of fast-food and instant everything, divorce is as simple as filing a one-page form at a courthouse, explaining a few details, paying a court fee, waiting a few days, standing in front of a judge who hears the case, and walking away a single person.

The current environment was sown by the Jesuits over the past nearly 500 years in nearly every country on the planet. It is no wonder why we place so little emphasis on remaining together as couples, and instead prefer a teflon exit.

This is not to say that people should be forced to stay together as one, which is what Jmmanuel preached. His was a simpler time in our history which, after his traveling on to India after his "death," descended into a morally corrupt atmosphere.

Jmmanuel's teachings were meant in good spirit, but they were left to rot in the streets because he chose not to spend more time with the people of the world. Instead, he made statements like, "Those who can grasp this, let them grasp it."

He is telling us that only those who can believe and understand his words will actually ascend to enlightenment and will find the knowledge and truth. Those ignorant or foolish souls who are not capable of this level of understanding are left to their own devices. In his language, this means they are condemned for all time.

Is this not a shallow way of thinking, particularly coming from a man who has first-line celestial blood from extraterrestrials? Were they not more evolved than we are? Could they not see the compelling need to take even more time teaching us on Earth and to ensure that we not only received their messages about The Laws of Creation, but also understood them well enough to implement them and pass them on to progeny, friends and followers?

Jmmanuel's philosophy appears narrow and unjust, and it suggests that he and his extraterrestrials were only interested in teaching to the small minority of people, those who had faith and were capable of understanding his teachings at first blush. The remainder of the population, which was the vast majority, the MOBsters, were left to drift toward false teachings from false prophets and those disciples who did not firmly grasp Jmmanuel's messages.

"Let the children be and do not hinder them from coming to me, because they are my most attentive listeners, and theirs is the realm of wisdom." And he laid his hands upon them and said, "Learn knowledge and wisdom to become spiritually perfect and true followers of the law. Truly, I say to you, inasmuch as I am called Jmmanuel, which means 'the one with godly knowledge,' you also shall bear this name when you grasp the wisdom of knowledge."

Again, Jmmanuel picks his students with great prejudice here, focusing on the children, i.e. those humans with open minds and hearts and souls, who are born to accept the requisite faith and who are capable of absorbing and learning on a level above typical adults.

This appears to be the message here and it is saddening because it immediately discards the majority of humans on Earth as if they were truly ignorant souls not worthy of teaching.

"Wisdom will only exist where the knowledge about the truth bears fruit, and where The Laws of Creation are followed and respected."

The teaching philosophy of Jmmanuel leaves much to be desired. Repeating words from chapters ago, how could such an advanced race of humans be so impatient with their own creation? Couldn't they have re-engineered us to be a smarter race like them? Why did they seemingly banish us Earth humans to an eternity of such ignorance and suffering?

Chapter 21: Two Blind Persons

On his journey to Jericho, Jmmanuel was accosted by two blind persons who insisted they be heard, even though Jmmanuel's followers shouted down the blind people.

Jmmanuel recognized something in the two blind persons and asked how they felt he could make them see again. To his surprise, they gave the answer he had sought from all his disciples and followers: "The power of Creation, which is in the laws."

Where did they learn this wisdom? We never learn how they came to understand it. Maybe they could have imparted their knowledge and wisdom on those ignorant disciples and followers of Jmmanuel who had failed to grasp the very basics.

Jmmanuel responded: "Truly, so far I have never found such faith and knowledge among these people. Be it done to you as you expect."

"Truly, truly, I say to you, if you are knowledgeable and comprehending and embrace wisdom, and if you practice love truthfully and do not doubt, not only will you do such things with blind eyes, but when you say to the fig tree, 'Dry up,' it will dry up. Or when you say to a mountain, 'Lift yourself up and throw yourself into the sea,' it will come to pass."

Jmmanuel is telling his new followers that anything can come to them if they accept and understand The Laws of Creation, although those laws specifically have yet to be mentioned in detail. When someone does not doubt their path, they will be rewarded.

A curious statement: "Do not suppose, however, that prayer is necessary, because you will also receive without prayer if your spirit and your consciousness are trained through wisdom."

Wouldn't it be grand if we modern-day humans could simply make a wish and have it come true? Would that ease our suffering on Earth? Would it bring an end to the current powers that be? Something so seemingly simple, yet so far out of reach.

The following statement is perhaps one of the most compelling and yet contradictory: "Do not delude yourself by heeding the falsified teachings that a person has a predetermined will, because this belief is wrong."

It goes against what is known about celestiophysics and the powers of the Universe, which mediate and modulate all geophysical and biophysical activity on Planet Earth. Jmmanuel's words strongly contradict what we see every day in all aspects of life: there is a strong and definite purpose to everything and the cycles of the Universe govern these events. Is this not a predetermined future? How often do we witness humans overcome their own evolutionary biology, written in their DNA? While we wish to believe that fate does not exist, we see it all around us, as if it binds us to its silent and mysterious laws and actions.

"Thus a person determines the course of their life, known as fate."

If this were in fact accurate, the world would be a far different place than we see. There is a small exception: people do have the power to change their course of action, but it is limited to short-term actions. A human being's fate or destiny is determined in great part by their date and time of birth. Their willingness to go "off-map" or away from their predestined life is determined by when they were first conceived and when their DNA was stimulated by the strange and mysterious forces of the Universe.

Jmmanuel says that the purpose of the spirit is to grow and learn and perfect itself, all in keeping with The Laws of Creation. Those who adhere to the false teachings shall cause everyone misery and suffering.

"Truly, I say to you, the princes suppress their people, and the mighty use violence against them; similarly, the forthcoming religious sects will use violence, when they adulterate my teachings and disseminate them. So beware of them and do not permit yourselves to be forced into carrying the yoke of these false teachings."

Jmmanuel foretells 2,000 years ago what we are seeing today, and he is 100% accurate, sad as that is to report. His final message is simple and poignant: "As I have come to teach truth and knowledge among the people, so you should keep on reaching, so the truth may indeed prevail." Jmmanuel challenges us to be curious, seek truth in everything, learn all we can about ourselves and life and all in it, and share our knowledge with others.

Chapter 22: Entry Into Jerusalem

Jmmanuel ventures into Jerusalem on a gifted donkey, and discovers the temple is inhabited by traders, vendors, dove merchants and moneychangers, who were profiting from the ignorance and misery of the people. In a fit of anger, Jmmanuel overturns the tables of the thieves and, using a donkey-driver's whip, forces them to flee the temple. His temper is now heightened to a new level. Previously, he had refused to engage in such a way with his enemies, choosing instead to run from them. What has changed here? Has Jmmanuel grown tired of those who oppose him? Have the Israelites, whom he has castigated in the past, angered him to the point of violence?

Jmmanuel's behavior is not uncommon among mentors and teachers whose students are often slow to understand. But Jmmanuel is half extraterrestrial and half human, and therefore possesses more-advanced physiology, neurochemistry and overall character traits. So how is it he is losing his temper with the thieves of the temple? Is this the only way to communicate with this lot and get his messages and parables across?

In the aftermath of Jmmanuel's violent outburst, the blind and lame visit him and are healed, all in the presence of the chief priests and scribes. The latter then confront Jmmanuel in anger and he replies, "Are you so afraid of the truth that it angers you?" He soon departs the city for Bethany and later returns to Jerusalem, to teach the people.

The chief priests, scribes, and the elders of the people approach Jmmanuel and ask why he is doing these things and on whose authority. Jmmanuel tells them he will answer their questions only if they will answer his.

He then recites another parable, which the chief priests, scribes, and the elders of the people do not understand or misinterpret, thus drawing Jmmanuel's wrath. He then recites another parable, which they also misinterpret.

Jmmanuel then refuses to answer their question and instead issues a dangerous warning:

"Therefore I say to you, peace and joy shall be taken from you and your people for all eternity, and all shall be given to a people who bring forth their fruits. If you disregard and trample on all the commandments of god, who is the ruler over this and the two other human lineages in the North and the East, you shall be disregarded and trampled upon for all time. The burden of the Israelite people will be like a heavy stone of the seven Great Ages. Whosoever falls upon this stone will be smashed to pieces, and whosoever it falls upon will be crushed."

Once again, Jmmanuel has warned the inhabitants of the Land of Israel, whom he holds in very low esteem. This is a land of thieves, he has stated over and over again, so why hasn't he made a good-faith effort to convert them? He has always taken the path of least resistance, focusing on those who understand his words by default or show great promise in understanding.

How should we further interpret Jmmanuel's methods? In modern-day teachings, we spend more time teaching and assisting those who understand the least, with the hope we can show them how to understand the subject material.

Jmmanuel appears to use a different approach to mentoring and teaching his disciples and followers.

Chapter 23: Taxes, Reincarnation, The Greatest Commandment

The Pharisees were actively plotting Jmmanuel's death, but first they sought to discredit him among his followers by posing provocative questions. One of them asked if it were "right" to pay tax to the emperor.

Jmmanuel saw through the veil of malice and deceit, and asked them to hand him a tax coin.

One obliged and gave Jmmanuel a denarius, a silver Roman coin.

He took the coin and asked, "Whose image and whose inscription are on this coin?"

They said it was the emperor's.

Jmmanuel said, "Therefore, give to the emperor what is the emperor's, give to god what is god's, and give to Creation what is Creation's. Yet beware and know that god and the emperor are men, above whom is the omnipotence of Creation, to which you must give the highest praise, for, although god is indeed ruler over humankind, and the emperor is indeed ruler over peoples, above them stands Creation as the highest authority, to which god and the emperor are subordinate in the Law, as is every human being and all life."

Jmmanuel's wisdom gave them nowhere to move in the conversation, so the would-be assassins of Jmmanuel's character departed.

This is not the first time Jmmanuel's enemies have baited him in public, but their jabs are becoming more sophisticated. They first seek to discredit him among his followers, using clever tactics that doubtless have worked on other enemies.

A Critical Analysis and Evaluation

Jmmanuel is a different kind of enemy: he holds an uncommon wisdom far above these mortal enemies, whose goals include enslavement of all good people, and at all costs. Each time they attempt to disgrace him in public, Jmmanuel eloquently illuminates their sinister nature while imparting his otherworldly wisdom on his followers. While Jmmanuel does not insult his enemies, he is actively revealing their true nature to his followers.

On that same day, the Sadducees accosted Jmmanuel and asked another baited question:

"Master, Moses has said, 'When a man dies and has no children his brother shall take the widow as his wife and begot descendants for his brother.' Once there were seven brothers among us. The first one was married and died, and because he had no descendants he left his wife to his brother, and so did the second and the third, until the seventh. At last the woman also died. Now, you teach there is a renewed life. Whose wife will she be among the seven in the new life, for she was the wife to all of them?"

Each question from the Pharisees, Sadducees and Herod's people reveal further details about the true nature of these malevolent rulers. In this particular instance, they show how they covet the wives (and daughters) of any deceased brother. This common practice also extends to neighbors and strangers, where these men use any means necessary to snare their helpless prey.

In Jmmanuel's answers, too, are details of his great wisdom and nature, and they also contain subtle clues about the future. Here, he suggests that, in the future, he will be the supreme judge of all those who followed a false god and his teachings.

He also answers their question directly: "Moses never gave this commandment; but he gave the commandment that a brother should take his brother's wife to himself in honor, so if one died the other would take care of the widow of his brother."

Another interesting clue, this one about the afterlife: those who are reincarnated do not recall their past lives, unless they are prophets, i.e. those who have the wisdom of knowledge of Creation and understand its Laws.

Perhaps the most damning of all Jmmanuel's replies to his enemies:

"But, since you and the Israelite people will continue to live in piercing darkness for an extended period, cognizance and wisdom of the spirit and of the consciousness will remain hidden from you for a long time. Other people will advance beyond you and will evolve greatly in spirit and consciousness, and will follow The Laws of Creation."

This statement is not simply a reply, but a formal condemnation of the Israelites for living such a cursed life. They will suffer for "a long time." The current inhabitants of the Land of Israel must be wondering how long that will last.

Jmmanuel's enemies were now tag-teaming him: the Pharisees came back with a new round of bait, this time enquiring about which commandment is the greatest and highest of all under the "law."

"Whose law do you speak of, the law of the emperor, the law of god, or the Law of Creation?" he replied.

They said all three: Creation's, god's (surely they mean their own God, not Jmmanuel's god, it's reference in lower case), and the emperor's.

"The highest directive in the Law of Creation is this: Achieve the wisdom of knowledge, so that you may wisely follow The Laws of Creation. But the highest commandment of the law of god is this: You shall honor god as the ruler of the three human lineages and obey his laws, for he is their king of wisdom and a good and just counselor. And the highest command of the laws of the emperor is this: You shall be obedient to the emperor, follow his laws and give to him the tithe, because he is the ruler over the people and their guardian and protector."

Again, we see Jmmanuel directing all his followers to obey the various entities above them. Why should all good people worship anything or anyone? Simply because we have been directed to by a higher intelligence? What are the true motives behind demanding such blind obsequious behavior? For one, Jmmanuel states it is a means for the emperor to control his subjects.

A rule of law is indeed necessary for an organized state to exist. Mindless obedience, however, is not.

He goes on to state again that Creation is omnipotent and, therefore, timeless. And while ephemeral man-made laws exist to control people, the permanent Laws of Creation are about the Laws of life and spirit.

In the end, Jmmanuel's enemies further plan for his death, because he jeopardizes their control over the people. And the more they bait Jmmanuel, the more he defeats their puerile games and reveals their true nature to everyone in attendance. These revelations are doubtless damaging to the enemies of Jmmanuel, so his enemies act quickly to end his life.

Chapter 24: Against the Scribes and Pharisees

Jmmanuel issues his harshest rebuke of all to the scribes and Pharisees, calling them liars, cheaters, thieves, deceivers, hypocrites and swindlers who intentionally confuse their followers for their own gain.

He also speaks directly to his own disciples and followers, cautioning them not to listen to the false teachings of the scribes and Pharisees, who make false public showings to fool the people and make their followers think they are more impressive than they really are.

The scribes and Pharisees order the people to refer to them as master and teacher, but they do not yet know the wisdom of knowledge of Creation and so cannot possibly be true masters or teachers.

Jmmanuel says, "It is unwise and foolish for people to allow others to consider them greater or smaller than they really are."

The scribes and Pharisees have distorted the teachings of previous prophets, who must have come long before Jmmanuel was brought into the world to deliver his messages and sermons. Did the ruler of the three lineages of human beings on Earth send messengers like Jmmanuel to impart the wisdom of knowledge of Creation, but ultimately failed?

This appears accurate, because god then commanded the stargod Gabriel to take an Earth female and impregnate her, to produce Jmmanuel, the new messenger of god. Jmmanuel, it appears, would take up where the other messenger(s) and prophets failed because they were murdered by the descendants of the Pharisees, who then distorted their teachings and messages, and enslaved the good people for their own gain.

How many times in the distant past has god, or any extraterrestrials, come to Earth with "messages" and "teachings" for us human inhabitants? The words of Jmmanuel give a slight clue, stating, in the words of the scribes and Pharisees, 'Had we lived at the time of our forefathers and fathers, we would not have become guilty with them in the shedding of the prophets' blood.'

"Shedding of the prophets' blood."

Is this an admission that their descendants did, in fact, murder previous messengers sent by god?

Jmmanuel then answers the question: "Thus you bear witness against yourselves that you are the children of those who killed the prophets and falsified their teachings."

Of course, it also brings on another question: Who exactly were these prophets? Were they half-stargods like Jmmanuel, whose mothers were Earth humans? Were these prophets sent by god, the same leader of the extraterrestrials who sent Jmmanuel to us?

One must feel the immediate raising of goosebumps of joy and hives of anger over this conundrum, as it brings on so many new questions and thoughts about god's previous prophets and their murder by the descendants of the Pharisees.

Perhaps this is the reason the world still feels such revulsion toward modern-day Jews, who continue to distort the teachings of Jmmanuel and god, and, along with the Jesuits, further enslave good people all over the world and destroy our life, livelihood and surroundings.

Curiously, Jmmanuel's public humiliation of the scribes and Pharisees leaves room for forgiveness, as he offers them a solution to their evil ways:

"You brood of snakes and vipers, how can you aspire to be great in spirit and in consciousness when you don't possess any understanding yet?"

The word "yet" calls for some form of hope, does it not? Jmmanuel is saying to his enemies that they cannot become great in spirit and consciousness if they carry on with the ways of their forefathers. But there is hope still that the descendants of the Pharisees will change significantly, though not likely.

This passage is Jmmanuel's olive branch to his enemies:

"There will be hatred against you in this world. Even the new age will bring you neither rest nor peace until you retreat from the land you took by force, or until you make a conciliatory peace, create brotherly trust and unity with your enemies, and renounce your wrongful and stolen rights."

Jmmanuel's words become a powerful sermon and plea:

"You brood of snakes and vipers, this will happen to you into the distant future. Yet not by accident will you have a fortuitous chance in the new age when my teachings on Creation's justice and Laws will again be disseminated, so you may then seize the opportunity to end and settle the world's hatred against you by means of an honest peace. Therefore, in the new age, heed my teachings, which are truly the teachings of the Laws and directives of Creation. Pay heed when they will be taught anew, because this will be the sign of the time at which many things will change. The power of the mighty and tyrants will crumble, so that the peoples of all humankind become free."

Do we see a possible end to all the strife we currently see in our beautiful world? Is it as simple as Jmmanuel shows us in the previous passage? Moreover, would the enemies of good people all over Earth take it upon themselves to renounce the evil deeds perpetuated by their forefathers, and make peace with those they have sought to manipulate, control and ultimately enslave?

Can it really be that simple a solution?

Would Earth's enemies ever even consider Jmmanuel's "advice"?

What will be the consequences for us good people if this brood of snakes and vipers chooses not to make peace with the good people of the world?

Chapter 25: The Prophecy

Jmmanuel's impatience shows clearly in this chapter, where he prophesies a series of worldwide calamities that result from the ignorance and irrational behaviors and actions of the people.

"The Israelites have ravaged this land through plunder and murder, they have killed their friends with whom they had drunk wine, and they have deceived and misled their fellow believers of the Jewish cult, who are truly not Israelites but merely believers in a cult. Thus the Israelites betrayed their own friends and murdered them because of their greed, but it shall likewise be done to them by the rightful owners of this land whom they have deprived of their rights and subjugated since ancient times."

Is this not Jmmanuel's fiercest condemnation of the Israelites? Moreover, is he telling of future events, actions we are seeing today in the Middle East?

In no other sermons does he castigate a class of people so much and with such passion. What were the sordid actions of the Israelites that gave rise to his anger? In modern readings and teachings, we are led to believe the Israelites and their descendants are just, they are the "chosen ones" and "children of God."

The gospel according to Jmmanuel tells a quite different story, however, one that has been whitewashed by Jewish and Jesuit scribes who continue to hold that the pen is truly mightier than any sword.

The results of modern history support this sad assertion of the current powers that be.

Jmmanuel then prophesies that in "two thousand and more years" these events will transpire.

Are we not in that general period of time now? Or will we be the lucky ones, spared the upcoming "end of days" and simply be left to contend with the current powers that be?

"Soon the knowledgeable people will be consigned to misery and will be killed ... but those who persist in the truth will survive."

Jmmanuel spells a measure of hope for the believers and those who spread what they know of The Laws of Creation.

"When the people see the horror of destruction in Jerusalem, of which the prophets have spoken, the end will come . . . Soon thereafter there will be a greater grief than there has ever been since the beginning of the world, and than will ever be again."

"Since the human populations will consist of far more than ten times five hundred million people at that time, great segments of them will be eradicated and killed. This is what the law ordains, because people have violated it and will continue to violate it into the distant future."

We good people will be punished for the deeds of those who have ruled our beautiful world for thousands of years and driven it into a state of living hell. And, as Jmmanuel states clearly, most of the world's population will be eradicated.

If the world truly understood the coming destruction, how would people react? In panic? Horror? Disbelief? What will become of the reasonable law and order we see today?

"For as lightning flashes and illuminates from start to finish, so will be my coming in the future, when I will bring the teachings anew and announce the legions of the celestial sons. At that time I will have a renewed life and will again be accused of deception and blasphemy across the entire world, until the teachings of truth will bring about insight and change in the people."

Is this the "biblical coming of Christ," which has been rewritten in so many different ways to frighten the believers of the current false religions and cults?

The prophecy appears to suggest that the end of days will truly be an end of Mother Earth, the moon, and our sun, as Jmmanuel states: "The makeup of the Earth's sky and air will be disturbed, and the land will burn because of the black oil of the Earth, ignited by people's craving for power. The sky will darken because of smoke and fire, which will rage for a thousand days, and everything above the burning land and far beyond will be covered with black soot. Consequently the weather will break down, and severe cold and much death will come over the people, plants and animals, and over the Earth, as a result of the senselessly unleashed forces of the people who live in lust for power, evil passions and vices."

We do know that most large-scale geophysical forces on Earth act relatively slowly: the celestiophysical modulation of the movement of tectonic plates, which produce earthquakes, and firing of even dormant volcanoes, which can change Earth's atmospheric chemistry in a matter of days.

But the cataclysm Jmmanuel speaks of would be unprecedented, eventually leading to the total collapse of the Earth as we know it. Such ungodly forces occur over millennia. Usually. Will there be a significant celestiophysical event, the aftershocks of which mankind has never seen or dreamed of?

"Humans owe their existence to god, who is the ruler over them; so they must follow his commandments and respect him as the greatest king of wisdom. In days to come, he will send forth his guardian angels who will sound their trumpets and call together his trusted followers from the four directions, from one end of the Earth to the other.

Isn't Creation the greatest King of Wisdom, as Jmmanuel has preached to his disciples and followers?

"And that generation will not pass away until all of this has happened."

Does this passage suggest that the last generation to witness these cataclysmic events will see them to the end, then begin anew? A modern generation is typically 25 years, so that group of humans will witness the greatest upheaval in humankind's history, then serve as the builders of a new world.

"No one knows the day or hour when this will all take place, not the guardian angels nor god himself nor I, Jmmanuel; but only providence and destiny know this through the Laws and directives of Creation, which possesses the greatest wisdom."

Jmmanuel contradicts himself here, and it is disturbing: he has said before that he knows the future, but he now states he does not know when these epic events will occur. If he knows the future, as claimed, then what part of it? How far into the future can he "see"?

The following passage provides a clue about the mysterious entity that stands above Creation itself:

"Creation alone stands far above all humankind, and it alone deserves honor and praise, just as it renders honor and praise to the absolute power above it."

What is this "power" he alludes to? Does Jmmanuel even know what it is and how it acts, who controls it? Will Jmmanuel reveal anything further to Earth-based humans about the existence of it? If so, when and how? Are there currently any clues about who or what this "powers" truly is? If so, where might we discover them?

Chapter 26: Laws and Commandments

"The Laws and directives of Creation and the laws and commandments of god should be considered as the true laws and commandments and should be followed, since they alone have lasting validity and correctness. When humans deviate from these laws and directives, however, they bring forth illogical and inadequate human laws and commandments that are based on false logic and, thus, are extremely faulty."

If you read only one chapter in this book, please make it Chapter 26, Laws and Commandments.

Jmmanuel issues his wisest and most poignant observations and directives about The Laws of Creation, and hurls thunder at man-made laws, which have been created and handed down by various powers that have controlled humankind over the millennia to control humanity.

Who are the "wise" and the "foolish"?

We see them each day in all life: rules and politicians, captains of industry and commerce, leaders of our military, and our social and education programs. Who are the wise and who are the foolish in these areas that govern the rest of us?

"The wise do not moan about lost things, about the dead and about events of the past. Fools, however, cry over things that are not worth crying over, and thereby they increase their grief, privation and misery."

Those leaders who lack wisdom are considered fools by the standards issued by Jmmanuel. And those who follow them perpetuate their foolishness.

Perhaps Jmmanuel's finest gift to use all, a concept that has been suppressed by the powers that be:

"Wisdom is the greatest asset of humanity and so is the created will, which is lord over love and happiness; but all of this is meaningless without the power of the spirit."

True happiness does not come from searching for happiness itself. It is discovered as a by-product or appears as a side effect when one searches and learns wisdom from experiential experience, that is, doing something important and worthy. And when one has the power of the spirit, which we humans call passion, then one is truly on the path to attaining wisdom, implementing those experiences, and passing them on to family, friends and followers.

Jmmanuel elaborates on this concept:

"There is no eye equal to wisdom, no darkness equal to ignorance, no power equal to the power of the spirit, and no terror equal to the poverty of consciousness. There is no higher happiness than wisdom, no better friend than knowledge, and no other savior than the power of the spirit."

A man named Saul accosted Jmmanuel and said his teachings were confusing to him and, therefore, Jmmanuel himself must be confused.

Jmmanuel then castigated him and condemned him to a life of false teaching among Saul's own ignorant followers. He also renamed him Paul and chased him away with a stick.

"Just as you will bind the land of the Greeks to an evil religious cult because of your false teachings, so you will call me 'the Anointed' in their language. It will be your fault, due to your lack of understanding, that they will call me Jesus Christ, which means 'the Anointed.'"

Here, Jmmanuel places full blame on the newly named Paul for falsely calling him Jesus Christ (a future event), which is how we know Jmmanuel today.

"You, however, will be the cornerstone of the folly by which I will be called 'Jesus Christ' and the 'redeemer' for a deluded religious cult."

After Paul had departed, he then joined forces with Juda Ihariot, son of the Pharisee, and they plotted how they would capture Jmmanuel and hand him to the henchmen who would later crucify him.

Jmmanuel tells his disciples and followers:

"My betrayer will be Juda Ihariot, the son of Simeon the Pharisee, because he is interested only in gold, silver, goods and chattels. He will betray me for thirty pieces of silver, because he has been misled by his father's greed. But his joy over the pieces of silver will not last long, because his mind is fickle and unstable, and he will soon feel the guilt. Since Juda Ihariot is without courage and has little knowledge, he will put his waistband around his neck and hang himself from a branch."

So Jmmanuel foretells the suicide of Juda, and then preaches to his disciples and followers how suicide breaks The Laws of Creation:

"Regardless of how much guilt a person may incur, or how heavy their load or burden is, they nonetheless have no right to determine their own death. Although Juda Ihariot incurs great guilt, he has no right to take justice into his own hands and decide over his life and his death."

The reason Creation forbids suicide is logical and sound: it prevents a human from learning from his mistakes and becoming wise. Faults and mistakes throughout life are to be expected among humans, and this is how we learn and attain our own wisdom, which we then pass on to others.

Jmmanuel says, "But if a person escapes from guilt or a mistake by committing suicide, he flees from cognizance and responsibility and must learn to be cognizant and accountable in another life."

Here, we are given another gift from Jmmanuel, the concept of an afterlife once we have passed on from our material life on Earth. It is not a place we can get to via some a series of shortcuts, but a long and often-painful journey of human life, where we experience it in our own way en route to becoming a wise being, one who understands The Laws of Creation and the Universe.

Chapter 27: The Disciples' Agitation

The disciples grow more uneasy because of their lack of understanding of Jmmanuel's words and teachings. And with the rising agitation, Jmmanuel grows more impatient.

His disciples cry to him: "Why don't we capture Juda Ihariot and stone him, so he can't betray you?"

Jmmanuel responds in anger: "Don't you know that the law says, 'You shall not kill out of degeneration,' and don't you know what I prophesied to you, that I shall be crucified to gain a special insight?"

To what insight does Jmmanuel refer here? He gives no clues, the same tack he takes in other instances when his disciples and followers lack enough understanding of his words.

Jmmanuel then explains that each person must follow their own path of destiny, regardless of the pain, suffering and consequences. The disciples do not appreciate this concept of destiny, when they think they can simply change the course of the future by stoning Juda Ihariot to death, for example.

Jmmanuel then reveals something new:

"Truly, I say to you, if I were not to follow my destiny, how could I be in position to fulfill my mission, which will lead me to India?"

In the false bibles and "prophecies" that followed Jmmanuel's death, there is no discussion of his passage to India, only his crucifixion and death, then the "resurrection of his spirit. There are many Indian scrolls that discuss Jmmanuel's passage to India, all of which have been suppressed by one Roman power or another. For the past nearly 500 years, the Jesuits have confiscated or destroyed most if not all accounts of Jmmanuel's travels outside Israel, and have rewritten history to "show" that Jmmanuel remained in Israel and the region and did not travel elsewhere.

Again, one must wonder why Jmmanuel does not acknowledge the concept of going off-map from one's Map of Destiny. We all have a destiny that is imprinted at or near the moment of conception by the Universe. But destiny and free will are not mutually exclusive. One can exercise free will and go off-map from one's personal Map of Destiny, experience many things, then return to his prescribed destiny, which is the real governing power over humans and their actions and behaviors in life.

Jmmanuel does not do this, nor does he even acknowledge it, although it certainly does exist in the Universe. Why did he choose not to venture off-map and just kill Juda Ihariot and all Jmmanuel's other enemies? Why did he not choose to teach his disciples and followers effectively, so they could understand him and his teachings?

There is another instance in modern-day culture where this curious behavior occurs: in the realm of storytelling through film and television and books. If the protagonist actually acted smartly all the time, then there would be no conflict and, therefore, no story.

With this in mind, one must wonder if Jmmanuel is simply telling a grand story based on his epic adventure in the land among Earth humans.

"How can it still be inconceivable to you that after my departure my teachings will be adulterated by you and disseminated in all directions as erroneous teachings and erroneous religious cults?"

Again, Jmmanuel did have the option to change his behavior, but he clearly chose not to, instead opting to live out his prescribed "destiny," as directed by the prophets before him.

"Because of what you will do, the world will resound with misguidance and false teachings. Many among you will bear the blame that humanity will not recognize the truth, although I certainly have taught it to you."

Jmmanuel clearly did not do a good enough job teaching his disciples and followers, because they are still ignorant and, as he said, will betray him and his words because of their ignorance. This is perhaps the most puzzling part of Jmmanuel: why he chose to teach his disciples and followers using such limited patience and understanding. After all, he was a half-extraterrestrial, possessing powers and knowledge that far exceeded those of mere Earth humans, so why didn't he use this otherworldly power to assist humankind in understanding and appreciating his words?

It's as if Jmmanuel were wired to be a rigid and impatient teacher who spoke a sermons only once, not caring whether his pupils understood the lesson, and simply moving on to the next lesson. To all good teachers and professors in modern-day society, this shows that this magnificent half-stargod was a very poor teacher, indeed.

I cannot belabor this point: why didn't Jmmanuel take the extra time to teach his students well enough so they understood him and could pass on his knowledge to others, to spread the Gospel of Jmmanuel to the world?

The fact he did not is most puzzling and troubling, is it not?

A further example of Jmmanuel's rising impatience with his own flock: "You are struck with blindness, like the legitimate people of this land who are held in darkness and oppression by the Israelites, just as the prophets predicted for these people, because they have forsaken the tenets of truth, like the Israelites who plundered this land and since then dominated and oppressed its legitimate owners."

It begs the question: Who are the legitimate people of the land? He gives no clue, except perhaps that they occupied the land before the Israelites invaded and took power, thus enslaving the original inhabitants and their descendants.

Again, who were these original inhabitants Jmmanuel speaks of? Assyrians? Babylonians? Egyptians?

And who are Jmmanuel's forefathers, the ones he refers to as "prophets," those who came before him?

Where can the answers to these questions be found? Certainly not in modern historical texts, which have been bastardized by the powers in control at various times in history. Did Jmmanuel or his people leave any clues whatsoever for us to uncover, other than his 36 sermons described in this book?

Jmmanuel's farewell revelation is lost in his harsh criticism of his disciples and followers:

"I have fulfilled my mission among this race. But, due to the fault of the Israelites and their false teachings, I was unable to teach any reason to this population, as their thinking is irrational because of confusing and mistaken teachings. I will leave, therefore, so that the teachings of truth can also be brought to two other populations in the North and East. Just as the legitimate owners of the land, who are governed by the violent rule of the Israelites, exist under the guidance of god, so also are the other two peoples under him. They are the people in the high north land where cold and ice cover the highest mountains and at the end of the Earth, and also the people in the land of India, because he, god, is the master over these three human populations."

The original inhabitants of the Land of Israel existed under the "guidance of god," but it is not mentioned specifically what this guidance is or who imparted it to them. Was it the prophets, i.e. extraterrestrials, who preceded Jmmanuel?

His statements encourage further questions: when he travels to the other two lineages, will he take the same half-baked approach to teaching them, as well? And then blame his ignorant flock for not understanding his words and teachings? If not, how will events be different? Will he be more successful in instructing his new disciples and followers?

The answers may never be known.

We are left only with his generalization:

"Therefore, I must walk on my path as predestined by Arahat Athersata and requested by god, since I also serve god's will and his laws, as god himself serves The Laws of Creation."

Bethany would be Jmmanuel's next sojourn, where he visited the house of Simon, a leper. Inside, a woman pours water on Jmmanuel's head and draws the ire of his disciples, who criticize her for wasting a valuable resource.

Jmmanuel scolds them by saying the old woman is right to have done this, because it shows that even though the water is valuable, she is willing to part with it to show her appreciation for Jmmanuel and his teachings. He then explains that her small act will be told throughout the world, even when the ignorant masses are betraying Jmmanuel's teachings.

While they are in the house, he tells them of Juda Ihariot's plot to hand him over to the chief priests in Jerusalem, who seek to murder him. His people do not believe him so he scolds them again.

"As Juda Ihariot, the son of the Pharisee, will turn me over to the henchmen, my disciple Judas Ish-Keriot will be considered the traitor."

The two disciples' names are so similar that people will be told by the chief priests that the scapegoat Judas is the true traitor to Jmmanuel, even though it is clearly Juda Ihariot.

Perhaps the most famous and memorable passage is The Last Supper, held in the house of Aaron, where Jmmanuel tells his disciples that he soon must leave them for good.

Jmmanuel took the bread, broke it and gave it to the disciples, saying, "Take it and eat; the body requires nourishment even in times of distress and grief." And he took his cup, gave it to them and said, "Drink from this cup, all of you; the throat becomes thirsty even on a rainy and cold day."

Oh, how this differs from the passages we read in the heavily edited, modern-day bibles.

His disciples were incredulous when hearing how they would soon pass on false teachings to their own students and followers, and even more so when Jmmanuel told them he would see them again after his near-death.

What is still puzzling about Jmmanuel's behavior is his seemingly being so arrogant and impatient. But, when one considers this is the stereotypical behavior of certain classes of extraterrestrials who see mankind as a very low life form, his attitude toward his disciples and followers is perhaps not out of line. Still, why did they choose such a poor tack of impatient teaching, one they knew would bring heartache and sorrow to the masses? It is now clear that it was planned in advance by the extraterrestrial prophets, but to what end? So people all over could learn these lessons painfully, which would leave a more-lasting impression on society? Their plan appears to have backfired.

Chapter 28: In Gethsemane

After leaving the house of Aaron, Jmmanuel and his disciples travel to Gethsemane (Latin for "olive press"), where the half-man, half-stargod is placed under tremendous life-death stress.

His truly human side then shows itself: he becomes anxious and fearful at the thought of fulfilling his destiny:

"My mind is deathly grieved. Remain here, therefore, and watch with me, so I will not feel so alone. It is easier to bear an adversity with one or two others at one's side than by oneself."

Jmmanuel's friend and disciple Judas Ish-Keriot told him he saw "veiled lights" near the city walls.

Jmmanuel said, "They may be the henchmen Juda Ihariot is bringing, because he has secretly followed us here to betray me." Returning to his disciples, he found them sleeping and so he said to Peter, "Can you not watch with me for one hour, so I'm not left alone in my difficult hour? Be awake and great in spirit and in consciousness so you will not fall prey to temptation: The spirit is willing but the flesh is weak!"

Is this a breakdown? If so, why did he share his thoughts with one of his disciples, whom he clearly saw as inferior? Jmmanuel begins to pace about, lie down for a time, then pace some more. Clearly he is anxious and wishes to share his thoughts, and even asks the other disciples to join him, to share in his misery. Such selfishness is evident when we consider that Jmmanuel was so impatient when teaching his disciples and followers.

It is often difficult, if not impossible, to witness one of our leaders and mentors in the midst of a moment of weakness, let alone a full-blown anxiety attack. How did his people see him in that moment? Had they lost any measure of faith in Jmmanuel because he appeared weak?

We are taught by BigMedia that this form of behavior is a sign of weakness. While it may be seen as weakness in the eyes of society as a whole, sharing one's pain and grief and asking for help is a sign of wisdom to those of us who have experienced and shared it with others.

I doubt Jmmanuel's disciples took his behavior for wisdom. They were doubtless frightened and confused.

Just as Jmmanuel had foreseen, Juda Ihariot, the son of the Pharisee, and a large group of chief priests and elders of the people arrived, bearing swords and long wooden poles.

Juda Ihariot had given them a sign, saying, "Behold, I will flatter him and mislead him into thinking I repent the sins of my life. As a sign of the false flattery, there shall be a kiss. And behold, whoever I kiss, he is the one; seize him."

In that unfortunate moment, Juda Ihariot gave Jmmanuel the kiss of betrayal, which would forever be known—inaccurately—as the "Judas Kiss."

In a surprise move, Jmmanuel asks Juda: "My friend, why have you come to lie to me when betrayal burns in your mind and in your actions?"

The henchmen then arrested Jmmanuel but, in a change of heart, one of them drew his sword and sliced off the ear of the servant of a chief priest.

Jmmanuel said to the man, "Put back your sword into its sheath, because anyone taking a sword without being in danger will perish by the sword. Or do you think that I could not have fled before your group arrived? But how could I fulfill my destiny had I done so?"

The thoroughly confused henchman broke down in tears and fled the house, but those remaining stayed their course. Jmmanuel argues with them about why they chose to avoid capturing him in daylight where everyone could witness the spectacle, calling them hypocrites and saying, "Truly, I say to you, darkness will become light, and everyone will speak of your deed for which you will be denounced for all time to come."

After further arguing, Jmmanuel states, "Truly, I say to you, for a long time you may succeed in accusing Judas Ish-Keriot as my betrayer before the people, but the truth will come out and be known by all people throughout the entire world, namely, that my betrayer is not Judas Ish-Keriot but is your son, Juda Ihariot, who bears the name of his father, the Pharisee."

In that heated moment, the Pharisee Simeon Ihariot punched Jmmanuel in the face, and Jmmanuel's disciples, now fearing for their own lives, turned away and fled.

Jmmanuel was then taken to the Pharisee high priest Caiaphas who, along with other members of the high council, were preparing to pass judgment on Jmmanuel Sananda.

At the trial, Caiaphas is unsuccessful in finding anyone who will give false testimony about the prisoner. The only item said was that Jmmanuel was begotten by the guardian angel Gabriel.

After considering all testimony, Caiaphas then asks Jmmanuel to respond to the statement about his being the son of Gabriel, and he refuses. After Caiaphas yells at him, Jmmanuel then gives the "court" a lesson in extraterrestrial history, including the revelation: "... god and his celestial sons are other human lineages who have come from the stars out of the depths of space in their machines of metal."

How could Caiaphas possibly have responded to this? True to his character, he yelled, "He has blasphemed God, the Creator. Why should we need further testimony against him? Behold, now you have heard his blasphemy for yourselves. What punishment do you think he deserves?"

They all responded, "He deserves death," and began beating Jmmanuel relentlessly.

At this point, how could this half-extraterrestrial not fight back against such lowly humans? His Map of Destiny preordained otherwise, but the option to fight back still remained. Is it not puzzling? If Jmmanuel had fought back, the story would have ended there we humans would not have learned the mandatory lessons brought to Earth by Jmmanuel.

During Jmmanuel's ordeal, one of his disciples, Peter, attempted to flee the scene, but was called out by a maid who asked him, "Aren't you one of the disciples of this Jmmanuel from Galilee?"

Peter strenuously denied the allegation, even after someone else accused him of speaking like Jmmanuel. Feeling he had no other recourse, Peter began to castigate Jmmanuel: "I don't know this crazy person or his blasphemous teachings of God!"

But soon thereafter a rooster crowed three times and Peter thought of Jmmanuel's previous statement that Peter would betray him. With that, Peter fled the house in tears, his own betrayal following him like an evil shadow.

Chapter 29: The Suicide of Juda Ihariot

One of the greatest lies told by the Pharisees, Sadducees and their Roman conquerors was that Jmmanuel was betrayed by his own disciple, Judas Ish-Keriot, when, in fact, his betrayer was the spy, Juda Ihariot, son of a Pharisee.

Upon witnessing Jmmanuel's torture, Juda became filled with guilt. So much so that he visited the chief priests and elders, and threw his bag of silver on the floor at their feet, proclaiming, "I repent that I have betrayed innocent blood, because his teachings do not seem evil to me."

The priests and elders were unmoved, asking how his words affected them.

Juda said, "Behold, it is up to you what you want to do, to live in peace with yourselves."

Soon after, Juda fled to the potter's field beyond the walls of the city, and hanged himself from a tree.

Thereupon Caiaphas, the high priest, said, "Well then, give this blood money to the potter and buy his field with it for the burial of strangers."

Immediately, the chief priests and elders of the council circulated a rumor that Jmmanuel's betrayer was his own disciple, Judas Ish-Keriot, and he was buried in the potter's field. Word of mouth soon took over and disseminated the story to everyone in the city.

Of course, this story was false:

Judas was not the betrayer of Jmmanuel, as modern history tells us. Judas is the man who studied the words and sermons of Jmmanuel and transcribed them to scrolls that were later discovered outside Jerusalem in 1963 by Markus-Isa Rashid and Eduard Albert Meier; the former, translated them from Aramaic to German between 1963 and 1970.

Following the suicide of Juda Ihariot in the potter's field, Jmmanuel was brought in front of Governor Pilate, who demanded to learn of Jmmanuel's background.

Jmmanuel gave little:

"Behold, eons ago, I returned from the realm of a higher world to fulfill a difficult task; and now I was begotten by a celestial son to be a prophet in this life. This came to pass, according to destiny and the desire of god, the ruler over the three lineages of terrestrial humans procreated by him.

"Through his kindness, I have added to my knowledge in this incarnation by gaining great insight and learning true wisdom, which was imparted to me by his teachers over a period of forty days and forty nights.

"Furthermore, I have traveled extensively to faraway places and lived for many years in the land of India. There I was taught much knowledge and many secrets by the great wise and knowledgeable men who are known as masters.

"When I have fulfilled my mission here, I will return there with Thomas, my brother, who is a faithful disciple of mine."

Pilate asked if Jmmanuel wished to justify himself and, without showing disrespect toward the governor and his people, Jmmanuel issued a thinly veiled slight, telling all that "It is also customary among humans that the most righteous person does not find justice, because it doesn't matter whether many or few testify against him, as long as they are highly regarded."

During the Passover feast, Governor Pilate asked the people which of the two prisoners should be released to them, Barabbas the criminal, or Jmmanuel who is said to be a King of Wisdom and the son of an angel?

The people voted that Barabbas should be released ... and Jmmanuel crucified.

The chief priests and elders sat proudly, knowing their machinations against Jmmanuel had worked as planned.

Was this "plan" of theirs really their own, or was it Jmmanuel's all along? After all, Jmmanuel had been manipulating all humans in his path since his arrival as a prophet of stargods to Mother Earth.

Chapter 30: Defamation of Jmmanuel

Jmmanuel was dragged into the courthouse by the Roman soldiers, and the entire boisterous crowd followed. He was stripped bare, then a purple shawl was draped over him, and he was fitted with a crown of thorns.

The crowd beat and spat on him until he was barely conscious, then the high priest Caiaphas asked Jmmanuel: "How are you doing now, great King of Wisdom?"

After more beatings, Jmmanuel then spoke a prophecy:

"And the time will come in five times a hundred years when you will have to atone for this, when the legitimate owners of the land, whom you have enslaved and deprived of their rights, will begin to rise up against you and fight against you into the distant future."

Jmmanuel introduced the prophet Mohammed to the Pharisees, scribes, priests and Roman soldiers, telling them all that this great and powerful prophet will start a new religion that will soon be bastardized and turned into a cult. He also foretold of a great and long-lasting battle between the true holders of the Land of Israel, the predecessors of Mohammed, and the Israelites, and that the true and legitimate owners of the land will persecute the Israelites well into the future.

We are seeing this epic battle play out in the Middle East and in America: so-called Christians and Jews vs. Muslims. Jmmanuel foretold of this battle and also how it ended: the defeat of the Israelites.

How will this defeat play out in the modern world? Will Israel fall? What will happen here in America? How will Mohammed's followers follow the prophecy of Jmmanuel? Are we seeing the worst of this ongoing crises or is more hell to come, and when?

Most likely, we are seeing only the beginning....

Jmmanuel was again beaten, stripped bare, dressed only in undergarments, and forced to carry a heavy wooden cross on his right shoulder. He had walked only so far when he collapsed and was aided by a stranger, Simon of Cyrene, who was then forced him to help carry the cross all the way to the place they called Golgotha.

This was, indeed a first, because instead of typing Jmmanuel to the cross, they nailed his hands and feet to it and hoisted it high, placing two murderers on opposite sides of him. The problem with this scenario is that a man of about 150 lbs., whose hands are nailed to a similar cross that is then raised vertically, will collapse because the weak tendons and flesh of his hands cannot hold his weight. To be properly secured, the nails much be driven between the bones of his wrists, just above his hand.

Jmmanuel was repeatedly mocked: "Since you are a King of Wisdom, get down from the cross and help yourself."

But he fell silent, only later begging for something to drink. His request was rebuffed by the crowd.

Following a thunderstorm, Jmmanuel fell into a deep stupor and was pronounced dead by a Roman soldier, after he had stabbed Jmmanuel in the loin and witnessed no reaction or movement.

This was Jmmanuel's and his closest followers' plan all along.

The next phase of the escape plan involved moving his body from the cross, covering him in a special linen cloth, then transporting him to a special tomb outside Jerusalem. The tomb had extra hidden entrances and exits known only to Jmmanuel's followers, including Joseph.

Now safely ensconced in the tomb, Jmmanuel rested and healed in relative peace, while Joseph set out to find Jmmanuel's friends from India. Were these friends already in the Land of Israel, and had they witnessed Jmmanuel's crucifixion? If not, were they actually in northern India, where Jmmanuel had lived and worked before coming to the Land of Israel? There is no documentation of Jmmanuel's friends from India having been present at his crucifixion, therefore, it is possible that they were in fact in Northern India.

Joseph's flight to India by Joseph of Arimathea. In sermons about Joseph of Arimathea's flight to India, we are given no evidence for how Joseph traveled to and from India, nor how long the journey actually took. But anecdotal evidence from other sources suggest that he was escorted to India by extraterrestrials in one of their spaceships. Since Joseph's journey took place over a short time, this hypothesis is the most compelling. Had he journeyed by foot or donkey, it would have taken him over 2,500 miles of hazardous terrain, two-thirds of which were mountainous, and doubtless under unpleasant weather conditions.

Joseph's flight via extraterrestrial craft suggests, too, that Jmmanuel's extraterrestrial leaders and handlers may have been present during his ordeals to ensure that Jmmanuel fulfilled his destiny and that no one interfered with it. After all, Jmmanuel was half-human and, therefore, subject to a weak mind when under severe stress and pressure, not to mention imminent death.

On the third day following Jmmanuel's crucifixion, he was well enough to walk....

Chapter 31: Jmmanuel's Flight From the Tomb

Jmmanuel had prophesied that, after three days and nights, he would return from his near-death experience, and he was accurate: he was up and about when dawn broke on the first day of the week after Passover.

In that moment, an extraterrestrial spacecraft appeared as a brilliant flash of light and landed, and an extraterrestrial being stepped from the aircraft and came out of the brilliant light. The being was bathed in light and his clothing was pure white.

As he approached Jmmanuel's tomb, he held out his hand and shot the soldiers with an incapacitating beam of light. Rolling the stone out of the way, he spoke to Mary and Mary Magdalene:

"Don't be afraid. I know you seek Jmmanuel, the crucified. He is not here, for he is alive just as he said he would be. Come here and behold the place where he has lain. Go quickly and tell his disciples that he has risen from near-death. Also tell them: He will walk before you to Galilee, and there you will see him. Behold, I have told you."

Mary questioned him about how Jmmanuel, who was pronounced dead, could now be alive, and she was rebuked by the being, who told her again to tell Jmmanuel's followers. A moment later, the being stepped back into the light and into his craft, and departed with a thunderous boom.

These are the words we have been waiting for: a suggestion that the extraterrestrials were in fact present at some time before, during and at least after the near-death of Jmmanuel. Sound logic suggests they had been present all along, ensuring that Jmmanuel's destiny was carried out as ordained by god, the creator and leader of the three human lineages on Mother Earth.

Extraterrestrials not only existed during the time of Jmmanuel, but they influenced and guided events surrounding some of Jmmanuel's actions and the events he himself initiated and/or influenced. Moreover, none of these events involving extraterrestrials made it into subsequent writings, including those of various bibles throughout the world.

When the Roman soldiers recovered, they met with the chief priests and elders of the council, who paid them off, spun a quite different version of events, and told the soldiers:

"Tell the people the King of Wisdom's disciples came at night while we were sleeping and stole his body."

As Mary and Mary Magdalene journeyed to Galilee, an extraterrestrial being accosted them and said, "Remember what you have been instructed to do. Be careful and do not inadvertently tell the people."

When Mary Magdalene reached out and tried to touch the being, he said, "Do not touch me, because I am of a different kind from you, and my garment is a protection against this world. If you touch me, you will die and be consumed by fire. Step back from me and be on your way, as you have been instructed."

Yet another dot of circumstantial evidence that the being was an extraterrestrial: his biology was different enough from ours so that he could not withstand the various atmospheric (or some kind of physical) effects, and had to wear a special protective suit.

The so-called Shroud of Turin may not be fiction after all. According to the events described in Jmmanuel's sermons, Peter and another of Jmmanuel's disciples went to his tomb and saw the linen body cloth and Jmmanuel's sweat cloth, which covered his head, both lying neatly in a pile on the ground, along with some very peculiar objects that Peter had never before seen or heard of. Some were described as clay figurines.

What were they? Did they depict extraterrestrials or their spacecraft? Similar figurines have since been discovered in South America and India, although they were made of gold.

That same evening, Jmmanuel's disciples were in a room, discussing the events of the day, when a stranger appeared and said, "Peace be with you."

It wasn't until he showed them his wounds that they recognized Jmmanuel. But Thomas was incredulous, so he said, "If I could touch your wounds, I would know that you are not a ghost."

Jmmanuel scolded Thomas by calling him "you of small minds," then ordered his disciples to guard the secret of his return so the people would not know he is alive. Only Jmmanuel's supporters were permitted to learn of his return from his near-death experience.

On the road to Galilee the next day, a group of followers were joined by a man they did not know. Spoke of how Jmmanuel had died on the cross, when Jmmanuel asked them why they were mourning. He is rather dramatic in his entrances, Jmmanuel, and the effect is strong and positive: the people react to him with great surprise, which creates an infectious energy that soon spreads among the crowd.

Does he do this for some other effect or to create this new energy?

Later on, Jmmanuel saw some of his followers on the banks of the Sea of Tiberias (Galilee), and asked for something to eat. When they lamented over not having caught anything, Jmmanuel told them, "Throw the net out to the right side of the boat, and you will have a large catch."

Moments later, they hauled in a great catch and feasted. During the meal, Jmmanuel broke the news that their time together will soon be at an end.

Drama seems to be a great part of Jmmanuel's character. Was he actually like this or was it carefully scripted by those who took down his sermons? Has any of his story been exaggerated by his scribes? This question could have been asked hundreds of times before.

The results suggest this: Jmmanuel performed certain actions for dramatic effect, because the lesson was forever emblazoned into the hearts and minds of his disciples and followers. Had he simply spoken softly his thoughts and ideas, the effect may have been lukewarm and not produced a lasting memory. High drama is often used by great orators to burn their words into firm memories of those who witness their speeches. Jmmanuel appears no different in his encounters with people.

One still must wonder why he spoke so little of his extraterrestrial family and friends, mentors and teachers. They would of course be of great interest to all human beings on Mother Earth. Was he withholding for a reason or was his method of storytelling simply rather mundane?

This notion contradicts his being dramatic, so we still must question why he didn't tell more in-depth stories about the extraterrestrials. It is possible he was not permitted to do so.

And, even though this entire tale is the grandest of all tales in human history, it is also possible that these stories are purely fiction....

But this is not likely, as there are too many events and points in the historical record that have been corroborated over 2,000 years.

Chapter 32: Jmmanuel's Farewell

Jmmanuel's most difficult yet exciting sojourn came at the end of his travels in the Middle East. He finally met with his followers at the specified mountainous area, where he broke his news:

"Behold, I will speak to you one last time, then I will leave and never return. My path leads me to the land of India where many of this human lineage also dwell, because they have left this land to live there. My mission leads me to them and to the human population that is born there. My path there will be long, for I have yet to bring my teachings, new and old, to many countries, and likewise to the shores of the great black waters to the north of here."

Did he travel by foot, donkey or spacecraft? Given he openly traveled in an extraterrestrial craft earlier, would it not make logical sense to travel to India in the same manner? He stated that he needed to speak with other followers along the way, but he still could have traveled smartly via spacecraft.

Jmmanuel has revealed his journeys via these extraterrestrial craft, so why doesn't he discuss these spacecraft in detail? Maybe just a few clues about their physical makeup, how they operate, where they travel to, who operates them and how, etc.

Jmmanuel's shares so little about his extraterrestrial family that it makes one wonder if this story is true at all. After more than 30 chapters of sermons, one might begin to question this man's integrity and logic, and the veracity of his story.

Throughout the sermons, Jmmanuel speaks of The Laws of Creation, but never once gives even a clue what those Laws really are. Should we infer them from his preaching, his sermons and parables? If so, how do we know if we're accurate? It is disturbing that the Laws are not explicitly presented to the audience.

His sermon was perhaps his longest and most profound, yet it revealed so little. For example, what did he truly mean when he stated, "No greater darkness rules within humans than ignorance and lack of wisdom. Greatness of personal victory requires uprooting and destroying all influences that oppose the Creational force, so that which is Creational may prevail. Humans should develop within themselves the power to judge over good and evil and to correctly perceive all things, so that they may be wise and fair and follow the Laws. It is necessary to be cognizant of what is real and what is unreal, what is valuable and what is worthless, and what is of Creation and what is not."

Such beautiful words, yet so enigmatic and distant, full of riddles and mysteries. How should one decipher and interpret such sentiments?

The most important question still remains: What are The Laws of Creation?

It is quite maddening to read such wisdom, yet lack the power to understand it in its intended spirit.

Jmmanuel said, "Humans gain experience in the use of their powers and capabilities only by trying daily to unlock them.

Fine. I personally would love to understand my powers and exercise them every day, become stronger and wiser and more fluent in my new-found wisdom. But even I beg Jmmanuel for further insight here, so that I may fully comprehend his wisdom. In this moment, I feel at a loss to explain exactly what he meant by his teachings in this chapter. They simply are too vague and leave too much to inaccurate interpretation. Jmmanuel castigated humans for being inaccurate in how they interpreted his words.

How can we possibly overcome such a scolding without proper guidance from the storyteller himself?

He cautions his followers: "As long as human beings do not become one with Creation, they will never be able to rise above death or near-death, since the fear of the unknown is within them."

Was this fear programmed into our DNA by Jmmanuel's genetic engineers, i.e. those extraterrestrials who designed and built us humans?

Jmmanuel tells us, "Instead of following instinctive and impulsive urges, humans should live by cognition and wisdom, so that they may live justly according to the Laws and directives."

Unfortunately, he seems to forget it was his mentors who programmed us to begin with, so why didn't they simply add a few lines of code to effect this desired outcome?

Is this also another way of saying that it's okay to go off-map and not necessarily follow one's Map of Destiny? He seems to be giving us humans permission to do so.

As we follow our own path, we will be guided by lights. What are those lights exactly? Is it a literal reference to lights or is it a metaphor for something of little weight, i.e. "light"? The connotation strongly suggests some sort of bright light that follows us as we traverse our Map of Destiny, but the true interpretation eludes us, like most of his other words, parables and teachings.

As if the previous rules and laws weren't enough, we are now encouraged to strive for perfection. Perhaps this is more easily interpreted than other passages, as it may mean that we must get better at everything we do and never stop trying to become better. As we move along, we learn countless lessons that we share with others. And as we share more and more, we learn even greater hidden truths from those very lessons.

Jmmanuel says, "There may be no limits to love, peace and joy, because the present state must always be exceeded. Truly, I say to you, a love that is unlimited, constant and unfailing is unconditional and is a pure love, in whose fire all that is impure and evil will burn. Such a love is Creation's love and, therefore, its Laws as well, to which humanity has been predestined to follow since the beginning of time."

In the end, humans must follow their own Map of Destiny, according to Jmmanuel:

"Since this is the ultimate destination for human beings, they must take steps to guarantee that this will come to be, for this is their destiny."

What happens when we are forced off our Map of Destiny by an evil wind? Jmmanuel tells us that it is because we do not understand the wisdom of Mother Earth, but this is inaccurate. He discounts the role of the Jesuits and their handlers in humans falling off their prescribed maps.

What's most exciting is that he tells us that, "in two times a thousand years they shall be taught anew without falsification, when humans become sensible and knowledgeable, and a new age heralds great upheavals. And it can be read in the stars (via celestiophysics) that the people of the new age will be great revolutionaries. Thus, some special predestined people, who will be the new proclaimers of my teachings, will preach them unfalsified and with great courage."

One must wonder who these revolutionaries are or will be. Is there any indication one or more of them are here among us now?

Answers will doubtless include Mandela and Ghandi, but we must remember that both men were controlled by the Jesuits and were given strict marching orders that resulted in further control of large populations of people. Mandela and Ghandi were traitors to us all, but they served their masters, the Jesuits, quite well.

What Jmmanuel states is someone far different than the vegetative beings the Jesuits have propped up to be our "leaders." When one shows up, we will know it, because the Jesuits and their minions will try to silence him (or her), discredit him, and when they fail, ultimately murder him to prevent any revolution that they cannot control completely.

The Jesuits murdered half a dozen US presidents, including Abraham Lincoln, and countless other government and civilian leaders over the past nearly 500 years. Their history of regicide, homicide, rape, pillage and plunder is legendary.

Jmmanuel warns us many times to beware of false teachings, which have been all around us for more than 2,000 years. Is it our lack of judgment that has emplaced these powers? Certainly not. They were forced upon us from the beginning, then advertised and marketed as being good for all, therefore, we must support and, in some countries, worship them.

During his final sermon, a great extraterrestrial spacecraft landed and Jmmanuel boarded. Suddenly, the craft was engulfed in a lenticular cloud. Soon after, a great flash of light and thunderous roar spread over them, and the spacecraft ascended and it was gone.

Soon, Jmmanuel's disciples returned to Jerusalem and started spreading the news to all his followers.

Chapter 33: Jmmanuel in Damascus

So, one mystery is solved: Jmmanuel did in fact fly to Syria in an extraterrestrial spacecraft, as stated here in this chapter. He lived in Syria for two years without anyone knowing who he was.

Did he pilot his own craft or did his extraterrestrial mentors provide him a limousine, equipped with pilot and security and entourage? It is likely that, since he traveled by spacecraft parts of the way, he had a protection detail to ensure his security and success.

Today, we see a similar type of behavior in all our leaders and those who would provide the distractions of entertainment so we do not question authority.

At the end of his stay there, Jmmanuel sent a messenger to Galilee, to find his brother Thomas and Judas Ish-Keriot, his dear disciple. Unfortunately, when they arrived two months later, they told Jmmanuel of a man who was blaspheming Jmmanuel and his teachings. Worse, the chief priests and elders were also punishing Jmmanuel's followers.

Why didn't Jmmanuel's disciples and followers rise up against the chief priests and elders? Why didn't they form a band of brothers and sisters that could effectively challenge the Pharisees and Sadducees and their descendants? Didn't Jmmanuel teach them how to protect themselves?

When Jmmanuel heard of Saul's persecution, he said, "Don't be afraid, the time will soon come when Saul will receive a lesson about his evil thinking."

He armed up with a special concoction given to him by a trusted friend, and lay in wait just outside Damascus for Saul and his men. When they appeared, Jmmanuel lit his concoction, which burned brightly and threw off multi-colored flashes that blinded the men. Fireballs shot off Jmmanuel's weapon and created thunderous booms and hissing sounds that frightened everyone.

Jmmanuel then scolds Saul about persecuting him in absentia, and orders him to return to Damascus, where he will learn a new way of life from one of Jmmanuel's disciples.

On the road to India, Jmmanuel began preaching again and felt a new strength and power not seen or felt before. Was this the beginning of his transition to a higher plane, as foretold in his prophecy? Clearly, he feels new powers and wishes to exercise them. What other powers will soon come to Jmmanuel and how will he use them? Will he again be hamstrung and unable to help his human subjects beyond his meager teachings?

While he sets off on roads, preaching his sermons, we do know that he also travels by extraterrestrial spacecraft at times. This is a revelation in that we do not see these stories in any modern-day bibles or religious teachings. There are no references to extraterrestrials in any modern bibles. History has effectively been rewritten by those who control the victors of wars, battles and conflicts.

The Jesuits certainly have been the most prolific ghostwriters in modern history and have created a dramatic fiction that most of us have swallowed hook, line and sinker.

Well, most of us. . . .

Chapter 34: Teaching About Creation

During Jmmanuel's transition to a higher plane, he began speaking about The Laws of Creation, which themselves are a true living spirit that continually strives to improve itself.

When a new spirit enters the body of human being, it is ignorant in the ways of humans, and lacks sufficient experiential experience, knowledge and wisdom. Its purpose is to learn by doing and become better through practice and further learning and ultimately teaching and mentoring to others. When the spirit moves on after the death of a human, it retains its new-found knowledge and wisdom, and perfects them even further in its next life inside that new human being.

As Jmmanuel says, "Thus, the human spirit perfects itself so extensively that it unfolds in a Creational manner and ultimately becomes one with Creation, as it was destined from the earliest beginning . . . Truly, I say to you, the time will never come when Creation ceases to create new spirit forms and to broaden itself."

Jmmanuel then begins to explain the seven levels of Creation, from highest to lowest Absoluta. These are quite confusing because there is no definition of each, nor is there a clear explanation of The Laws of Creation.

We are left wondering several things:

1. What are the actual Laws of Creation, so that we may learn, understand and follow them?

2. What are these arcane terms and definitions that, we are told, define who and what we are in the Universe?

3. Since the Laws are never clearly stated, where do we find them

and how do we apply them in our simple human lives?

4. Are we to be left with metaphors and parables, which we must interpret on our own, leaving much room for misinterpretation and misapplication, not to mention never reaching that desired and covetous state of wisdom?

5. Who among us will explain these things to us ignorant humans?

Nonetheless, here are the seven levels of Creation, 1 being the highest:

1. Being Absolutum
2. Zohar Absolutum
3. Super Absolutum
4. Creative Absolutum
5. Central Absolutum
6. Ur [primal; original, prime] Absolutum
7. Absolute Absolutum

We are told in this chapter that when we reach "perfection," we will understand these arcane matters. Until then, how are we to conduct ourselves? There is no road map for this, let alone to achieve success, according to Jmmanuel and The Laws of Creation.

Creation, we are told, runs in cycles of seven, when it alternates between creating and "slumbering." Do these cycles follow well-defined celestiophysical events? If so, then we can discover and study them, and ultimately predict their occurrence in the future. Since The Laws of Creation are an intimate part of the Universe, it is highly likely that they follow the physical laws of celestiophysics and run and flow in definite cycles that can be measured.

During certain periods, Creation is the only thing in existence, and humans and all life forms cease to exist. We are not in one of those periods now, but it would be wise to know when it will commence. Hundreds, thousands or millions of years from now? What will be the harbingers? How will we prepare for the "end of times" when living things cease to be?

Jmmanuel tells his followers that Creation is one body and all in it are one with each other and with Creation. This is in keeping with there not being any vacuum in space, but a continuous and seamless liquid (sliq) of some form of matter, perhaps quantoretta, that permeates the entire Universe. Quantoretta are the smallest known unit of matter in the Universe and have no defined boundaries. There are no gaps between individual quantoretta, only a seamless flow of matter and energy that permeates every part of the Universe.

This explains how Earth-based physics and all sciences are dumbed-down and inaccurate, to say the least.

"When a wise man says there are always two of everything, he means that they are one within themselves and one together. It is only two in appearance, because in itself and also together it is always one. Therefore evil is one in itself because it is also good in itself. Likewise, good is one in itself because it is just as much evil in itself.

Perhaps this is the greatest Law of Creation, that everything is one with everything else.

And when you see two or three of something, it is actually only one and the same thing, with all items coexisting within one entity.

Within the human body, there are two parts: the spirit and the body. And the spirit is comprised of wisdom and power. Thus, within each of us there is wisdom and power, but we do not yet know how to tap into it. We live according to a Map of Destiny that tells us where to go, how to live, and with whom.

But ultimately we ourselves define who and what we are and will become, and along our journey we discover new knowledge and wisdom, and share our lessons learned with others, and in turn learn new things that create an even larger and more expansive wisdom.

The take-home message is that, according to The Laws of Creation, we have everything inside us right now. Through false teachings and cults, we have been taught otherwise.

The time has come for all humans to wake up and realize this important Law of Creation: everything we need to know and learn about Creation is deep inside us, whether buried with our DNA or ancient reptilian brainstem or inside each of our bones. We have all the tools necessary to perfect ourselves and become one with Creation and the entire Universe, because we are intimately connected to both all the time and in every way.

As Jmmanuel says, "So when the scribes teach that a person lives in a trinity, this teaching is erroneous and falsified, because it is not taught in accordance with The Laws of Creation."

Chapter 35: Cults Around Jmmanuel

After his crucifixion and subsequent rising, Jmmanuel began his transition to the higher spiritual plane, which gave him new special powers and greater wisdom. But he was still half-human, which made him vulnerable in mind and body.

When he and his mother Mary and brother Thomas traveled northwest, they met quite different races of people who were hostile toward them, so Jmmanuel disguised himself and stopped his preaching for some time.

In the far western seaside town of Ephesus, which is now Turkey, Jmmanuel was recognized by a man who reported his presence to a secret society, The Association of Essenes, which purported to be followers of Jmmanuel. He agreed to attend one of their meetings, where they invited him to become a member and to teach them his extraterrestrial knowledge and wisdom.

Jmmanuel politely said, "Even if I were to teach you my knowledge, it would not agree with your teachings, because you follow incomplete human wisdom, whereas I adhere to spiritual wisdom. Therefore, I think that our different teachings would be incompatible with each other. It is also not my inclination to spread my knowledge and teachings in secret, as you do, since your secret Association of Essenes is unauthorized. But let me think over the pros and cons for three days, and whether I will then tell you 'yes' or 'no', because I must first think about everything before I give you my last word on it."

Instead of thinking about it for three days, Jmmanuel and his entourage fled the city. His concern was that the Essenes would use his name and claim that Jmmanuel was one of theirs, and they would use this false information to gather followers and enslave them via

A Critical Analysis and Evaluation

their false and distorted teachings.

We see this as an example of exactly what has occurred over the past 2,000 years, with the rise of hundreds of religions and cults that have hijacked the good name of Jmmanuel to further their own causes. These false religions and cults always spread half-truths so the people will be attracted to them, but they also spread lies and deceit, which are cleverly mixed with small truths.

Jmmanuel tells us that it will be 2,000 years before these false religions and cults will reach their peak, and then they will be destroyed. Are we in this period of history now? What will become of Catholicism and Protestantism? Of Islam and Judaism? And all other false religions and cults? When will Jmmanuel return to us, as he promised more than 2,000 years ago? Did he mean he himself would return, or did he suggest that another stargod like himself would come to Mother Earth?

The more Jmmanuel reveals, the more questions he leaves us. But he did leave us one important clue, which was revealed in the chapter on The Laws of Creation:

"But the truth lies deep within The Laws of Creation, and there alone should humankind seek and find it. Those who seek shall not stop seeking until they find, and when they find, they will be profoundly shocked and astonished, but then they will rule over the Universe. May humans recognize from this that the kingdom is within them and outside of them."

Once again, Jmmanuel tells us that we have all the answers inside each of us, and he encourages us to discover these Laws, implement them, and teach others what we have learned.

But first we must learn to distinguish the truth from all the various half-truths and lies disseminated by false religions and cults.

Chapter 36: Humankind and Creation

Once again, Jmmanuel traveled in a caravan, but was this a human-built mode of transportation or did his extraterrestrial mentors and security entourage assist them? There exist many independent accounts of a man like Jmmanuel who traveled over thousands of miles to many places, and preached many a sermon to the people. This man was said to have traveled via some brilliant light, which we now assume is an extraterrestrial spacecraft. What other explanation is there? It was certainly far more advanced than any craft of the day, and ordinary people were at a loss to explain its make and origin, method of movement, etc.

So, the man the world knows as Jesus Christ was a traveler, a preacher, a healer, and a very impatient and fearful young man who fled at the earliest sign of danger. With all his powers, he could have destroyed his enemies and those who posed any threat to him or his disciples and followers.

A strange man, indeed....

On his new travels, Jmmanuel gives us a new clue about what we should do in the future:

"Humans should look upward to the stars, for majestic peace and grandeur rule there."

The heavens hold many a key to the unlocking the secrets of the Universe and of Creation. Yes, there are many answers on Mother Earth, but clearly he encourages us to get out and explore. What is he not telling us? If his short history on Mother Earth is any indication, there is a lot he is not sharing. Again, he communicates to us in simple language, sometime parables, sometimes metaphors, sometimes riddles, but never in the complete, logical and understandable language we are accustomed to.

Mother Earth also holds so much for us, which is why he also encourages us to look here for answers. It is here where we will begin to heal ourselves, once we get rid of the evil Jesuits and their minions that permeate our global society.

Yes, we will learn some of the laws of Universal physics, just enough to cause untold destruction everywhere and to further enslave our population, but this scant knowledge is not enough to understand Creation, let alone respect it and implement its Laws.

The current powers that enslave us all speak of "honor, freedom and knowledge, but in truth these will be only hypocrisy, coercion and false teachings. Thus, in the future, humankind will lose its face and display an evil and false mask . . . Human ambitions and desires will be directed only toward acquisition, power, lust, addiction and greed.

Through all this deception, there will come a time when we turn things around and begin to learn The Laws of Creation.

He further encourages us with these words:

"Initially only a few will know that humans live not only on Earth but also in the endless expanse of the Universe, and that they live not only in the material world but their spirits reach into another world that cannot be grasped by the ordinary physical senses. This other one, the ethereal world, is the true home of the spirit. Therefore, humans should try without ceasing to broaden and deepen their knowledge, love, truth, logic, true freedom, genuine peace, harmony and wisdom, so that the spirit may be perfected and lifted up into its true home, becoming one with Creation."

Many of his teachings are harsh and seemingly negative, but there is a message in each one and it needs to be heard, interpreted, analyzed and implemented. Only a smart, thinking and discerning human can do all these things, and then share his new-found knowledge with others.

In his final sermon (as far as is known), Jmmanuel leaves on a high note, one of faith and hope, with the understanding that someday we humans will begin to grasp The Laws of Creation so that we will appreciate that we are all connected as one and, therefore, anything and everything we do affects all others and things.

"Truly, I say to you, those who understand the truth of this message and attain insight through wisdom, will awaken to the obligation of aligning their lives with their destiny of eternal change toward Creation . . . So let humankind beware and awaken, for The Laws of Creation state: Only that which is timeless and everlasting is of permanence, of truth and of wisdom, and so it is. . . ."

Part Two

The Original 36 Sermons of Jmmanuel

> It's not a question of whether extraterrestrials exist on Mother Earth, but when they will reveal themselves to humankind, and how we will react.
> —William Garner

7

The Biological/Adoptive Genealogy of Jmmanuel

1. These are the *Sermons of Jmmanuel*, who is called *The one with godly knowledge*. Jmmanuel was the adoptive son of Joseph and the biological son of extraterrestrial Gabriel, a stargod. He also was the adoptive grandson of Jacob, a distant descendant of David. Therefore, Jmmanuel was half-human and half-extraterrestrial.

David was a descendant of Abram, whose genealogy traces back to Adam, a half-extraterrestrial who was the father of a lineage of white terrestrial humans.

2. Semjasa, the celestial son and guardian angel of god, the great ruler of extraterrestrial voyagers who travelled here through vast expanses of the Universe, took a human Earth female and begot Adam.

3. Adam took for himself a human Earth female and begot Seth.
4. Seth begot Enos.
5. Enos begot Akjbeel.
6. Akjbeel begot Aruseak.
7. Aruseak begot Kenan.
8. Kenan begot Mahalaleel.

9. Mahalaleel begot Urakjbarameel.
10. Urakjbarameel begot Jared.
11. Jared begot Henoch.
12. Henoch begot Methusalah.
13. Methusalah begot Lamech.
14. Lamech begot Tamjel.
15. Tamjel begot Danel.
16. Danel begot Asael.
17. Asael begot Samsafeel.
18. Samsafeel begot Jomjael.
19. Jomjael begot Turel.
20. Turel begot Hamech.
21. Hamech begot Noah.
22. Noah begot Sem.
23. Sem begot Arpachsad.
24. Arpachsad begot Batraal.
25. Batraal begot Ramuel.
26. Ramuel begot Askeel.
27. Askeel begot Armers.
28. Armers begot Salah.
29. Salah begot Eber.
30. Eber begot Peleg.
31. Peleg begot Regu.
32. Regu begot Serug.
33. Serug begot Araseal.
34. Araseal begot Nahor.
35. Nahor begot Thara.
36. Thara begot Abraham.
37. Abraham begot Jsaak.
38. Jsaak begot Jacob.
39. Jacob begot Juda.
40. Juda begot Ananj.
41. Ananj begot Ertael.
42. Ertael begot Perez.

The Biological/Adoptive Genealogy of Jmmanuel

43. Perez begot Hezron.
44. Hezron begot Ram.
45. Ram begot Amjnadab.
46. Amjnadab begot Savebe.
47. Savebe begot Nahesson.
48. Nahesson begot Sahna.
49. Sahna begot Boas.
50. Boas begot Obed.
51. Obed begot Jesse.
52. Jesse begot David.
53. David begot Solomon.
54. Solomen begot Asa.
55. Asa begot Gadaeel.
56. Gadaeel begot Josaphat.
57. Josaphat begot Jora.
58. Jora begot Armeneel.
59. Armeneel begot Usja.
60. Usja begot Jothan.
61. Jothan begot Gadreel.
62. Gadreel begot Ahas.
63. Ahas begot Jtjskja.
64. Jtjskja begot Manasse.
65. Manasse begot Amen.
66. Amen begot Josja.
67. Josja begot Jojachjn.
68. Jojachjn begot Sealthjel.
69. Sealthjel begot Jequn.
70. Jequn begot Serubabel.
71. Serubabel begot Abjud.
72. Abjud begot Eljakjm.
73. Eljakjm begot Asor.
74. Asor begot Zadok.
75. Zadok begot Achjm.
76. Achjm begot Eljud.

77. Eljud begot Eleasar.

78. Eleasar begot Matthan.

79. Matthan begot Jacob.

80. Jacob begot Joseph.

81. Joseph was the husband of Mary, the mother of Jmmanuel who was impregnated by extraterrestrial Gabriel, a distant descendant of the celestial son, Rasiel, who was the guardian angel of the secret.

82. When Joseph heard of Mary's secret impregnation by a descendant of the celestial sons from the lineage of Rasiel, he was filled with wrath and thought of leaving Mary before he would be married to her before the people.

83. While Joseph was thinking in this manner, a guardian angel sent by Gabriel appeared and said,

84. "Joseph, Mary is betrothed to you, and you are to become her spouse. Do not leave her, because the fruit of her womb is chosen for a great purpose. Marry her in all openness, so that you may be husband and wife before the people.

85. "Behold, the impregnation of Mary occurred 11,000 years after the procreation of Adam through the celestial son Semjasa, to fulfill the word of god, the ruler of those who travelled from afar, who conveyed these words through the prophet Isaiah:

86. "Behold, a virgin will be impregnated by a celestial son before she is married to a man before the people on Earth.

87. "They will name the fruit of her womb Jmmanuel as a symbol and honor to god. Through god's power and providential care, Earth was made to bear intelligent human life when the celestial sons, the travellers from the far reaches of the Universe, mated with the human females of Earth.

88. "Behold, god and his followers came far from the depths of the Universe, where they delivered themselves from a strong bondage, and created here a new human race and home with the early females of Earth.

89. "God deserves the honor of the people of Earth, because he is the true originator and engineer of the white and colored Earth humans.

The Biological/Adoptive Genealogy of Jmmanuel

90. "Except for him, there is nothing equal in form for these human lineages created by him. The people should worship no other gods who created other human lineages in other parts of Earth.

91. "Except for god, there is nothing of comparable form worthy of veneration. Over him and his celestial sons reigns only the omnipotence of all Creation, which should be revered by all.

92. "Behold, over the Earth reigns god, the master of the celestial sons and the people of the white and colored terrestrial lineages.

93. "God is the lawgiver for these human populations and, therefore, his wishes should be fulfilled by man and woman.

94. "God, the lord, is generous in his love, but also terrible in his wrath when his laws are disobeyed.

95. "Mary's impregnation is god's law. You, Joseph, are to be her husband in matrimony."

96. When Joseph heard this, he was mindful of his devoutness to god's laws, so he brought Mary home and married her before the people.

97. At this time, a decree went out from Emperor Augustus, that all the world should be counted.

98. This census was the first of its kind and occurred at the time that Cyrenius was governor in Syria.

99. All went to be assessed, each to his own town.

100. Joseph of Galilee, of the town of Nazareth, also went with his wife Mary into the Judaic land to the city of David, which is called Bethlehem, because he was of the house and lineage of David,

101. To be assessed with his wife, Mary, who was pregnant by the celestial son Gabriel from the lineage of Rasiel.

102. When they were there, the time came for her to give birth.

103. Since they could find no shelter, they spent the night in a stable.

104. And Mary bore her first son on the straw, wrapped him in cloth, and laid him in a manger near the animals, because there was no other room for her in the inn.

2

The Wise Men from the Orient

1. When Jmmanuel was born in the stable at Bethlehem, in the shelter in the land of the Jews during the time of Herod Antipas, Tetrarch of Galilee and Peraea, behold, wise men arrived in Jerusalem from the Orient and asked:

2. "Where is the newborn king of wisdom of the Jews?

3. "We have seen a bright light in the sky and heard a voice saying,

4. "Follow the tail of the light, because the king of wisdom of the Jews is born, who will bring great knowledge.

5. "Therefore we have come to worship the newborn king of wisdom.

6. "He shall possess the knowledge of god and be a son of the celestial son Gabriel.

7. "His knowledge will be boundless, as will be his power to control human consciousness, so that humans may learn and serve Creation."

8. When Herod Antipas heard of this, he was frightened, and with him everyone in Jerusalem, because they feared that the newborn child would wield dreadful power.

9. Herod Antipas called together all the chief priests and scribes

from among the people and inquired of them where Jmmanuel had been born.

10. And they replied: "In Bethlehem, in the Jewish land; for thus it was written by the prophet Micah:

11. "And you, Bethlehem, in the land of the Jews, are by no means the least among the cities in Judea, for from you shall come forth the king of wisdom, who will bring great knowledge to the people of Israel so that they may learn and serve Creation."

12. Thereupon, Herod Antipas called the wise men secretly and diligently asked them when the bright light with the long tail had appeared in the sky.

13. He later directed them to Bethlehem, and said, "Go and search diligently for the young child and when you find him, let me know, so that I may also come and adore him.

14. After they had listened to Herod Antipas, they departed. And behold, the light with the long tail, which they had observed in the Orient, moved ahead of them with a high singing sound until it reached Bethlehem and stood directly over the stable where the infant was born.

15. When they saw this they were filled with great joy.

16. They then went into the stable and found the young child with his mother, Mary, and with Joseph. And they fell down and worshiped the infant and offered their treasures, which were gold, frankincense and myrrh.

17. However, the voice again rang out from the light high above, saying that they should not return to Herod Antipas because he planned evil for the young child.

18. And they returned to their homeland by another route.

19. After the three wise men had left, behold, the celestial son Gabriel appeared to Joseph, saying:

20. "Arise and take the infant and his mother Mary with you and flee to Egypt. Stay there until I beckon you, because Herod Antipas is planning to seek out the young child and kill him, since he fears that this babe might wield terrible power.

The Wise Men from the Orient

21. "While you are in Egypt, I will send my messenger to Herod Antipas to teach him the truth."

22. And Joseph arose and took the young child and his mother by night and escaped under the guidance of the celestial son Gabriel in the descending light, which fled with them to Egypt.

23. Here they remained until Herod Antipas had a change of mind and his inner fear abated.

24. When Herod Antipas realized that he had nothing to fear from the young boy, who was credited only with great wisdom and knowledge, he felt safe in his realm. Thus, he promised the messenger of the celestial son Gabriel he would no longer pursue Mary, Joseph and Jmmanuel.

25. Now that Herod Antipas and his followers had changed their attitude, behold, the celestial son Gabriel appeared again before Joseph in Egypt, and said,

26. "Arise and take the young child and his mother Mary and move to the land of Israel; all those who sought the child's life have had a change of heart."

27. And Joseph stood up, took the child and his mother, and returned into the light which once more had appeared. It brought them to Israel.

28. The celestial son Gabriel brought them back to the land of Galilee.

29. There they dwelled in the city called Nazareth, so that what had been spoken by the prophets would be fulfilled, "Jmmanuel shall be called the Nazarene."

John the Baptist

1. In due course, John the Baptist came to the edge of the wilderness and preached at the banks of the Jordan.

2. John the Baptist preached of baptism in accordance with the old laws of god, according to which the way to knowledge was to be prepared.

3. He preached that god's laws shall be followed because he is the sole ruler of this human lineage.

4. He preached that above god, however, stands Creation, the source of the worlds, Universe and all living creatures.

5. And so he taught that the genderless Creation is the mystery of all mysteries; death and life, light and darkness, being and non-being.

6. And so he taught once again that god, the lord and ruler of this human lineage and of those who travelled from afar, the celestial sons, holds Creation in high esteem.

7. All Judea and all the people of Jerusalem went forth to John the Baptist, acknowledging the wisdom of the old laws of god, and let themselves be baptized by him in the river Jordan.

8. John wore a garment made from camel's hair and a leather belt around his loins. His food consisted of locusts and wild honey.

9. While he was baptizing many of the people, many Pharisees and Sadducees came to him and humiliated him with malicious talk.

10. But John the Baptist spoke, "You brood of vipers, who told you that you will escape from future wrath, once your false teachings are revealed?

11. "See to it that you bear righteous fruit of repentance and learn the truth.

12. "Turn away from the evil of your false teachings, which you carry out with arrogance and pursuant with your greed for power and fortune.

13. "Do not think just of saying to each other, 'We have Abraham as father.'?

14. "I say to you, with his knowledge and his power, god is able to raise up children to Abraham out of these stones, because he has knowledge of the mystery of Creation.

15. "Already the axe has been laid at the root of the trees. Therefore, any tree that does not bring forth good fruit will be hewn down and thrown into the fire.

16. "You brood of vipers, in two times a thousand years you and your followers, who pursue false teachings out of your own arrogance in your greed for power and fortune, shall be vanquished and, on account of your lies, punished.

17. "So it shall be when humankind begins to comprehend, and when the chaff is separated from the grain.

18. "It will be at the time when your false teachings will be laughed at and humankind discovers the truth.

19. "This will come to pass when humankind builds singing lights and chariots of fire, with which they can escape into the cosmos, as is done by god and his followers, the celestial sons,

20. "namely those who taught us the wisdom and knowledge of Creation,

21. "and who urged us to obey the laws of nature and live according to them.

22. "Oh you renegades, you brood of vipers, get away from this place, because you are impure and cursed in your false teachings.

23. "Get away from this place, because I can by my own accord baptize you into repentance only with water; but he who comes after me is stronger than I, and I am not worthy of removing his sandals. He will baptize you with the knowledge of the spirit and with the fire of truth.

24. "He has his winnowing fork in his hand; he will sweep his threshing floor and gather the wheat into his granary, but he will burn the chaff with unquenchable fire.

25. "The lie can never withstand the truth, which destroys evil in its fire."

26. As John the Baptist thus spoke, behold, Jmmanuel of Galilee then approached John at the Jordan, to be baptized by him.

27. John, however, refused him and spoke, "It is I who need to be baptized by you because you possess greater knowledge than I. And you come to me?"

28. But Jmmanuel answered him, "Let it happen so now, because it is fitting for us to fulfill all justice, since we are both sons of the Earth."

29. So John consented and baptized him.

30. When Jmmanuel had been baptized, he soon came out of the water of the Jordan, and behold, a metallic light fell from the sky and rushed over the Jordan.

31. Consequently they all fell on their faces and pressed them into the sand while a voice from the metallic light spoke:

32. "This is my beloved son with whom I am well pleased. He will be the king of truth, through which terrestrial humans shall rise as wise ones.

33. Behold, after these words Jmmanuel entered into the metallic light, which climbed into the sky, surrounded by fire and smoke, and passed over the lifeless sea, as the singing of the metallic light soon faded away.

34. After that, Jmmanuel was not seen for 40 days and nights.

Jmmanuel's Arcanum of Knowledge

1. From this day on, Jmmanuel no longer lived among the sons and daughters of these Earth humans.

2. Jmmanuel was lifted up from the Earth, and no one knew where he had been taken or what had happened to him.

3. But then he was set down by the metallic light between North and West, in a place where the guardian angels had received guidelines by which they were to evaluate the site for the chosen ones.

4. Thus, he lived for forty days and nights between the winds of the North and the West, where he received the *Arcanum of Knowledge*.

5. During this instruction period, he spent his days with the wise saints of god and the guardian angels, the celestial sons.

6. They taught him the wisdom of knowledge,

7. The dominion of god over terrestrial humans and over his celestial sons,

8. The omnipotence of the Creation of the Universe,

9. And about the immortality of the human spirit through rebirth.

10. There he saw the initial forefathers, the saints of ancient times,

who were the celestial sons and the fathers of the terrestrial humans.

11. From there he went to the North towards the ends of the Earth, where the metallic lights and chariots of fire came down from the sky or shot upwards with a singing sound, enveloped in smoke and fire.

12. There, at the ends of the entire Earth, he saw a great and marvellous wonder.

13. In that place, he saw the celestial portals open, of which there were three different ones.

14. The celestial portals radiated in the most brilliant Zohar or radiant energy, an area as large as the lifeless sea on the river Jordan.

15. Actually gleaming therein was the entire land of Israel, alive and true, humans and animals and everything that was there.

16. In this first celestial portal, no secret was concealed, because the Zohar entered into the smallest spaces in the cottages and revealed the last intimate detail.

17. Inside the second celestial portal, there rose mighty mountains, whose peaks reached into the sky and disappeared into the clouds.

18. Far below lay deep masses of snow, at whose edges a different, brown-skinned human population built their huts.

19. The third celestial portal revealed a land of gigantic dimensions, mountainous and interspersed with rivers, lakes and seas, where yet another human population dwelled.

20. Not far from these three celestial portals had been built the palace of god, the ruler of these terrestrial humans and of those who had travelled from afar, the celestial sons, the guardian angels.

21. In his palace, god ruled over the three human lineages created by him and over his following, the celestial sons.

22. He was immortal, ancient and of giant size like the celestial sons.

23. In the palace of god, there appeared to Jmmanuel two very tall men, the likes of whom he had never seen on Earth.

24. Their faces shone like the sun, and their eyes looked like burning torches. From their mouths issued fire. Their clothing resembled a covering of foam, and their arms were like golden wings.

25. They inhabited an environment of their own, because the air of this earthly world would have been fatal to them.

26. These two men from the constellation of the seven stars were venerable teachers, and they were together with two smaller men who said that they were from Baawi.

27. They said, "People have come from the heavens to Earth, and other people have been lifted from Earth into the heavens; the people coming from the heavens remained on Earth for a long time, and they created the intelligent human lineages.

28. "Behold, humans begotten by the celestial sons were different in a unique way from other people on Earth.

29. "They were not like Earth humans but like the children of the celestial angels, and of a different kind.

30. "Their bodies were white as snow and red as the rose blossom, their hair at the top of the head white as wool and their eyes beautiful.

31. "Earth humans will now retain their inherited beauty and propagate it further.

32. "But in the course of centuries and millennia, they will mix with other human populations and the heavens, so as to generate a new humankind and special lineages, as the celestial sons did with the Earth people.

33. "Jmmanuel, you are an informed insider, begotten from among our ranks by a celestial son.

34. "With your knowledge, you will make the impossible possible and accomplish things that Earth humans will deem miraculous.

35. "You know the power of the spirit, but beware of abusing it.

36. "Your own wisdom and the knowledge obtained through us should contribute to the well-being of humankind, though the road leading thereto will be very difficult for them and for you.

37. "You will be misunderstood and denounced, because Earth humans are still ignorant and addicted to delusional beliefs.

38. "They believe that god is Creation itself and not the ruler of the celestial sons and these human lineages.

39. "Earth people attribute to him the omnipotence of Creation

and glorify him as Creation itself.

40. "But god is a human being, like all the celestial sons and the terrestrial humans, except that he is vastly greater in consciousness than they are.

41. "Creation, however, is of immeasurably higher standing than god, the lord over the celestial sons and terrestrial humans, because Creation is the immeasurable enigma.

42. "Jmmanuel, you will also be slandered as god and as his only begotten son, and you, too, will be equated with the mysterious Creation.

43. "Do not heed these false teachings, however, because millennia will pass before the people of these human lineages are capable of recognizing the truth.

44. "Much human blood will be shed because of you, including your own and that of countless generations.

45. "Notwithstanding, fulfill your mission as the king of wisdom, as the son of Gabriel, the celestial son.

46. "The law for your creation was issued in the name of god, so that you may serve as prophet and pioneer of wise knowledge for these human lineages.

47. "Fulfill your mission unperturbed by the irrationality and all false teachings of the scribes and Pharisees, and despite the disbelieving people.

48. "**Hence, following the fulfillment of your mission, centuries and two millennia will pass before the truth of the knowledge you brought to the people will be recognized and disseminated by a few humans.**

49. "Not until the time of space-travelling machines will the truth break through and gradually shake the false teachings that you are the son of god or Creation.

50. "And this will be the time when we celestial sons begin to reveal ourselves anew to Earth humans, when they will have become knowing and will threaten the structure of the heavens with their acquired power."

51. Thus they spoke, the celestial sons between the North and the West, before bringing Jmmanuel in the metallic light back to Israel, to the land of Galilee.

52. When Jmmanuel heard that John the Baptist had been imprisoned, he left the town of Nazareth, came to and lived in Capernaum, which lies by the sea in the land of Zebulon and Naphtali.

53. From that time onward, Jmmanuel began to preach, saying, "Repent and turn to the truth and knowledge, because they alone bring you life!"

54. When Jmmanuel went by the Sea of Galilee, he saw two brothers, Simon, who is called Peter, and Andrew, casting their nets into the sea because they were fishermen.

55. And he said to them, "Follow me; I will teach you knowledge and make you fishers of people.

56. Thereupon, they left their nets and followed him.

57. As he went on, he saw two other brothers, Jacob, the son of Zebedee, and John, his brother, in the boat along with their father, Zebedee, mending their nets.

58. And he called them.

59. Soon they left the boat and their father, and followed Jmmanuel.

60. Jmmanuel went about in the entire land of Galilee, teaching in their synagogues, preaching the knowledge of the spirit, and healing all diseases and infirmities among the people.

61. News of him spread through the entire land of Syria, and they brought to him all the sick afflicted with various diseases and torments, the possessed, the lunatics, and the paralytics, and he made them well.

62. And many people followed him. From Galilee, from the Decapolis, from Jerusalem, from the land of Judea and from beyond the Jordan.

The Sermon on the Mount

1. When Jmmanuel saw the people following him, he went up a hill and sat down, and his disciples came to him.

2. And he taught them, saying:

3. "Blessed are those who are rich in spirit and recognize the truth, for life is theirs.

4. "Blessed are those who endure hardship, for they shall thus recognize truth and be comforted.

5. "Blessed are the spiritually balanced, for they shall possess knowledge.

6. "Blessed are those who hunger and thirst for truth and knowledge, for they shall be satisfied.

7. "Blessed are those who live according to the laws of nature, for they live according to the plan of Creation.

8. "Blessed are those who have a clear conscience, for they need not fear.

9. "Blessed are those who know about Creation, for they are not enslaved by false teachings.

10. "Blessed are the righteous, for nature is subject to them.

11. "Blessed are you if, on my account and because of our teachings, people revile and persecute you and speak all manner of evil against you; thus they lie about the teachings.

12. "Be of good cheer and take comfort; this life and the next life will reward you. For so have the belittlers of the truth persecuted the prophets who were before you, and so will they also persecute you.

13. "You are the salt of the Earth, and if the salt loses its flavor with what would one salt? It is useless henceforth, except it be thrown out and stepped on by the people.

14. "You are the light of the world, and consider: the city that lies on top of a mountain cannot be hidden.

15. "One does not light a candle and place it under a bushel, but on a candlestick; thus it shines for all those who are in the house.

16. "Likewise your light shall shine before the people, so they see your good deeds and recognize the truth of your knowledge.

17. "Do not think that I have come to do away with the law or the prophet; I have come not to undo, but to fulfill and to reveal the knowledge.

18. "Truly, I say to you: Until the heavens and the Earth vanish, neither a letter nor a dot of the Law of Creation and the laws of nature will vanish, until all is fulfilled.

19. "Whosoever violates one of the smallest of the laws or directives and teaches the people falsely, will be called the smallest; but whosoever spreads the teachings truthfully will be called great and will receive the reward of the spirit.

20. "I tell you: if your righteousness does not exceed that of the scribes and Pharisees, you will not receive the reward of the spirit and of life.

21. "You have heard that it was said to your ancestors: 'You shall not kill; but whosoever kills shall be found guilty by the courts.'

22. "However, I say to you: exercise justice according to the natural Laws of Creation, so that you find the judgment in logic.

23. "Guilty are all those who kill when not acting in self-defense or

according to legal verdict based on self-defense. Likewise, guilty are all those who engage in evil speech and actions.

24. "Only justice according to the natural Laws of Creation produces a logical judgment.

25. "Do not accommodate your adversaries if you are in the right, and the judge will probably have to decide in your favor.

26. "Truly, I say to you: you will attain justice only when you find it yourself and can make your fellow humans understand it.

27. "You have heard that it was said: 'You shall not commit adultery.'

28. "But I say to you: whosoever has sexual intercourse with someone other than their spouse shall be delivered to the courts, for it is an act unworthy of humans, contemptible and an offense against the laws of nature.

29. "If, however, your right or left eye causes annoyance, tear it out and throw it away, because it is better for you that just one of your members be destroyed than your whole body.

30. "If a thought causes you annoyance, eradicate it and ban it from your brain. It is better to destroy a thought that incites annoyance than to bring the whole world of thought into an uproar.

31. "It has also been said, 'Whosoever divorces his spouse shall hand over a certificate of divorce.

32. "However, I say to you: whosoever separates from their spouse, except in response to adultery, commits adultery; whosoever marries a person who is guilty in a divorce also commits adultery.

33. "You have further heard it said to your ancestors: 'You shall take no false oath, and you shall keep your oath to god.'

34. "However, I say to you that you shall not swear at all; do not swear by the heavens, because they are infinite and immeasurable.

35. "Neither swear by the Earth, because it is impermanent, nor swear by Jerusalem, because it is an impermanent city built by human hands.

36. "You shall also not swear by your head, because you cannot change the color of a single hair.

37. "Also do not swear by the memory of a person or a thing, for

they are all impermanent.

38. "Let your speech at all times simply be: 'Yes, yes' or 'no, no.' Anything beyond that goes against the laws.

39. "You have heard it said: 'An eye for an eye, and a tooth for a tooth.

40. "But I say to you, exercise justice according to the natural Laws of Creation, so that you find the verdict in logic.

41. "Offer your love wherever it is warranted, and punish wherever the law of nature demands punishment.

42. "Give to them who ask of you, if they make their requests in honesty, and turn away from them who want to borrow from you in a dishonest way.

43. "You have heard it said, 'You shall love your neighbor and hate your enemy.

44. "However, I say to you: Practice love and understanding according to the natural Laws of Creation, so that through logic you find the right action and perception.

45. "Offer your love where it is warranted, and despise where the law of nature demands it.

46. "You shall be wise and acquire knowledge, because you shall become perfect in spirit as the Creation which created you.

47. "Over the course of incarnations, you shall train your spirit and your consciousness and allow them to develop to perfection, so that you become one with Creation.

Alms, Fasting, Treasures, Concerns

1. "Be mindful of your piety, that you practice it before the people with correct words, lest you be accused of lying and thereby find no reward from them.

2. "Choose your words using natural logic, and draw upon the knowledge and behavior of nature.

3. "When you give alms, you shall not proclaim it, as do the hypocrites in the synagogues and on the streets, that they may be praised by the people; truly, I say to you, they have forfeited their reward, because their alms serve only their selfishness.

4. "And when you pray, you shall not be like the hypocrites, who enjoy standing and praying in the synagogues and on the corners of the streets, because they pray only for the sake of their selfishness and the impression they have upon the people.

5. "When you pray, you shall call upon the omnipotence of the spirit and not babble misleading nonsense like the idol worshippers, the ignorant and the selfish, because they think they are heard when they use many words.

6. "The Creation-spirit part of the human has no need for many words, however humans need the knowledge of how powerful it is.

7. "Pray therefore to the omnipotence of the spirit, in the knowledge that its greatness and power are infinite.

8. "If you do not know how to pray directly to the almighty power of the spirit, make use of something sacred by which you can reach the spirit.

9. "But be never like the ignorant, the hypocrites, the idol worshippers and the selfish, who worship something sacred in the belief that the omnipotence of the spirit dwells in it.

10. "Be aware, however, that the almighty power of the spirit always dwells within you regardless of your usage of a sacred object or place.

11. "Therefore pray as one who knows; thus you should pray as follows:

12. " 'My spirit, you exist within omnipotence.

13. " 'May your name be holy.

14. " 'May your kingdom incarnate itself within me.

15. " 'May your power unfold itself within me, on Earth and in the heavens.

16. " 'Give me today my daily bread, that I may recognize my wrongdoings and the truth.

17. " 'And lead me not into temptation and confusion, but deliver me from error.

18. " 'For yours is the kingdom within me and the power and the knowledge forever. Amen.

19. "When you pray to your spirit, it will give you what you request; have trust in this knowledge and you will receive.

20. "However, if you believe in the false teachings that the power and spirit do not dwell within you, then you will be without knowledge and will live in spiritual poverty.

21. "Now and then you will receive what you in your false belief request from misused sacred things, or from idols and gods; but you will receive only because of your strong false belief, without knowledge of the real truth.

22. "Truly, I say to you: Blessed are only those who serve the actual truth and knowledge, because only they receive in honesty.

23. "When you fast, do not look sour like the hypocrites, for they put on pretentious faces to shine with their fasting before the people.

24. "Truly, I say to you, they forfeit their reward, because they fast only for the sake of their selfish impression upon others.

25. "But when you fast, anoint your head and wash your face, so that you do not shine before the people with your fasting, but before your own spirit, which is hidden.

26. "You fast for the sake of your health and for the expansion of your consciousness, spirit and your knowledge.

27. "Neither should you amass great treasures on Earth, where moths and rust consume them and thieves break in and steal them.

28. "But collect treasures in the spirit and in consciousness, where neither moths nor rust consumes them and where thieves neither break in nor steal.

29. "For where your treasure is, there your heart is also; and the true treasure is wisdom and knowledge.

30. "The eye is the light of your body.

31. "When your eye is clear, your entire body will be a light.

32. "But if your eye is evil, your whole body will be dark.

33. "If now the light within you is dark, how great then will be the darkness?

34. "No one can serve two masters; either he will hate the one and love the other, or he will adhere to the one and despise the other.

35. "You cannot serve your good spirit and the devil of covetousness.

36. "Therefore, I say to you, concern yourself about the knowledge of your spirit, and what you will eat and drink, and be concerned about your body and how you will clothe it.

37. "For are not the spirit, life and body more important than all the treasures of the world?

38. "The human spirit, which is thirsting for truth and knowledge, is incapable of preserving its earthly life without the body, because both body and spirit together are one.

39. "Thus you should be concerned about increasing your knowledge for your spirit's sake, about the laws of life and about food, drink and clothing for your body.

40. "Look at the birds in the sky: they do not sow, they do not reap, they do not store their food in barns, and yet Creation feeds them.

41. "Are you not much more than they?

42. "Look at the birds in the sky: they devour the harmful insects, and they have plumage for clothing, yet they have no spirit capable of ongoing evolution.

43. "They work to fulfill their duty, and they are fed and clothed by Creation.

44. "Are you not much more than they?

45. "You can think independently through your free consciousness; you can work independently and you can prepare food and drink and clothe your bodies independently.

46. "Behold the lilies in the marsh as they grow: they neither toil nor spin, yet truly, I say to you, the lilies also fulfill their mission, when they give pleasure to the eye with their beauty.

47. "I tell you, even Solomon in all his splendor was not arrayed as one of these.

48. "Creation nourishes and clothes the grass in the field, which today is standing and tomorrow is thrown into the stove. Should not you then do much more for yourselves?

49. "The grass fulfills its mission by serving as fodder and fuel; but are you not of much greater value than grass, oh you of little knowledge?

50. "Therefore, you shall care for the wisdom and knowledge of your spirit, and take care that you do not suffer from lack of food, drink and clothing.

51. "Truly, I say to you, if you suffer from hunger, thirst and nakedness, then wisdom and knowledge will be crowded out by worry.

52. "First seek the realm of your spirit and its knowledge, and then seek to comfort your body with food, drink and clothing.

53. "Therefore, take care for the next day, for tomorrow will not take care of you by itself.

54. "It is enough that each day has its own troubles, therefore you must not also be at the mercy of the need for your physical welfare."

7

The Spirit of Judgment

1. "Judge not falsely, lest you be falsely judged.

2. "For with whatever judgment you judge, you will be judged, and with whatever measure you measure, you will be measured.

3. "Judge according to the logic of the laws of nature, which are from Creation, because only they possess its truth and correctness.

4. "Why do you see the splinter in your brother's eye and are not aware of the beam in your own eye?

5. "Or, how dare you say to your brother: 'Wait, I will take the splinter out of your eye!' And behold, there is a beam in your own eye.

6. "You hypocrite, first take the beam out of your own eye, then see how you can take the splinter out of your brother's eye.

7. "Learn first the Laws of nature and of Creation, their logic, before you judge and condemn and wish to see the faults of your neighbor.

8. "Through the Laws of Creation and nature, learn first how to recognize your own faults, so that you can then correct the faults of your neighbors.

9. "You shall not give sacred things to the dogs, nor throw your

pearls before the swine, lest they trample them with their feet and turn on you and tear you apart.

10. "Truly, I say to you: Do not throw your spiritual treasure into the dirt and do not waste it on the unworthy, because they will not thank you and will tear you apart, for their understanding is small and their spirit is weak.

Response to Prayer

11. "Ask, and it will be given to you; seek and you will find; knock, and it will be opened to you.

12. "For whosoever asks of their spirit, will receive; and whosoever seeks through the power of their spirit, will find; and whosoever knocks at the door of their spirit, to that person will it be opened.

13. "Who among you would hand your son a stone if he asks for bread?

14. "Or offer him a snake if he asks for a fish?

15. "So if you, now, though being wicked, can nevertheless give your children good gifts, how much more will your spirit give you, if you ask for it.

16. "Everything that you wish people would do to you, do likewise to them.

17. "This is the law delivered through the prophets.

18. "Enter through the narrow portal.

19. "The portal is wide and the path is broad which leads to damnation, and many are those who travel thereon.

20. "And the portal is narrow and the way is slender which leads to life and knowledge, and there are only few who find it.

21. "Beware of false prophets and scribes who come to you in sheep's clothing, but inwardly are like ravenous wolves, preaching to you about submissiveness before shrines, false deities and gods, and preaching submissiveness to idols and false teachings.

22. "Beware of those who forbid you access to wisdom and knowledge, for they speak to you only to attain power over you and to seize your goods and belongings.

23. "You will recognize them by their fruits.

24. "Can one gather grapes from the thorns, or figs from the thistles?

25. "Hence, every good seed brings forth a good harvest, but a rotten seed brings forth a bad harvest.

26. "A good tree can never bear bad fruit, and a rotten tree can never bear good fruit.

27. "Thus, by their fruits you will recognize them.

28. "Therefore, whosoever hears these words of mine and acts upon them will be like an intelligent man who built his house on the rock.

29. "Now when a downpour fell and the waters came and the winds blew and beat upon the house, it did not fall because it was founded on rock.

30. "Whosoever hears these words and does not act upon them is like a foolish man who built his house on sand.

31. "When a downpour came and the waters and the winds beat upon the house, it collapsed and great was its fall."

32. It happened that after Jmmanuel had finished his talk, the people were shocked by his teachings.

33. He taught with authority a new doctrine unlike that of the scribes.

The Healing of the Leper

1. When he descended from the mountain, many people followed him.

2. Behold, a leper came and knelt before him and said, "Master, if you will it, you can make me clean."

3. Jmmanuel stretched out his hand, touched him and said, "I will do it. Be cleansed." And immediately the leper was cleansed of his leprosy.

4. And Jmmanuel spoke to him, "See to it that you tell no one. Instead, go and present yourself to the priest.

5. "You were healed through the power of the spirit and the wisdom of knowledge."

The Centurion at Capernaum

6. When Jmmanuel went to Capernaum, a centurion walked up to him with a request, saying,

7. "Master, my servant lies at home incapacitated with gout and is in great distress.

8. "Master, I have heard your new teachings and I know the truth of

your wisdom, which states that the human spirit can perform miracles through knowledge of the truth."

9. Jmmanuel spoke to him, "I will come and make him well."

10. The centurion replied, "Master, I am not worthy to have you enter under my roof, but only say the word and my servant will be well."

11. "I, too, am a man subject to authority, and I also have soldiers under me. If I say to one, 'Go!' he goes, and to another, 'Come here!' he comes, and to my servant, 'Do this!' he does it."

12. When Jmmanuel heard this, he marvelled and spoke to those who followed him, "Truly, I say to you, such trust I have found in no one in Israel.

13. "But I say to you, many will come from the east and the west, from the south and the north, and they will understand my teachings and recognize their wisdom in knowledge.

14. "However, the children of Israel will be expelled into darkness; there will be wailing and the chattering of teeth.

15. "The false teachings of Israel will bring bloodshed over the millennia, because the power-hungry selfishness and high-handedness of Israel will bring death and destruction over the land and all the world.

Jmmanuel in the House of Peter

16. "Turn away from the false teachings of the Israelite authorities and their scribes, because they will bring destruction to successive generations.

17. "The Israelites believe themselves the "chosen people." By no means is this the case, because they are more disloyal and unknowing than the ignorant who lack the secret of Creation's laws."

18. And Jmmanuel spoke to the centurion, "Go, be it done for you as you have expected." And his servant became well that same hour.

19. Jmmanuel came to Peter's house and saw that his mother-in-law lay sick with a fever.

20. He touched her hand, the fever left her and she got up and served him.

21. In the evening, however, they brought to him many who were

possessed; and he drove out the evil spirits through his word and made all the sick well.

22. So it came to pass that what was said through the prophet Isaiah would be fulfilled, who spoke, "He has brought us new teachings of knowledge and has taken our infirmities upon himself, and he has healed our sick."

On the Seriousness of Discipleship

23. When Jmmanuel saw many people around him, he gave the order to go across to the other shore.

24. A scribe walked up to him and said, "Master, I will follow you wherever you go.

25. Jmmanuel spoke to him, "Foxes have dens and birds of the air have nests, but I have no fixed place where I can lay my head.

26. "I have the mission to preach wisdom and knowledge, therefore , I am moving restlessly through the lands.

27. And another, one of his disciples, said to him, "Master, permit me to go and bury my father who just died."

28. But Jmmanuel said to him, "Follow me and let the dead bury their dead."

The Healing of Two Possessed Persons

29. He arrived at the other shore, in the region of the Gadarenes. There, two possessed persons ran up to him; they came out of the burial caves and were very dangerous, so that no one could walk on this street.

30. And behold, they cried out, saying, "What do you want of us, you son of Gabriel, the celestial son?

31. "Have you come to torment us before it is even time?"

32. Then the evil spirits within the possessed asked him, "Master, if you intend to drive us out, then let us go into the herd of swine, grazing just over there."

33. And he spoke, "So go there."

34. Then they went out into the swine, and behold, the whole herd

rushed down to the water and drowned.

35. The swineherds fled and went into the town and told everything, including what had happened to the possessed.

36. The whole town came out and approached Jmmanuel.

37. And when they saw him, they asked him to leave their area.

9

The Healing of the Paralytic

1. Then he stepped into the boat, returned to the other side again and came into his town.

2. And behold, they brought to him a paralytic lying on a bed. When Jmmanuel saw their faith, he spoke to the paralytic, "Be comforted, because your faith in the power of my spirit and your confidence in my teachings of wisdom, which are the teachings of nature and of Creation, have helped you.

3. And behold, some of the scribes began stirring up talk among the people: "This man blasphemes God and our holy teachings."

4. But since Jmmanuel understood their thoughts, he spoke, "Why do you think such evil thoughts against your better knowledge?

5. "Yet, what is easier to say, 'Your faith has helped you,' or, 'Stand up and walk!'

6. "So that you may know that I am a person like you and yet know how to use the power of my spirit through my knowledge, I command the paralytic, 'Get up, pick up your bed and go home!'"

7. And he stood up, took up his bed, and went home.

8. When the people saw this, they became fearful and praised the new wondrous teachings of Jmmanuel, which could give such power to humans.

Matthew

9. As Jmmanuel was leaving, he saw a man named Matthew sitting at the tax office and spoke to him, "Follow me!" And he stood up and followed him.

10. And it came to pass as he was eating at home, behold, many tax collectors, ignorant people and seekers of the truth came and ate at the table with Jmmanuel and his disciples.

11. When the Pharisees saw this, they spoke to his disciples, "Why is your master eating with the tax collectors and the ignorant?"

12. When Jmmanuel heard this, he spoke, "The healthy do not need a physician but the sick do; and the knowledgeable do not need the teachings but the ignorant do. Those who were not misled do not need the teachings, but those who were misled do.

13. "Go, therefore, and recognize the falseness of your wrong teachings, so you do not mislead those people who thirst for the truth.

Fasting

14. Then the disciples of John came to him, saying, "Master, why do we and the Pharisees fast while you and your disciples do not?"

15. Jmmanuel said to them, "How can the ignorant fast and suffer while they are being taught knowledge?

16. "And how can the teacher fast when he must teach knowledge to the ignorant?

17. "Truly, I say to you, your teachings are false if you fast according to a religious dogma; fasting serves only the health of the body and the growth of the spirit.

18. "No one mends an old garment with a new patch of cloth, because the patch will tear again from the garment, and the rip will become worse.

19. "Neither is new wine poured into old wineskins, for the skins

will tear, the wine will spill, and the wineskins will be ruined. Instead, new wine is put into new wineskins so both are preserved.

The Daughter of Jairus and the Woman with Hemophilia

20. While he was talking with them, behold, one of the community leaders came and knelt before him, saying, "My daughter has just died, but come and lay your hand on her so she will live.

21. And Jmmanuel stood up and his disciples followed him.

22. And behold, a woman who had hemophilia for twelve years stepped up behind him and touched the fringe of his garment.

23. She spoke to herself, "if only I could touch his garment, I would be cured."

24. Then Jmmanuel turned around and saw her, and he said, "Be comforted, your faith has helped you," and the woman was well from that hour on.

25. When he came into the community leader's house and saw the pipers and the turmoil of the people, he spoke,

26. "Depart, because the maiden is not dead but is asleep." And they laughed at him.

27. But after the people were driven out, he entered and took her by the hand and spoke, "I order you to get up and walk!"

28. And the maiden stood up and walked, and soon the news of this spread through the entire land.

A Blind Man and Two Mutes

29. As Jmmanuel left and continued on from there, a blind man followed him, crying, "Oh Lord, you son of wisdom and knowledge who can use the power of your spirit, take pity on me."

30. And as he arrived at his house, the blind man stepped up to him, and Jmmanuel spoke to him, "Do you have confidence that I can do this?" And he answered him, "Yes, Master."

31. Then Jmmanuel touched his eyes, saying, "Be it done to you according to your faith."

32. And his eyes were opened and he saw.

33. Then Jmmanuel warned him, saying, "See to it that no one learns what happened to you."

34. However, the man went out and spread the news of him throughout that land.

35. After the man had left, behold, they brought to him two people who were mute and possessed.

36. And after the evil demons of self-delusion were cast out, behold, the mutes could speak.

37. And the people were amazed, saying, "Such things have never been seen in Israel; how mighty are these new teachings about the power of the spirit that they can accomplish such miracles."

38. However, the Pharisees said, "He drives out the evil spirits through their supreme chief, and he blasphemes God, our Lord."

39. But among themselves they said, "Who is this Jmmanuel, who possesses greater wisdom and greater knowledge than we?

40. "His teachings are mightier and truer than ours, and therefore he endangers us.

41. "We must try to seize him, so that he will suffer death."

The Great Harvest

42. And Jmmanuel went about in all the cities and villages, taught in their synagogues and preached the mystery of Creation and of the laws of nature, so that the spirit could attain omnipotence.

43. He preached about the spiritual kingdom within humans and healed every type of sickness and infirmity.

44. When he saw the people, he took pity on them, for they were languishing and scattered like a flock of sheep without a shepherd.

45. Then he spoke to his disciples, "The harvest is great, but there are few laborers to bring it in.

46. "Seek and pray in your consciousness that more laborers will be found for the harvesting."

47. And so it came to pass that workers for the harvest were found, who gathered around Jmmanuel to become disciples.

70

Commissioning of the Disciples

1. He called his twelve disciples to him and gave them the knowledge for controlling the unclean spirits, so they could drive them out and heal every sickness and infirmity.

2. These are the names of the twelve disciples: Simon called Peter, and Andrew, his brother; James, the son of Zebedee, and John, his brother;

3. Philip and Bartholomew; Thomas and Matthew, the tax collector; James, the son of Alphaeus, and Thaddeus;

4. Simon Canaaeus, and Judas Ish-Keriot, the only one other than Jmmanuel who understood handwriting.

5. Jmmanuel sent forth these twelve, commanding them and saying, "Do not go into the streets of Israel, and do not go to the scribes and Pharisees, but go into the cities of the Samaritans and to the ignorant in all parts of the world.

6. "Once I have left you, go to those who lack understanding, to the idol-worshippers and the ignorant, because they do not belong to the house of Israel, which will bring death and bloodshed into the world.

7. "Go out and preach and say, 'The laws of nature are The Laws of Creation, and the power of the Creational spirit within humans embodies life.

8. "Heal the sick, raise the dead, cleanse the lepers, drive out evil spirits. Because you received without having to pay, give therefore without compensation.

9. "You shall not amass gold, silver or copper in your belts.

10. "Also, on your travels, you shall not take large bags with you in which to carry food, water and clothing.

11. "Go on your way with only the bare essentials for eating and sleeping, for keeping yourselves clean, and for a change of clothing.

12. "Never carry too much with you, because you would only burden yourselves and become welcome victims of waylaying bandits.

13. "Remember furthermore, all labor is worthy of its reward, and you will not be wanting if you diligently preach and teach the true knowledge.

14. "When you go into a city or village, inquire if someone is there who is worthy; and stay with him until you depart.

15. "And when you enter a house, greet it.

16. "If the house is worthy, your peace will pass onto the occupants. But if it is not worthy, your peace will return to you.

17. "And if someone will not take you in or listen to your words, leave that house or that city and shake the dust from your feet.

18. "Truly, I say to you, do not stay in such places, because they are abodes of the ignorant and evil; people there will not recognize the words of truth and knowledge.

19. "Flee from those places, because their residents are disloyal to Creation and the laws of nature; the people there worship shrines, false gods and idols, but not Creation, nor do they follow its Laws.

20. "Flee from those places, for people there will try to take your life, because they do not want to forsake their false teachings.

21. "Flee from such unrighteous people, because you must not lose your life for the sake of truth and knowledge. No law demands this of you, nor is there one that endorses such recklessness.

22. "Truly, I say to you, many, nevertheless, will die and shed their blood into the sand, because later my teachings will be turned into false teachings that I never preached and which originate in the minds of the scribes and priests.

23. "Thereby, they will bring the people under their control through belief in their false teachings, in order to rob them of their goods and belongings.

24. "Throughout the world, there will be wailing and chattering of teeth when the blood flows from all those who have made my teachings of wisdom and knowledge into false teachings, and when the blood flows from all of those who, in their false belief and through evil seduction, believe and advocate these false teachings that certainly are not mine.

25. "Many of these false believers will lose their lives, including many Israelites, who will never find their peace until the end of the world, because they are ignorant and unwise and deny the power of the spirit, of love and of knowledge.

26. "Truly, I say to you, the people of Israel were never one distinct people, and they have always lived by murder, robbery and fire. They gained possession of this land through guile and murder in reprehensible, predatory wars, where the best of friends were slaughtered like wild animals.

27. "May the people of Israel be cursed until the end of the world, and never find their peace.

28. "Behold, like sheep among the wolves, I am sending you among the ignorant and the idolaters. Therefore, be wise as serpents and innocent as doves.

29. "But beware of the people, for they will turn you over to the courts and scourge you in their synagogues.

30. "And you will be led before sovereigns and kings because of my teachings, as witnesses to them and to all other ignorant people.

31. "If you cannot flee and they turn you over to the courts, do not be concerned; the power of your spirit will not leave you, and your knowledge will tell you what you should say.

32. "It will not be you who speaks, but the power of your spirit with its knowledge.

33. "And you will come to be hated for the sake of my teachings. But those who persevere to the end will be great.

34. "When they persecute you in one city, however, flee to another.

35. "Do not go to too much trouble with the cities of Israel, for truly, I say to you, you will get nowhere with the people of Israel until the end of the world.

36. "The disciple is never above the teacher, nor the servant above the master.

37. "It is enough for the disciple to be like his teacher and the servant like his master.

38. "If they have called the master of the house Beelzebub, how much more will they malign those of his household?

39. "Therefore, beware of Israel because it is like a festering boil.

40. "However, do not be afraid of them, because there is nothing hidden that will not be revealed and nothing secret that will not be known.

41. "What I tell you in darkness, speak in the light; and what is whispered into your ear, proclaim from the rooftops.

42. "Do not be afraid of evil slander, nor fear those who take life and limb.

43. "Do not think that I have come to bring peace on Earth.

44. "Truly, I have not come to bring peace, but the sword of knowledge about the power of the spirit, which dwells within the human being.

45. "For I have come to bring wisdom and knowledge and to provoke mankind: son against his father, daughter against her mother, daughter-in-law against her mother-in-law, servant against master, citizen against government and believer against preacher.

46. "The people's enemies will be their own house mates.

47. "The path of truth is long and the wisdom of knowledge will only penetrate slowly.

48. "Dark ages will follow, centuries and millennia, before the truth

of the spirit will penetrate to the people.

49. "The unrighteous and the ignorant, including the scribes, priests and the authorities, will hate those who have the knowledge and will, therefore, persecute them and sow enmity."

11

The Baptist's Question

1. It happened that after Jmmanuel had finished giving such directives to his twelve disciples, he continued on from there, teaching and preaching in their cities.

2. When John in prison heard about the works of Jmmanuel, he sent forth his disciples to him and had them say,

3. "Are you the one who is to come, the king of wisdom, as foretold by the prophets, or should we wait for another?"

4. Jmmanuel answered and said to them, "Go back and report to John what you hear and see:

5. "The blind see, the lame walk, the lepers are cleansed, the deaf hear, the dead rise, and the truth of knowledge is proclaimed to those who seek it.

6. "And blessed are those who are not offended by my teachings.

Testimony About the Baptist

7. As they were leaving, Jmmanuel began to speak to the people of John, "What did you go out into the wilderness to see?

8. "Did you expect to see a reed blowing to and fro in the wind?

9. "Or, what did you go out to see?

10. "Did you expect to see a man clothed in soft raiment?

11. "Behold, those who wear soft raiment are in kings' houses with the rulers and the rich, and with the hypocrites, scribes and priests.

12. "Or what did you go out for?

13. "Did you expect to see a prophet?

14. "Yes, I tell you, he is more than a prophet.

15. "This is he of whom it is written, 'Behold, I will send my messenger before you, who shall prepare your way before you.

16. "Truly, I say to you, among all those born of women, no one has arisen who is greater than John the Baptist.

17. "But now, in the days of John the Baptist, the Earth suffers from violence, and those who commit violence are devastating it.

18. "For all prophets and the law have foretold up to the time of John.

19. "And if you wish to accept it, he is Elisha, who was to come again in his next life.

20. "Those who have ears, let them hear!

In Praise of the Spirit and the Knowledge

21. "But to whom shall I compare this generation?

22. "It is like the children who sit at the market and call to their playmates, saying,

23. "'We struck up a tune for you, and you would not dance; we wailed before you, and you would not mourn.

24. "John, who is Elisha, has come neither eating nor drinking; so they say, 'He is possessed.'

25. "But I have come, eating and drinking, and so they say, 'Behold, what a glutton and winebibber this man is, a companion of the tax collectors and the unjust.'

26. "Yet wisdom is justified through the acknowledged deeds

27. But at this time Jmmanuel began to speak, "Praise be to Creation, maker of the heavens, the Universe and the Earth for keeping the

knowledge and power of the spirit hidden from the unwise and the misguided who spread the false teachings, and for revealing this knowledge to sincere seekers now.

28. "Yes, it has been good of Creation, and of god and his celestial sons as well, that they have thwarted until now the misuse of power among Earth humans.

29. "All things have now been given over to mankind, and no one knows the secret of Creation, not even one person, and therefore neither god nor his followers.

30. "And all things have now been given over to me by god, whose guardian angels taught me the laws and knowledge of nature and the Laws emanating from Creation.

31. "So come to me, all you who are seeking and thirsting for knowledge and truth; I will refresh you.

32. "Take upon yourselves the yoke of having to learn the new teachings, for they offer enlightenment; within them you will find peace for your life,

33. "because the yoke of spiritual development is gentle, and its burden is light."

12

Regarding Marriage and Cohabitation

1. And it came to pass that Jmmanuel began to speak of the laws of marriage and related topics, and he said:

2. "You have been given the directive: 'You shall not commit adultery.'

3. "Despite this, people commit adultery and fornication, thus violating the laws of nature.

4. "It is written, however, 'Whosoever commits adultery and fornication shall be punished, because the fallible are unworthy of life and its laws; thus they shall be castrated or sterilized.

5. "If unbetrothed men and women bed down with one another in disgrace and without loving each other, they shall be punished also, for the fallible are unworthy of life and its laws; thus they shall be castrated or sterilized.

6. "And if two men bed down with each other, then they shall be punished, for those fallible are unworthy of life and its laws and behave heretically; thus they shall also be castrated, expelled and banished before the people.

7. "If, however, two women bed down with one another, they shall not be punished, because they do not violate life and its laws, since they are not inseminating but are bearing.

8. "When inseminator and inseminator join together, life is desecrated and destroyed. But if conceiver and conceiver join together, there is neither desecration nor destruction nor procreation.

9. "Truly, I say to you, there is no animal beneath the heavens that would behave like humankind and violate The Laws of Creation and nature. Are you not much more than the animals?

10. "No animal is found under the heavens for which males cohabit with other males, but females are found together with females, because male and female animals follow the laws of nature.

11. "Whosoever indulges in fornication for the sake of pay or pleasure shall be castrated or sterilized, expelled and banished before the people.

Regarding Marriage and Cohabitation

12. "Whosoever sexually abuses a child is unworthy of life and its laws and shall therefore be punished by castration or sterilization, and be deprived of freedom through lifelong confinement and isolation.

13. "Whosoever indulges in incest is unworthy of life and its laws and shall therefore be punished by castration or sterilization, and be deprived of freedom through lifelong confinement and isolation.

14. "Whosoever has sexual intercourse with an animal is unworthy of life and its laws and shall be castrated or sterilized, and be expelled and banished before the people.

15. "Whosoever marries a man or woman divorced in guilt shall be castrated or sterilized, because he or she is unworthy of life and its laws. They shall both be expelled and banished before the people.

16. "He who begets a child without being married to the woman and leaves her unmarried is unworthy of life and its laws and shall therefore be punished by castration and loss of his freedom.

17. "Whosoever rapes a woman or a man is unworthy of life and its laws and shall therefore be punished by castration or sterilization, and

be deprived of freedom through lifelong confinement and isolation.

18. "Whosoever commits violence against another person's body, life or mental health is unworthy of life and its laws and shall therefore be punished with loss of freedom through lifelong confinement and isolation.

19. "Truly, truly, I say to you, these laws are rational and were established by nature, and they shall be obeyed, or humans will bring death to themselves in great masses.

20. "This Earth can nourish and support five hundred million people of all human populations. But if these laws are not followed, in two times a thousand years there will exist ten times five hundred million people, and the Earth will no longer be able to support them.

21. "Famines, catastrophes, worldwide wars and epidemics will rule the Earth; Earth humans will kill each other, and only a few will survive.

22. "Truly, I say to you, there will be wailing and chattering of teeth when so much human blood drenches the sands of Earth that new life forms arise from it, bringing the final horror to mankind.

23. "But on this day you have been allowed to receive all good things, and have been given the laws by which you shall live.

24. "And you shall adhere to additional laws, so that you will have prosperity on Earth and peace within your families.

25. "Do away with enforcing the old law that subjects woman to man, since she is a person like the man, with equal rights and obligations.

26. "But when a man marries a woman, he shall pay to the most trusted steward of her possessions a price as security, so that she will not suffer from lack of necessities.

27. "The price shall be calculated whereby a hundred pieces of silver will be required for each year of the woman's age, if her health is not lacking. Thus she will be measured according to her knowledge, abilities and strength.

28. "The price shall not be considered that of a purchase, but as security for the woman, so she will not suffer from want.

29. "The bond of matrimony between man and woman shall

be permitted only if both are mentally competent and capable of conducting a marriage according to the laws.

30. "A marriage agreement between man and woman shall be concluded only when the price for the woman is paid.

31. "If, according to prearranged agreement, no price is paid, the law applies that the man must provide for all of the wife's necessities.

32. "A wife's infertility is no cause for divorce, nor for any other judgment or action.

33. "The only valid grounds for divorce, aside from adultery, are the destruction or endangerment of the material consciousness, the body or the life of a member of one's own family.

34. "A person who is to blame for a divorce shall be castrated or sterilized, expelled and banished before the people, because he or she is unworthy of life and its laws.

35. "If all is done and adhered to in this way, justice and peace will come to all humankind and life will be preserved."

13

Jmmanuel and the Sabbath

1. At that time, Jmmanuel walked through a field of grain on the Sabbath, and his disciples, being hungry, began to pluck ears of grain and to eat.

2. When the Pharisees saw this, they spoke to him, "Behold, your disciples are doing what is not allowed on the Sabbath."

3. But he spoke to them, "Have you not read what David did when he and those with him were hungry?

4. "How he went into the temple and ate the shewbread, which neither he nor those with him were permitted to eat but only the priests?

5. "Or have you not read in the law, how on the Sabbath the priests in the temple violate the Sabbath and yet are without guilt?

6. "Truly, I say to you, you brood of snakes and vipers, a stone will turn into bread before no work may be done on the Sabbath.

7. "For the law that the Sabbath be kept holy is only a man-made law without logic, as are many man-made laws that contradict The Laws of Creation.

8. "False prophets and distorters of the scriptures are the guilty ones responsible for these false laws that contradict The Laws of Creation and of nature.

9. "It is, therefore, a human law that the Sabbath be kept holy and that no work be done on that day, but it is a law that escapes logic, since this law is a false teaching, emanating from the human mind.

10. "Truly, I say to you, no Sabbath is holy and no Law of Creation dictates that no work may be done on the Sabbath.

11. "Thus, the Sabbath is a day like any other day on which the day's work may be done.

12. "Humans are creatures with wills of their own; thus they alone are masters over the Sabbath, as was previously written in those ancient scriptures and laws that were not adulterated by false prophets, distorters of the scriptures and Pharisees."

13. And he walked on from there and came into their synagogue, where he continued to teach the people.

14. And behold, there was a man with a withered hand, and they asked him, "Is it also lawful to heal on the Sabbath?" in order that they would have further cause against him.

15. But he spoke to them, "You hypocrites, if only you had eyes, ears and minds so you could see, hear and understand; but you are blind and without reason, because you lack the knowledge to see, hear and understand nature. Therefore, you lack insight into The Laws of Creation that would enable you to see, hear and understand that Creation does not keep the Sabbath holy.

16. "Every Sabbath day, Creation rotates the stars through the heavens, regulates the sun, winds and rains and nourishes all creatures on Earth.

17. "It keeps the rivers flowing in their beds, and everything goes its normal way on one Sabbath as on another, just as Creation made it.

18. "But are not humans much more than all the creatures and plants? Thus they are masters over them all when they follow the true laws.

19. "You brood of snakes and vipers, you distorters of the scriptures

who, because of your greed for money and power, spread false teachings; had you but one sheep that fell into a pit on the Sabbath day, who among you would not take hold of it and pull it out?

20. "How much more is a person worth than a sheep or your deceitful and false teachings?"

21. Then he spoke to the man, "Stretch out your hand!"

22. And he stretched it out and it became sound again just like the other hand.

23. Then the Pharisees went out and held counsel about Jmmanuel, on how they could destroy him, since he made known their lies and false teachings in front of the people.

24. When Jmmanuel learned of this, he withdrew from there, and many people followed him, including many sick people; and he healed them all.

25. He warned them, however, not to spread the news about him, because he was afraid he would be captured and put to death by torture.

26. But his dedication to the truth prevailed, and so he continued to reveal his teachings and wisdom to the people.

The Wrongdoings of Judas Ish-Keriot

1. It came to pass that Jmmanuel and his disciples went to Bethlehem, where he taught and instructed the people.

2. However, Judas Ish-Keriot had become disloyal to the teachings of Jmmanuel and lived only for his own gratification.

3. Secretly, he was collecting from Jmmanuel's audiences, accumulating gold, silver and copper in his money bag so he could live vainly.

4. And it happened that Juda Ihariot, the son of Simeon the Pharisee, informed Jmmanuel of Judas Ish-Keriot's wrongdoings, since he hoped to be compensated for this.

5. But Jmmanuel thanked him and did not repay him with any gifts, so Juda Ihariot thought of revenge, for he was greedy for gold, silver and goods.

6. But Judas Ish-Keriot was led into the desert by Jmmanuel where, for three days and three nights, he taught him the concept of right and wrong, whereupon the disciple repented and forthwith followed the teachings of Jmmanuel.

7. When Judas returned to the city, he distributed all his possessions and collections among the poor and became a trusted disciple of Jmmanuel.

8. However, at the same time, it transpired that the writings, in which Judas Ish-Keriot had reported on the teachings of Jmmanuel, were stolen from him. So he told Jmmanuel about it.

9. But he spoke, "Truly, truly, I say to you, Judas Ish-Keriot, you will have to suffer even greater evils than the mere loss of your writings about my teachings and my life.

10. "For over two thousand years, you will be wrongly accused of betraying me, because Simeon the Pharisee wants it so.

11. "But his son, Juda Ihariot, is the real culprit; like his father, Simeon Ihariot, he is a Pharisee who seeks my life.

12. "It is he who stole the writings from you and brought them to the scribes and Pharisees, so they could thereby judge me and put me to death.

13. "He received seventy pieces of silver for your writings and will receive another thirty when he makes it possible to hand me over to the executors.

14. "Truly, I say to you, he will certainly succeed in this, and for two times a thousand years, you will innocently have to pay the penalty for it; consequently, you will become a martyr.

15. "But write down my teachings and my life story another time, for the time will come, in two times a thousand years, when your writings will be revealed.

16. "Until then, my teachings will be falsified and will turn into an evil cult, which will cause much human blood to flow,

17. "because the people are still not prepared to comprehend my teachings and to recognize the truth.

18. "Not until two times a thousand years will an unassuming man come who will recognize my teachings as truth and disseminate them with great courage.

19. "He will be vilified by the established cult religions and advocates of the false teachings about me, and be considered a liar.

20. "But you, Judas Ish-Keriot will until then be innocently reviled as my betrayer and thus be condemned, as a result of the deceitfulness of the chief priests and the ignorance of the people.

21. "But pay no attention to this, for the teaching of the truth demands sacrifices that must be made.

22. "The people are still not very great in their spirit, consciousness and knowledge. Therefore, they must first take upon themselves much guilt and error before they learn to accumulate knowledge and wisdom, so as to recognize the truth.

23. "For all of this to take place, however, and for the knowledge of the truth to bring forth a rich harvest within people, write down my teachings and my life story once again. In this way, my teachings will be available for later generations and bear fruit to the truth.

24. "Remain with me from now on, follow me and faithfully carry out your duty as the transcriber of my teachings, namely the teachings of the laws of nature, which are the original Laws of Creation.

25. "Never will there be a will greater than the will of Creation, which reveals itself through these laws.

26. "But The Laws of Creation have been valid for yesterday and today, and therefore for tomorrow, the day after tomorrow, and for all time.

27. "Thus the Laws are also a determination and hence a predetermination for things of the future that must happen."

The Meaning of the Parables

1. That same day, Jmmanuel went out and walked to the sea, where he sat down.

2. Many people gathered around him, so that he stepped into a boat and sat down, and all the people stood on the shore.

3. He talked to them in parables about various things, saying, "Behold, a sower went out to sow.

4. "While he sowed, some seeds fell on the pathway; then the birds came and ate them up.

5. "And some fell on the rocks, where there was not much soil.

6. "And as the sun rose high, they withered, and because they had no roots, they dried out.

7. "Some fell among the thorns; and the thorns grew up and smothered them.

8. "Some fell on good ground and bore fruit, some hundredfold, some sixty-fold, some thirty-fold.

9. "Those who have ears, let them hear."

10. The disciples stepped up to him and said, "Why do you speak in

parables, when they do not understand your teachings!"

11. He answered, saying, "It has been given to you to understand the secrets of the spirit, but it has not been given to them.

12. "They certainly hear my words, but they still live and think according to the false teachings of their scribes and Pharisees.

13. "Their consciousness is unknowing and empty, therefore they must first learn to live and think.

14. "What would be better to make them come alive and think, if not through speaking in parables?

15. "Truly, I say to you, life and the knowledge of truth are only valuable and good when they are achieved through one's own thinking or through the resolving of mysteries that are recounted in parables.

16. "As yet humans have little knowledge and no insight, and they are not yet conscious of The Laws of Creation and the power of the spirit.

17. "First, humans must learn to recognize the truth and thus to live according to The Laws of Creation, so they may become knowledgeable and strong in spirit.

18. "For to those who have, more will be given so they may have in abundance; but from those who have not, from them will be taken what they have.

19. "Therefore, I speak to them in parables, because with seeing eyes they do not see, and with hearing ears they do not hear; nor do they understand.

20. "And in them the prophecy of Isaiah is fulfilled that says, 'With your ears you will hear and not understand; and with open eyes you will see and not perceive.'

21. "For these people are stubborn in their minds and endeavors. The ears of these humans hear poorly and their eyes slumber, so they neither see with their eyes nor hear with their ears, nor understand with their intelligence. Nor do they try to comprehend the truth and the acknowledged Laws of Creation, although they would thereby attain help and knowledge.

22. "For the people of Israel are unfaithful to The Laws of Creation

and are accursed, and never will they find peace.

23. "Their blood will be shed, for they constantly transgress against The Laws of Creation.

24. "They presume themselves above all humankind as a chosen people and thus as a separate race.

25. "What an evil error and what an evil presumption, for inasmuch as Israel was never one people or one race, so it was never a chosen people.

26. "Unfaithful to The Laws of Creation, Israel is a mass of people with an inglorious past, characterized by murder and arson.

27. "Only a few fathers in the masses of these unfaithful have an honorable past and a traceable family tree.

28. "These, however, are not part of the brood of snakes and vipers who have pledged themselves to the false Judaic faith,

29. "to the false beliefs and false teachings they adopted from Moses who, in turn, had stolen them from the Egyptians.

30. "These few fathers are knowers of the truth and of true knowledge, and they recognize only The Laws of Creation.

31. "They became rare in this land, however, and so can be counted on just one man's hand.

32. "They are only a few, and no one's eyes may recognize them, and no one's ears may hear them.

33. "But blessed are your eyes, for they see, and your ears, for they hear.

34. "Truly, I say to you, many prophets and righteous men have wanted to see what you see but did not see it, and to hear what you hear but did not hear it.

35. "So listen now to the hidden meaning of this parable about the sower:

36. "If someone hears the word of truth about the spirit and the laws, and does not understand it, then the evil one comes and snatches away what is sown in their mind. That is for whom it is sown on the pathway.

37. "But for whom it is sown on the rocks, that is the one who hears

the word and promptly accepts it with joy.

38. "But this person has no roots within, so that which is heard cannot take hold and grow. Rather, this one is fickle and becomes annoyed when misery and persecution arise because of the truth.

39. "But for whom it is sown among the thorns, that is the one who hears the word, but the woes of the world and the deception of material riches smother the truth and the knowledge; thus this one brings forth no fruit.

40. "But for whom it is sown on good ground, this is the one who accepts the word and seeks and finds the truth, so as to be able to live according to the laws of truth; thus the fruit is allowed to grow and ripen, bringing in a rich harvest. One person bears a hundredfold, another sixty-fold and another thirty-fold.

41. "These are the meanings of the parables, whose secrets must be deciphered by the people, in order that they learn to think and develop insights.

42. "Nevertheless, the path to wisdom and finding the truth is long, as is compliance with The Laws of Creation, even though these are so obvious."

The Weeds Among the Good Fruit

43. But he put before them another parable and said, "The spiritual kingdom is like a man who planted good seeds in his field.

44. "But while he slept, his enemy came and sowed weeds among the good seeds and went away.

45. "As the plantings grew and bore fruit, the weeds also appeared.

46. "Then the servants came to the sower and said, 'Master, did you not sow good seed in your field? Where have the weeds come from?'

47. "He spoke to them, 'An enemy has done this.' Then the servants said, 'Do you want us to go out and pull up the weeds?'

48. "He replied, 'No, lest you uproot the good fruit when you pull up the weeds.

49. " 'Let both grow together until the harvest, and near harvest time I will tell the reapers: First gather the weeds and bind them in

bundles, that they may be burned and the ashes strewn over the field so that the soil will be nourished; but gather the good fruit and stack it for me in my barn.'

50. "For behold, said Jmmanuel, "Both grow side by side, the weeds and the good fruit.

51. "The weeds hinder the good fruit from growing, yet later the weeds will become compost and nourish the ground.

52. "Were it not for the weeds being made into nourishment for the soil, the good fruit could not grow, since it needs nourishment."

The Mustard Seed

53. He presented the people with another parable, saying, "The spiritual kingdom is like a mustard seed that a man took and sowed in his field.

54. "It is the smallest among the seeds, but when it is grown, it is bigger than all the shrubs and becomes a tree, so that the birds of the sky come and dwell in its branches.

The Leaven

55. He told the people another parable, "The spiritual kingdom is like leaven, which a woman took and mixed into three bushels of flour until it was thoroughly leavened."

56. Jmmanuel told the people all of this in parables, and he did not speak to them without using parables,

57. So that what is said through the prophet would be fulfilled, who states, "He will open his mouth in parables and will proclaim what has been hidden since the beginning of the world." This was so that people might learn from it, find the truth, and recognize and follow the laws.

The Treasure in the Field and the Priceless Pearl

58. "Those who have ears, let them hear: The spiritual kingdom is like a hidden treasure in the field, which a person finds and conceals; and in his joy over the discovery he goes out and sells everything he has and buys the field.

59. "Once more, the spiritual kingdom is like a merchant who was searching for fine pearls. When he found a precious pearl, he went and sold everything he had and bought it.

The Fish Net

60. "Again, the spiritual kingdom is like a net that was thrown into the sea and caught all manner of fish.

61. "When it was full, the fishermen pulled it ashore, sat down and sorted the good fish into containers, but threw the useless ones away.

62. "Such is the spiritual kingdom, which rules within humans and whose king is the human being itself.

63. "Pay heed to the parables accordingly, and learn to solve their secrets, so that you learn to think and to recognize and follow The Laws of Creation.

64. "Have you understood all this?" And they said, "Yes."

65. Then he said, "Therefore, every scribe who has become a disciple of the spiritual knowledge, and the spiritual kingdom is like the father of a household who retrieves from his treasure the new and the old.

In Nazareth

66. It happened that after Jmmanuel had finished these parables, he went away from there.

67. Arriving in his hometown of Nazareth, he taught in the synagogue. The people were appalled and they said, "How did he come by such wisdom and deeds?

68. "Is he not the son of Joseph, the carpenter whose wife became pregnant by a guardian angel?

69. "Is not his mother named Mary?

70. "Are not his brothers Judas, Joseph, Simeon and Jacob?

71. "And his sisters, are they not all with us?

72. "From where does he get all this wisdom and the power for his deeds?"

73. So they took offense to him and threatened to turn him over to the courts.

74. But Jmmanuel spoke, "Nowhere is a prophet valued less than in his own country and in his own house. This will prove true for all time, as long as humanity has little knowledge and is enslaved by the delusional teachings of the scribes and distorters of scripture.

75. "So it will come true in two times a thousand years, when humans have become knowledgeable and thinking, and when my actual unfalsified teachings will be revealed anew.

76. "The new prophet of that distant future will not possess as much strength and power over evil and sickness.

77. "But his knowledge will surpass mine, and his revelations about my real teachings will shake the foundations of the entire Earth, for in his time the world will be inundated by my teachings, as falsified by the distorters of the scriptures, and it will be living in false religious cults that bring death.

78. "It will be a time when wars from space begin to threaten, and many new gods will seek to rule over the Earth.

79. "Truly, truly, I say to you, the new prophet will be persecuted not only by a wrong-minded people, as will happen to me, but also by the whole world and by many deluded religious cults, which will bring forth many false prophets.

80. "Yet, before the end of two times a thousand years, the new prophet will reveal my unfalsified teachings to small groups, just as I teach the wisdom, the knowledge and the Laws of the spirit and of Creation to small groups of trusted friends and disciples.

81. "Nevertheless, his path will be very difficult and full of obstacles, because he will begin his mission in a peace-loving country in the North which will be dominated, however, by a strict and false religious cult based upon scriptural distortions of my teachings.

82. "Thus I prophesy, and thus it shall be."

83. And he did not there show great signs of his power, nor did he impart his great wisdom because of their disdain for the truth.

Herod and the Baptist

1. At the time when Jmmanuel was staying in Nazareth, news about him reached Herod.

2. And he spoke to his people, "Surely this is John the Baptist, who has arisen from the dead and who therefore possesses such mighty powers."

3. For Herod had seized John, bound him and put him into prison because of Herodias, the wife of his brother Philippus, and had him beheaded.

4. However, it had come to pass previously that John reprimanded Herod, saying, "It is not good that you have taken Herodias, because you have committed adultery with your brother's wife and therefore you must be punished according to the law."

5. For this he wanted to kill the Baptist, but was afraid of the people, because they considered this man to be a prophet.

6. However, as Herod was celebrating his birthday, the daughter of Herodias danced before them, and Herod was greatly pleased.

7. He therefore promised her, with an unlawful oath, that he would

give her whatever she would demand of him.

8. And as she had been induced accordingly by her mother, she said, "Give me the head of John the Baptist on a silver platter."

9. But the daughter of Herodias wept while saying this, not just because she was inspired with love for John the Baptist, but also because she was devoted to his teachings.

10. The king was pleased that Herodias had persuaded her daughter to demand the head of John the Baptist, because this way he was not guilty in the eyes of the people, inasmuch as he had taken an oath.

11. But Herodias' daughter did not know that Herod and her mother had agreed, even before the dance, to demand the head of John the Baptist through her.

12. Thus Herod sent someone and had John beheaded in prison.

13. His head was carried in on a silver platter and given to the girl.

14. She kissed the brow of the decapitated head, wept bitterly and said,

15. "I did not know that love tastes so bitter."

16. Then she brought the head of the Baptist to her mother.

17. His disciples then came, took the body and buried it. Then they went to Jmmanuel and told him of the event.

18. When Jmmanuel heard this, he was overcome with fear and retreated by boat to a deserted area. However, when the people heard that, they followed him on foot from the towns.

19. Jmmanuel saw the large crowd from the water, and feeling sorry for them, he went ashore and healed their sick.

The Feeding of the Five Thousand

20. In the evening, his disciples came to him and said, "This area is deserted and night is falling over the land. Tell the people to go away so that they can buy food and drink in the villages."

21. But Jmmanuel said, "It is not necessary that they go away. Give them food and drink."

22. They replied, "We have nothing here but five loaves of bread and three fish.

23. And he said, "Bring them to me."

24. And telling the people to stay put, he took the five loaves of bread and the three fish, spoke secret words, broke the loaves of bread, cut up the fish and gave them to his disciples; and the disciples gave them to the people.

25. They all ate and were filled, and they saved what was left over: twelve baskets full of pieces.

26. And there were about five thousand who had eaten.

Walking on the Sea

27. Soon afterward, Jmmanuel directed his disciples to enter the boat and to cross over to the city in advance of him, so he could dismiss the people.

28. After he had sent the people away, he climbed up a small mountain alone to rest and regain his depleted strength. And so he was there alone in the evening.

29. The disciples' boat was at that time in the middle of the sea and being threatened by the waves, for the wind was against them and the storm was over them.

30. However, on the fourth watch during the night, Jmmanuel approached them, walking on the water of the sea.

31. When his disciples saw him walking on the water, they were terrified and said, "He is a ghost!" And they screamed in fear.

32. But soon Jmmanuel came closer, spoke to them and said, "Be comforted, it is I, do not be afraid."

33. "Master, is it you!?" Peter asked.

34. "Truly, it is I," said Jmmanuel.

35. But Peter answered him and said, "Master, if it is you, then let me come to you on the water."

36. And Jmmanuel said, "Come here to me and don't be afraid.

37. "Understand and know that the water is carrying you, and it will carry you.

38. "Do not doubt your knowledge and ability, and the water will be a firm foundation."

39. And Peter stepped out of the boat, walked on the water and approached Jmmanuel.

40. But when strong thunder ripped through the howling storm, he was startled and began to sink, screaming, "Jmmanuel, help me!"

41. Jmmanuel quickly went to him, stretched out his hand and grabbed him, saying, "Oh, you of little knowledge, why are you frightened and why do you become doubtful in your fright?

42. "The power of your knowledge gives you the ability, as you have just witnessed.

43. "You trusted in my words before the thunder came, but then you were frightened and began to doubt, and so the power of knowledge left you and your ability disappeared.

44. "Never doubt the power of your spirit, which is a part of Creation itself and therefore knows no limits of power.

45. "Behold, there was a little bird that circled at great heights and sang, rejoicing about life, when a strong gust of wind came and made it waver. It then suddenly doubted its power to fly, plummeted down and was killed.

46. "Therefore, never doubt the power of your spirit and never doubt your knowledge and ability when logic proves to you The Laws of Creation in truth and correctness."

47. They stepped into the boat and Jmmanuel commanded the storm to stop. It abated and the winds ceased.

48. Those who were in the boat marvelled and said, "You are indeed a master of the spirit and someone who knows The Laws of Creation.

49. "No one like you has ever been born among us, nor has any prophet known to us had such power."

50. But Jmmanuel answered, "I tell you there are greater masters of spiritual power than I, and they are our distant forefathers of Petale." Petale is the highest level of spiritual development that a pure-spirit form can attain before it ultimately melds with Creation and becomes one with it.

51. "And great are they also, who came from the depths of space, and the greatest among them is god, and he is the spiritual ruler of three human lineages.

52. "However, above him stands Creation, whose Laws he faithfully follows and respects; therefore, he is not omnipotent, as only Creation itself can be.

53. "Thus, there are also limits set for him who allows himself to be called god, and who is above emperors and kings, as the Word says.

54. "But humans are ignorant and immature, thus they believe god to be Creation and serve an erroneous doctrine, as was falsified by the distorters of the scriptures.

55. "Thus, since people believe in god, they do not know about the reality of Creation, but god is human as we are.

56. "But the difference is that in his consciousness and knowledge, and in wisdom, logic and love, he is a thousand times greater than you and greater than all people of Earth.

57. "But he is not Creation, which is infinite and without form.

58. "Thus, god is also one of Creation's creatures who, according to illogical human opinion, has no beginning and no end."

59. And they went across the sea and came ashore at Gennesaret.

60. And as the people in that region became aware of him, they sent word throughout the land and brought to him all who were sick.

61. Then they asked him if they might just touch the hem of his garment, so they would be healed.

62. And thus it came to pass, those who touched the hem of his garment became well.

Human Commandments and The Laws of Creation

1. Pharisees and scribes from Jerusalem came to Jmmanuel and said,

2. "Why do your disciples disregard the statutes of the elders?"

3. He answered, saying to them, "Why do you violate The Laws of Creation by following your statutes?

4. "Moses said, according to the laws of mankind, 'You must honor your father and mother, but those who unjustly dishonor their father and mother shall die.'

5. "The teaching of The Laws of Creation is this: You shall honor your father and mother, but whosoever does not honor their father and mother shall be expelled from the family and from the society of the righteous.

6. "But you teach, 'Say to one's father or mother: I donate to the religious cult what I owe on your behalf, thus I am no longer indebted to you.'

7. "Therefore you wrongly teach that people no longer need to honor their father or mother. Thus you have traded The Laws of Creation for your own statutes and lust for power.

8. "You hypocrites, Isaiah has prophesied quite accurately about you when he said,

9. " 'The people of Israel profess to follow and obey The Laws of Creation, but their hearts and their knowledge are far from it.

10. " 'They serve their cult in vain, because they teach such falsified and untruthful teachings, which are no more than man-made laws.' "

11. And Jmmanuel called the people to him and said, "Listen and understand!

12. "The teachings of the scribes and Pharisees are false and untruthful, for they preach to you only man-made statutes, which are not The Laws of Creation."

13. Thereupon, his disciples came to him and said, "Are you aware that the scribes and the Pharisees were offended by your words when they heard them?

14. "They went out to bear witness against you and to have you killed because of your teachings."

15. But he answered and spoke, "All plants that do not live according to The Laws of Creation will dry up and rot.

16. "Leave them be, they are blind leaders of the blind; but when a blind man leads another blind man, both will fall into the pit.

17. "But let us go away, so that the henchmen remain without booty."

18. Then Peter answered him, saying, "Please interpret your speech about the plants and the blind men for us."

19. But Jmmanuel reprimanded his disciples and said, "Are you, too, still without wisdom and, therefore, also ignorant and doubting in recognition, comprehension and understanding?

20. "You have been with me for a long time now, but you still lack the ability to think and recognize the truth.

21. "Truly, I say to you, you yourselves will do much toward falsifying my teachings in the future.

22. "In your knowledge, you barely exceed the other people.

23. "Haven't you realized yet that all the parables and speeches have a spiritual meaning and are, therefore, about the spiritual life of humans?

24. "Oh, you of little knowledge, does your understanding still not extend beyond the stupidity of the people?

25. "Beware, lest you see me in a false light and accuse me of an origin from which I could not have descended."

The Pharisees Demand a Sign

1. Jmmanuel departed and escaped to the region of Sidon and Tyre.

2. And behold, the Sadducees and Pharisees approached him and demanded that he demonstrate a sign of his spiritual power.

3. But he answered, saying, "In the evening you say, 'Tomorrow will be a fair day, because the sky is red.'

4. "And in the morning you say, 'Today will be foul weather, because the sky is red and cloudy.' So you can judge by the appearance of the sky, why then can you not also judge by the signs of the time?

5. "This wicked and unfaithful generation is seeking a sign; no sign shall be given to it except for the sign of Jonah, who disappeared alive into the belly of the fish, dwelled alive in its belly and emerged alive again into the light."

6. And he left them and went away.

The Leaven and the Pharisees

7. When they sailed across the sea and arrived at the other shore, they had forgotten to take along some bread.

8. But Jmmanuel said to them, "Take care and beware of the leaven of the Pharisees and the Sadducees."

9. They spoke to each other and said, "This must refer to our not having brought along bread or anything else to eat."

10. When Jmmanuel heard this, he was angry and said, "Oh, you of little knowledge, why does it worry you that you have no bread?

11. "Don't you yet understand, and can't you imagine the meaning of my words?

12. "Are you then of such little knowledge and without understanding that you can't recognize the meaning?

13. "Do you still not understand, and do you intend not to understand for all times?

14. "Don't you remember the five loaves of bread and the three fish divided among the five thousand and how many basketfuls you then saved?

15. "How is it you don't understand that I am not speaking to you about the bread you eat every day? But I tell you this: Beware of the leaven of the Pharisees and the Sadducees."

16. Then they finally understood that he had not said for them to beware of the leaven of the bread, but of the false and adulterated teachings of the scribes and Pharisees.

Peter's Faith

17. Jmmanuel came into the area of Caesarea Philippi and asked his disciples, "Who do the people say that I am?"

18. They said, "Some say that you are John the Baptist, others that you are Elijah, and still others that you are Jeremiah or one of the old prophets."

19. And he said to them, "But who do you say that I am?"

20. Simon Peter answered, saying, "You are the prophesied Messiah and a son of the living god who is the spiritual ruler of the three human lineages."

21. Jmmanuel became angry and answered, "Oh, you unfortunate one, my teachings have not revealed this to you, for I instructed you in the truth.

The Pharisees Demand a Sign

22. "And I also tell you, you certainly are a faithful disciple, but your understanding must be compared to that of a child.

23. "You are Peter, and I cannot build my teachings on your rock. You will open the portals of misunderstanding, so that the people will be overcome by your mistakened interpretation of my teachings and will follow them and live according to falsified teachings.

24. "I cannot give you the key to the spiritual kingdom, otherwise you would open false locks and wrong portals with it.

25. "I am not the son of a spiritual ruler of three human lineages and, therefore, not the son of god; furthermore, the sole spiritual power is Creation and never a human being; therefore, free yourself from these erroneous teachings and learn the truth.

26. "My mother is Mary, who truly conceived me through a guardian angel, a descendant of our ancestors, who travelled here from the far reaches of the Universe; and my earthly father is Joseph, who only acts as my paternal guardian."

27. Then he warned his disciples never to tell or wrongly assume such things, and that they were not allowed to spread Peter's confusing teachings.

Proclamation of the Passion

28. From that time onward, Jmmanuel began to tell his disciples that he would have to go to Jerusalem and suffer much from the elders, scribes and chief priests, because he could not help but bring his teachings to them.

29. And Peter took him aside and spoke to him angrily, "May god or Creation prevent that!

30. "This must not happen to you, because they will catch and torture and kill you."

31. But he turned to Peter, became angry and said, "Get away from me, Satan, for you are an annoyance, because you are thinking not in spiritual but in human terms.

32. "Simon Peter, again you make me angry and show your ignorant thinking.

33. "Truly, I say to you, owing to your lack of understanding, the world will shed much blood because you will falsify my teachings and spread them erroneously among the people.

34. "You will be to blame for the deaths of many people, as well as for the origin of a false name for me and for the evil insult of calling me the son of god, and calling god Creation itself.

35. "But you are still under the grace of my long-suffering patience, so you can still measurably improve upon your irrationality."

36. Then Jmmanuel said to his disciples, "Those who desire to follow my teachings should take upon themselves the burden of the search for truth, insight and understanding,

37. "Because those who live their lives in truth and knowledge will be victorious, but those who live their lives in untruth and ignorance will lose.

38. "What would it profit them if they should gain the whole world, yet still damage their consciousness?

39. "Or, how can one help one's spirit if unable to think?

40. "Truly, I say to you, there are several here who will not taste the power of spiritual knowledge in this life, and so they will learn in the next life.

41. "The human spirit is ignorant until it has gained knowledge through thinking and inquiry.

42. "The spirit of a person is not a human product but is a part of Creation given to humans. It must be made knowledgeable and perfected,

43. "So that it proceeds to become one with Creation, since Creation, too, lives in constant growth.

44. "Creation is timeless, and so is the human spirit.

45. "The teaching of this knowledge is extensive and not simple, but it is the way to life that is diverse in its nature.

46. "The human life is destined for perfection of the spirit, so that life be lived in fulfillment thereof.

47. "Even when humans burden themselves with mistakes, they act according to The Laws of Creation, because they learn from them and

gather insight and knowledge, whereby they develop their spirits, and through their spirits' strength they are able to act.

48. "Without making mistakes it is impossible, therefore, to gather the logic, insight, knowledge, love and wisdom necessary to develop the spirit.

49. "Truly, I say to you, the teachings of the chief priests, Pharisees and scribes are erroneous and false when they tell you that a mistake would be punished by god or Creation when, in fact, the mistake serves the insight and knowledge, and hence the progress, of the spirit.

50. "Therefore, there is no punishable mistake, if it serves the insight, knowledge and progress of the spirit; likewise, there is no inheritable mistake or punishment in this world or another world.

51. "Punishment of such a mistake would contradict all the laws of nature and thus all The Laws of Creation.

52. "When one makes a mistake that serves the insight, knowledge, and progress of the spirit, there is no punishment, neither in this life nor in any subsequent life.

53. "Thus, humans live with the mission of perfecting their spirits and obtaining insight and knowledge through mistakes, so that they may lead the lives to which they were destined.

54. "Humans, however, neither learn consistently nor in accordance with the greatness of their spirit, which is guided by The Laws of Creation and introduced to situations that must sequentially ensue, for they are destined. Thus humans mislead their consciousness, their thinking, feeling and actions; they burden themselves with guilt and expose their inner selves to attacks from outside forces.

55. "In this manner, the power of consciousness of others affects the life of the individual, for better or worse.

56. "Because humans at this time are beginning to think and perceive, they are in need of the teachings. Thus, the prophets have been sent by the celestial sons to teach humankind about the true Laws of Creation and the knowledge regarding life.

57. "But the people are still ignorant and addicted to the false laws of the chief priests and distorters of the scriptures. Consequently, they

do not recognize the new teachings as truth.

58. "Lacking understanding, the people curse the truth which yet must come; they curse, stone, kill and crucify the prophets.

59. "But since the teachings of the truth must be brought to the people, the prophets have to bear great burdens and suffering under the curse of the people.

60. "Just as they persecuted many prophets, they are now after my life.

61. "The prophecy of the inexorable destiny says that it shall come true for me, insofar that I, an innocent man, will be declared guilty.

62. "However, it will not come to pass that I am killed, but while in a state of near-death, I will be considered dead for three days and three nights. I will be placed in a rock tomb, so that the sign of Jonah will be fulfilled.

63. "My friends from faraway India, who are well versed in the art of healing, will be my caretakers and will help me flee from the tomb on the third day, so that I then may finish my mission among the people of India.

64. "It shall come to pass that I will attain a certain insight, increase my knowledge and generate a new strength in spirit and consciousness."

19

The Nature of a Child's Thinking

1. It came to pass that the disciples stepped up to Jmmanuel and asked, "Who is the greatest in spirit?"

2. Jmmanuel called a child to him, placed the youth in their midst,

3. And spoke, "Truly, I say to you, unless you change and become like the children, you will not become great in spirit.

4. "Those who search, seek and gather insights and thirst for knowledge like this child will be great in spirit.

5. "Those who search, seek and find like such a child will always reach their fullest potential within themselves.

6. "But whosoever does not heed this truth and embraces erroneous teachings, and neither searches nor finds, would be better off with a millstone hung around the neck and drowned in the deepest part of the sea.

7. "Truly, there is no sense in life and no fulfilment of its meaning without searching, seeking and finding.

8. "It would be better to expel those who lack understanding from the company of the true seekers and of those who search for true life, so that

they do not hinder those willing to seek the truth.

9. "The unreasonable ones will surely be willing to heed The Laws of Creation in their lives after their expulsion.

10. "Woe to the world for troubles, because trouble must come through troublemakers; but woe to those who cause troubles.

11. "Don't be concerned if your hand or foot troubles you and falls off. It is better to lose a limb and grow great in spirit than to have two hands and two feet and a consciousness that remains small, or even wastes away.

12. "Don't be concerned if an eye troubles you and becomes blind. It is better for you to see The Laws of Creation in the power of your spirit and consciousness than to have two eyes and yet be spiritually blind in consciousness.

13. "See to it that you are not one of those who is sound in body but sick and lacking in consciousness.

The Errors of Your Neighbor

14. "Search for the meaning and truth in my teachings. Since I am human like you, I, too, have had to search and perceive.

15. "Since I am human like you and have gathered my knowledge, you are also capable of learning, searching, perceiving and knowing; in so doing you may grasp and observe The Laws of Creation.

16. "If your neighbor errs and embraces a falsified teaching, go and reveal their error in private.

17. "If they listen to you, you have won your neighbor.

18. "If your neighbor does not listen and continues to be enslaved by a lack of understanding, leave that person be, for they are not worthy of your teaching, once you have done everything possible.

19. "It is better to let an unreasonable person walk on the path of misery than to bring confusion to one's own consciousness.

20. "Truly I say to you, the heavens will collapse before an unreasonable person can be taught reason; therefore, beware of such persons.

21. "Sow the seeds of wisdom on fertile soil where they can germinate,

22. "Because only the germinated seed will bring forth fruit."

20

Marriage, Divorce and Celibacy

1. It happened that after Jmmanuel had concluded these talks, he departed from Galilee and entered the land of Judea beyond the Jordan.

2. Many people followed him, and he healed the sick there.

3. The Pharisees approached him and tempted him by asking, "Is it right for a man to divorce his wife on any grounds?"

4. He answered, saying, "Truly, I say to you, stars would sooner fall from the sky than for divorce to be permissible.

5. "Truly, a person will leave father and mother for the sake of marriage and will cling to their spouse, so as to become one flesh and blood.

6. "So they are now no longer two, but one flesh and blood, which is uniquely theirs.

7. "From one flesh and blood, they bring forth offspring, who again are of the same flesh and blood as their father and mother.

8. "What has been joined together in this way, man shall not part, because it is against the laws of nature."

9. Then they asked, "Why did Moses command that a decree of annulment be issued in case of divorce?"

10. He spoke to them, "Moses gave you permission to divorce because of the hardness of your hearts and his dominion over you. But such has not been the case from the beginning of humankind, for Moses has broken a law in this instance.

11. "But I say to you, whosoever divorces, except for fornication or the other stipulated transgressions, and marries someone else, commits adultery."

12. And the disciples said to him, "If this is the way it is between a man and his spouse, then it is not good to marry."

13. But he spoke to them, "Not everyone understands this message, except those to whom it is given.

14. "Some do not enter into marriage because from the time of their birth they are incapable of it; some do not enter marriage because other people have made them unsuited for it; and still others do not enter marriage because they renounce it for the sake of spiritual strength.

15. "Those who can grasp this, let them grasp it."

Blessing of the Children

16. Then children were brought to him, so that he would lay his hands on them and bless them, but the disciples rebuked them.

17. However, Jmmanuel spoke, "Let the children be and do not hinder them from coming to me, because they are my most attentive listeners, and theirs is the realm of wisdom.

18. And he laid his hands upon them and said, "Learn knowledge and wisdom to become spiritually perfect and true followers of the law.

19. "Truly, I say to you, inasmuch as I am called Jmmanuel, which means 'the one with godly knowledge,' you also shall bear this name when you grasp the wisdom of knowledge."

20. And to his disciples he said, "Truly, truly, I say to you, seek knowledge and recognize the truth, so that you will become wise.

21. "Being named 'the one with godly knowledge' indicates that I stand spiritually above kings and emperors; therefore it says that

wisdom is among us.

22. "Thus I am the king of wisdom among Earth humans, as god is the king of wisdom among the sons of heaven who, together with god, are the creators of the three human lineages.

23. "As I was born of an Earth woman and speak her language, I am called Jmmanuel, as god in his language is called god, which also means king of wisdom, and he is often a ruler over a human population and master over a people.

24. "Seek and understand the meaning of my speech, lest you may be so bold as to call me the son of god or the son of Creation, or assign to me the power of Creation, or insult me by calling me the lord over good and evil.

25. "Behold the little children, they are not like you; they trust in the truth and wisdom of my speech, and therefore wisdom shall be theirs. So why do you push them away?"

26. And he laid his hands upon them and departed from there.

27. As they were walking, Peter said to him, "Behold, we have forsaken everything to follow you; what will we get in return?"

28. But Jmmanuel replied to them, "Truly, I say to you, some of you who have followed me will embrace the wisdom of my teachings, so you will be spiritually great in reincarnations to come. But some of you will not recognize the wisdom of my teachings and will disseminate erroneous teachings about me. Those will have difficulty finding the truth in future incarnations.

29. "So it will be among all Earth humans everywhere from east to west, and from north to south.

30. "My beneficial teachings will be brought to many, but they will not recognize them.

31. "Many will follow erroneous teachings about me and therefore not find the truth, because they mistake me for god or his son, or perhaps even the son of Creation.

32. "They will speak big words and insist that they alone know the truth, because they will have fallen prey to an evil error and thus will follow evil and falsified teachings.

33. "Many will be first among the people because they will think as humans in their deluded teachings, but they will be last in spiritual knowledge and small in their wisdom.

34. "Wisdom will only exist where the knowledge about the truth bears fruit, and where The Laws of Creation are followed and respected.

21

Two Blind Persons

1. When they set out on their way to Jericho, many people followed him.

2. And behold, two blind persons sat by the wayside; and when they heard Jmmanuel going by, they cried out, saying, "Oh, lord, son of a celestial son, have mercy on us!"

3. The people threatened them to be quiet, but they screamed even louder, saying, "Oh, lord, son of a celestial son, have mercy on us!"

4. And Jmmanuel stood still and called out to them, asking, "What do you want me to do for you?"

5. They said to him, "Lord, open our eyes so we can glimpse the splendor of the world."

6. And he had pity on them and asked, "Whose power, do you suppose, is it that can make you see?"

7. They replied, "The power of Creation, which is in the Laws."

8. Jmmanuel was astonished and said, "Truly, so far I have never found such faith and knowledge among these people. Be it done to you as you expect."

9. And he touched their eyes and immediately they could see; and they followed him.

10. As they went on their way, Jmmanuel taught the people with sincerity, and he spoke,

11. "Truly, truly, I say to you, if you are knowledgeable and comprehending and embrace wisdom, and if you practice love truthfully and do not doubt, not only will you do such things with blind eyes, but when you say to the fig tree, 'Dry up,' it will dry up. Or when you say to a mountain, 'Lift yourself up and throw yourself into the sea,' it will come to pass.

12. "Be knowledgeable in truth and wisdom, so that your spirit and your consciousness will become powerful.

13. "And when you are knowledgeable and live in the truth of wisdom, your spirit and your consciousness will be filled with infinite power.

14. "Then everything you command or ask for in prayer, you will receive if you trust in it.

15. "Do not suppose, however, that prayer is necessary, because you will also receive without prayer if your spirit and your consciousness are trained through wisdom.

16. "Do not delude yourself by heeding the falsified teachings that a person has a predetermined will, because this belief is wrong.

17. "Know this: Whatever a person may wish to accomplish, they must always first create the will to do so, because this is the law of nature.

18. "Thus a person determines the course of their life, known as fate.

19. "But it is a fact that one must acquire knowledge and learn the truth to engender a will that is imbued with the laws.

20. "Consider yourselves as people who live to learn and perfect the spirit,

21. "Because you were born with the task of becoming perfect in spirit.

22. "Pay no attention in the future when the erroneous teaching will be spread that humans must once again perfect themselves in spirit

because they have fallen away from Creation.

23. "Beware of this false teaching, because it is wrong down to the final dot on the 'i.'

24. "Truly, truly, I say to you, humans were never perfect in spirit and thus they have never fallen away from Creation.

25. "The spirit of each person is created specifically for the task of perfecting itself and gaining wisdom.

26. "This is to become one with Creation as destined by the laws, whereby Creation grows and expands within, and thus perfects itself.

27. "And as the spirit within a person is a unity, so is Creation a unity within itself, and no other powers exist besides it.

28. "Within itself, Creation is pure spirit and therefore infinite power, because it is one within itself, and nothing exists outside of it.

29. "Therefore, beware of the false and adulterated future teachings that will insult me when they call me the son of Creation and the son of God.

30. "From these false teachings, lies will be spun and, because of them, the world will suffer much deprivation and misery.

31. "Pay no attention to the erroneous future teachings that will endeavor to combine the spirit and Creation and me into one, creating from them a threefold entity, which in turn should be a unity again.

32. "Beware of these false and adulterated teachings of the future, because a trinity is impossible according to the logical Laws of Creation.

33. "Truly, I say to you, the princes suppress their people, and the mighty use violence against them; similarly, the forthcoming religious sects will use violence, when they adulterate my teachings and disseminate them.

34. "So beware of them and do not permit yourselves to be forced into carrying the yoke of these false teachings.

35. "But this does not have to happen to you; instead, you should be great and learn and teach the truth.

36. "As I have come to teach truth and knowledge among the people, so you should keep on reaching, so the truth may indeed prevail.

22

Entry Into Jerusalem

1. As they approached Jerusalem at Bethphage near the Mount of Olives, Jmmanuel sent forth two of his disciples and said to them,

2. "Go into the village that lies ahead, and you will find a female donkey tied to a post along with a foal. Untie her and bring her to me, as she is a gift to me and is only being kept there at the stable temporarily.

3. "And if anyone questions you, say, 'Jmmanuel of Nazareth needs her,' and right away he will let you take her."

4. The disciples went there and did as Jmmanuel had told them.

5. They brought the female donkey and the foal, and they laid their clothes on the old animal, and Jmmanuel mounted it.

6. When the people heard that Jmmanuel, the king of wisdom, was coming, they spread their clothes on the path. Others cut branches from the trees and scattered them on the path.

7. And the people who walked ahead of him and those who followed him shouted and said, "Hail to the descendant of David. Praise be to him who comes to proclaim anew the teachings of truth."

8. And when they entered Jerusalem, the whole city became excited

and asked, "Who is coming?"

9. The people replied, "It is Jmmanuel, the prophet from Nazareth in Galilee, who brings anew the teachings of truth.

Purging of the Temple

10. Jmmanuel went into the temple in Jerusalem and became furious when he saw that traders, vendors, dove merchants and moneychangers had established themselves there.

11. Jmmanuel was very upset and said to them, "It is written: 'The temple is to be a place of teaching and a place of contemplation. But you make it into a den of thieves.'"

12. In his anger, he overturned the tables of the moneychangers and the chairs of the dove merchants, and he drove them all out with a donkey-driver's whip.

13. And the blind and lame came to him in the temple and he healed them all.

14. But when the chief priests and scribes saw the great deeds he was performing, and the people as they shouted in the temple, saying, "Hail to the descendant of David!" they became indignant.

15. When they asked him, "Do you hear what these people are saying?" Jmmanuel said to them, "Are you so afraid of the truth that it angers you?"

16. And he left them there and departed from the city for Bethany, where he stayed overnight.

Back in Jerusalem

17. And when Jmmanuel returned again to the temple and taught, the chief priests, scribes, and the elders of the people came to him and asked, "By what authority are you doing these things?"

18. But Jmmanuel answered, saying to them, "I too wish to ask you a question and, if you answer it, I will tell you by whose authority I am doing everything.

19. "Whence came the baptism of John? From Creation or from men?"

Entry Into Jerusalem

20. They pondered the question and spoke among themselves. "If we say it was through Creation, then he will reply, 'Why don't you trust in it, and why aren't you following its Laws?'

21. "But if we say it was through men, then we must fear the people because they consider John a prophet."

22. And so they answered Jmmanuel, saying, "We don't know."

23. Thereupon he replied to them, "You brood of snakes and vipers. I will not tell you by whose authority I act.

24. "But what do you think? A man had two sons and went to the first one and said, 'My son, go and work today in the vineyard.'

25. "He answered, saying, 'Yes father, I will go.' Yet he did not go.

26. "So he went to the other son and said, 'My son, go and work today in the vineyard.'

27. "But he answered and said, 'I don't want to do it and therefore I will not go.' However, he soon felt remorse and went.

28. "Now I ask you, which of the two did the will of the father?" And they said, "The latter, of course."

29. But Jmmanuel spoke to them, "Truly, truly, I say to you, the publicans and prostitutes will recognize the wisdom of knowledge before you do.

30. "John and the prophets came to you and taught you the right way, and you did not trust them, but the publicans and prostitutes did trust them. And although you recognized it, you nevertheless did not do penance and change your mind, so that you would trust them from that time on.

31. "You know the truth, and yet you deny it to profit in gold, silver and goods and enrich yourselves at the expense of the poor, misguided people. You mislead and exploit them in the name of the faith.

32. "But listen to another parable about a vineyard, and perhaps you will understand, if you have not lost your minds.

33. "There was a lord of a large property who planted a vineyard, built a fence around it and dug a cellar therein. He built a tower, leased the vineyard to vine-dressers and left the country.

34. "When the time for the grape harvest arrived, and with it the

payment of the lease, he sent his servants to the vine-dressers so that they would collect the lease payment due him.

35. "The vine-dressers seized his servants, beat one, tortured the other and stoned to death the third one.

36. "Again the lord sent out other servants, more this time than the first, however, the vine-dressers treated them the same way as they did the servants before.

37. "Finally he sent the son of his administrator to them and said, 'They will be afraid of the administrator's son.'

38. "But when the vine-dressers saw the son of the administrator they spoke among themselves, 'This is the heir, come, let's kill him and take over his inheritance.'

39. "They seized him, pushed him out of the vineyard and killed him ... so they thought. While presuming him dead, they put him in a tomb where he remained in a state of near death for three days and three nights, and then he fled. Thereupon the son of the administrator returned to the lord of the vineyard and reported to him.

40. "Now when the lord of the vineyard heard what had happened to the son of the administrator, what do you think he did?"

41. They replied to him, "He probably had the villains punished and banished and turned his vineyard over to other vine-dressers who paid his lease at the proper time and, surely, he turned over the inheritance to the administrator's son in advance."

42. Jmmanuel spoke to them, "You have recognized the meaning, and you have also read it in the scriptures: 'The stone that the builders threw away became the cornerstone.'

43. "Therefore I tell you, I am like the son of the administrator of the vineyard, and you are like the vine-dressers that leased the vineyard.

44. "My teachings truly are not foreign to you and you are well acquainted with them, for they have already been given, handed down, and made known to you by the prophets.

45. "But if you disregard, falsify and interpret them to your advantage, you are also calling me a liar. Therefore, you also call god a liar, upon whose resolve I was begotten by one of his kind, and stand before you as a prophet.

46. "Therefore, I say to you, peace and joy shall be taken from you and your people for all eternity, and all shall be given to a people who bring forth their fruits.

47. "If you disregard and trample on all the commandments of god, who is the ruler over this and the two other human lineages in the North and the East, you shall be disregarded and trampled upon for all time.

48. "The burden of the Israelite people will be like a heavy stone of the seven Great Ages. Whosoever falls upon this stone will be smashed to pieces, and whosoever it falls upon will be crushed."

49. When the chief priests and Pharisees heard what Jmmanuel had said, they understood he cursed them and the Israelite people for all future time.

50. And they conspired on how they could seize Jmmanuel, but they were afraid of the people, who believed him to be a prophet.

23

Taxes, Reincarnation, the Greatest Commandment

1. When the Pharisees held counsel on how they could snare Jmmanuel in his speech, they sent their followers to him, including some of Herod's people.

2. They then said, "Master, we know that you are truthful and teach the way of the laws rightly, and don't enquire about anyone, since you do not care about people's reputations, but only about the laws of god and, in fact, The Laws of Creation.

3. "Therefore, tell us your opinion. Is it right to pay tax to the emperor?"

4. But Jmmanuel sensed their deceit and said, "You deceivers, hypocrites and swindlers, how low in intelligence and understanding are you that you want to tempt me in such a sick and foolish manner?

5. "Show me a tax coin so that I can heal you from your sick folly." And so they gave him a denarius, a silver Roman coin.

6. And Jmmanuel said to them, "Whose image and whose inscription are on this coin?"

7. They replied, "The emperor's."

8. He then said to them, "Therefore, give to the emperor what is the emperor's, give to god what is god's, and give to Creation what is Creation's.

9. "Yet beware and know that god and the emperor are men, above whom is the omnipotence of Creation, to which you must give the highest praise,

10. "For, although god is indeed ruler over humankind, and the emperor is indeed ruler over peoples, above them stands Creation as the highest authority, to which god and the emperor are subordinate in The Laws of Creation, as is every human being and all life."

11. When they heard this, they were astonished, left him alone and departed.

Rebirth

12. On the same day, the Sadducees, who hold the opinion there is no reincarnation, came to him.

13. They asked him, "Master, Moses has said, 'When a man dies and has no children, his brother shall take the widow as his wife and begot descendants for his brother.'

14. "Once, there were seven brothers among us. The first one was married and died, and because he had no descendants, he left his wife to his brother;

15. "And so did the second and the third, until the seventh.

16. "At last, the woman also died.

17. "Now, you teach there is a renewed life. Whose wife will she be among the seven in the new life, for she was the wife to all of them?"

18. Jmmanuel, however, answered, saying, "You are mistaken and do not know the unadulterated scriptures of the elders, nor do you know The Laws of Creation.

19. "Truly, I say to you, Moses never gave this commandment; but he gave the commandment that a brother should take his brother's wife to himself in honor, so if one died the other would take care of the widow of his brother.

20. "How is it possible for a brother to begot descendants for his

brother, since everyone's seed is different?

21. "In the next incarnation, they all will be strangers because they will not recognize each other; therefore, no law says the wife then belongs to one or the other.

22. "In each new life, the person determines for himself whom he wishes to marry; thus he can marry whoever is not spoken for.

23. "Take heed of The Laws of Creation, which teach that in a new life people do not remember their former lives. Thus your question is irrelevant.

24. "At this point, it is only the prophets who remember former lives, since they follow The Laws of Creation and, therefore, live in wisdom.

25. "But, since you and the Israelite people will continue to live in piercing darkness for an extended period, cognizance and wisdom of the spirit and of the consciousness will remain hidden from you for a long time.

26. "Other people will advance beyond you and will evolve greatly in spirit and consciousness, and will follow The Laws of Creation.

27. "Therefore, other people will be superior to you in spirit and in consciousness and gather great wisdom, so that many among them will soon be like the prophets and have recollections about their former lives.

28. "But you and the Israelite people shall remain poor in consciousness, and thus drift in piercing darkness.

29. "To wit: whoever incurs punishment shall also endure it."

30. When the people heard that, they were aghast and afraid.

The Greatest Commandment

31. But when the Pharisees heard that Jmmanuel had silenced the Sadducees, they gathered and deliberated.

32. And one among them, a scribe, tested him by asking, "Jmmanuel, which is the foremost commandment in the law?"

33. Jmmanuel asked in return, "Whose law do you speak of, the law of the emperor, the law of god, or The Laws of Creation?"

34. The scribe said, "The laws of all three."

35. But Jmmanuel said, "The highest directive in The Laws of Creation is this: Achieve the wisdom of knowledge, so that you may wisely follow The Laws of Creation.

36. "But the highest commandment of the law of god is this: You shall honor god as the ruler of the three human lineages and obey his laws, for he is their king of wisdom and a good and just counselor.

37. "And the highest command of the laws of the emperor is this: You shall be obedient to the emperor, follow his laws and give to him the tithe, because he is the ruler over the people and their guardian and protector.

38. "These are the foremost and greatest commandments in the laws of the three, as applied to their categories.

39. "But the other directive, equal to the first, is this: You shall consider only Creation as omnipotent, for it alone is constant in all things and therein is timeless.

40. "The emperor and god are transitory, but Creation is eternal.

41. "Upon these two directives depend the entire Law and the prophets.

42. "The laws of god and those of the emperor are human laws and are intended to maintain law and order among the people.

43. "But The Laws of Creation are the laws of life and the spirit and, therefore, they are eternal and constant.

44. "Likewise, eternal is a person's spirit, which is a tiny fragment of Creation's spirit, for how could Creation itself ever cease to be?

45. "Hence, when a person dies, their spirit lives on and leaves this side of existence for the other side, where it continues to gather the wisdom of knowledge.

46. "The greater the spiritual wisdom gained through the learning of the consciousness, the more the spirit itself determines its future, its return, and its subsequent activities.

47. "Since I am also a prophet and know the future, I tell you that I shall return as representative of god for the purpose of instructively rendering judgment over all those who live according to false teachings

and who degrade the wisdom of the spirit.

48. "Therefore, the words of truth will be harsh and without mercy, and many a person will seethe in rage because of them.

49. "The harsh words of truth themselves will be the instructive judgment and penalty for all those who live according to false teachings and degrade the wisdom of the spirit."

50. Since the Pharisees were together, Jmmanuel asked them, "Whose son am I?"

51. They said, "The son of David."

52. But he spoke to them, "How can I be the son of David, when he has been dead for a long time and I was begotten by Gabriel, the guardian angel?

53. "And haven't you read that David called me Lord when he said,

54. " 'The Lord said to my lord, sit down at my right side, until I can place your enemies beneath your feet, because you are my foster son and my successor.'

55. "Since David calls me Lord, how can I be his son?"

56. And no one could give him an answer, but secretly they said, "He blasphemes God and the prophets. Let's try to catch and kill him, because he endangers our position, in that we will no longer be respected by the people."

Against the Scribes and Pharisees

1. And Jmmanuel spoke to the people and the disciples, saying, "The scribes and Pharisees sit on the chairs of the prophets.

2. "Refrain, however, from doing and accepting anything they tell you, and also do not act on their works: their contrived words and actions.

3. "They teach you confusing teachings, which they and their forefathers have falsified for their own selfish interests.

4. "They contrive heavy burdens and place them upon the shoulders of the people, yet they themselves will not lift a finger.

5. "They do all their works to be witnessed by the people and impress them.

6. "They make their prayer-belts wide and the tassels on their clothing long.

7. "They like to sit at the heads of tables and in the best places in the synagogues.

8. "And they like to be greeted in the marketplace and to be called master by the people.

9. "But don't let anyone call you *master* until you have become cognizant of the wisdom of knowledge.

10. "And don't let anyone call you *teacher* until you follow The Laws of Creation yourselves,

11. "Because those who allow themselves to be called master and teacher, but do not possess the wisdom of knowledge, will be denounced as liars.

12. "For those who unjustly exalt themselves will be abased, and those who unjustly abase themselves will be disdained.

13. "Let those who are great in consciousness consider themselves great, and those who are small in consciousness consider themselves small, and those who are in between in consciousness consider themselves in between.

14. "It is unwise and foolish for people to allow others to consider them greater or smaller than they really are.

15. "Woe to you, scribes and Pharisees, you deceivers, hypocrites and swindlers who block the development of people's spirits and consciousness with your lies and false teachings.

16. "You will not achieve advancement easily and, through your false teachings, you deprive those who wish to advance from doing so.

17. "Woe to you, scribes and Pharisees, you deceivers, hypocrites and swindlers, who devour the homes of widows and engage in long prayers for the sake of appearance; therefore, you shall live in piercing darkness all the longer.

18. "Woe to you, scribes and Pharisees, you hypocrites who travel across land and sea to win a fellow believer; and once he becomes one, you turn him into an unreasonable and irrational child who indulges in twice as many false teachings as you.

19. "Woe to you, you blind proponents of false teachings who say, 'if a person swears by the temple, the oath is not valid, but if he swears by the gold on the temple, the oath is binding.'

20. "You fools and blind people, you are the offspring of evil; why do you let people swear, knowing that an oath is not binding and is a worthless act?

Against the Scribes and Pharisees

21. "Or you say, 'if one swears by the altar, it is not valid; but if a person swears by the sacrificial offering, it is binding.'

22. "You blind and mistaken teachers, who gave you the right to demand or take an oath since The Laws of Creation state that oaths should not be taken?

23. "Your words should always be only 'yes, yes' or 'no, no.'

24. "Therefore, those who swear by anything on Earth or in the Universe swear by something fleeting, which is without permanence.

25. "Hence, an oath is also without permanence.

26. "And those who swear by Creation or its Laws swear by something over which they have no power. Therefore, such an oath is also without permanence.

27. "Whoever swears by anything, therefore, commits an offense against the truthfulness of their word and makes it untrustworthy.

28. "Woe to you, scribes and Pharisees, you hypocrites who tithe mint, meramie [a type of medicinal sage], dill and caraway seeds, but neglect the most important things in the law: justice, freedom of knowledge, and the truth of Creation. Thus you ignore the law of love and the laws of logic and justice.

29. "Woe to you, you blind leaders of a horde of blind who say, 'This should be done and that should not be left undone.'

30. "You only spread confusing teachings and ignore The Laws of Creation.

31. "You blind leaders, you are gnats who swallow camels, which you cannot digest.

32. "Woe to you, scribes and Pharisees, you hypocrites who keep cups and bowls outwardly clean, yet inside they are full of rapaciousness and greed.

33. "You blind ones, you scribes and Pharisees, you hypocrites and distorters of the truth, first clean what is inside the cup, so that the outside may become pure and light up with its brilliance.

34. "Woe to you, scribes and Pharisees, you hypocrites who are like whitewashed tombs that appear beautiful on the outside, but inside they are full of stench, bones and filth.

35. "So, on the outside you also appear pious and good before the people, while inside you are full of hypocrisy, deceit and transgression.

36. "Woe to you, scribes and Pharisees, you hypocrites who build monuments to the prophets and decorate the graves of the righteous and say,

37. " 'Had we lived at the time of our forefathers and fathers, we would not have become guilty with them in the shedding of the prophets' blood.'

38. "Woe to you, scribes and Pharisees, you deceivers, hypocrites and swindlers. You secretly call upon the dead people of high and of common standing, and you deceive yourselves by disbelieving you were speaking with them and believing in your own delusion.

39. **"You cannot talk with the dead, and even if you could, the departed could tell you only the erroneous thoughts they previously held during their lifetime.**

40. "You are not great enough to call upon those dead who have wisdom and can tell the truth.

41. "Thus, you bear witness against yourselves that you are the children of those who killed the prophets and falsified their teachings.

42. "Well then, fill up the measure of your forefathers and fathers; thus you will end your lives without understanding and will have difficulty learning until the distant future.

43. "You brood of snakes and vipers, how can you aspire to be great in spirit and in consciousness when you don't possess any understanding yet?

44. "All the righteous blood that was shed by your doing on Earth will befall you, beginning with the first prophet your fathers and forefathers murdered, to the blood of Zacharias, the son of Barachias, whom you killed between the temple and the altar, as well as all the blood that will be shed in the future because of your guilt.

45. "You will be outcast among human peoples, and then you will alternately lose the land you took by force, regain it and lose it again well into the most distant future.

46. "Truly, I say to you, your existence will be a continual struggle

and war, and so the human peoples will smite you with their hostile thinking and enmity.

47. "You will find neither rest nor peace in the country stolen by your ancestors by way of falsehood, deceit and fire, because you will be haunted by the inherited burden of these murders, through which your forefathers assassinated the ancient inhabitants of this part of the Earth and deprived them of life and material goods.

48. "Hence, all of this righteous blood will fall upon you—this blood that was shed by your forefathers and through you, and which will still be shed by you and your close and distant descendants into the faraway future.

49. "There will be hatred against you in this world. Even the new age will bring you neither rest nor peace until you retreat from the land you took by force, or until you make a conciliatory peace, create brotherly trust and unity with your enemies, and renounce your wrongful and stolen rights.

50. "You brood of snakes and vipers, this will happen to you into the distant future. Yet not by accident will you have a fortuitous chance in the new age when my teachings on Creation's justice and Laws will again be disseminated, so you may then seize the opportunity to end and settle the world's hatred against you by means of an honest peace.

51. "Therefore, in the new age, heed my teachings, which are truly the teachings of the Laws and directives of Creation. Pay heed when they will be taught anew, because this will be the sign of the time when many things will change. The power of the mighty and tyrants will crumble, so that the peoples of all humankind become free.

52. "In the coming distant new age, heed the renewed presentation of my teachings of the spiritual and Creational forces and Laws and directives, which are valid for all times and throughout the universe, so that you may act according to my counsel and that there may be tranquility and peace among you and all human beings in this world.

53. "Truly, truly, I say to you, all this shall be fulfilled and come upon you and upon your people long into the future, as I have told you.

The Prophecy

1. And Jmmanuel walked out of the temple, and his disciples approached him because they wanted to show him the temple's structure.

2. He, however, spoke to them, "Look at all this. Truly, I say to you, not one stone here will remain upon the other without being broken.

3. "The Israelite people trespass against life and the truth, and they built this city on human blood. These people are divided into Israelites who call themselves sons and daughters of Zion, with whom I do not identify, those who want to kill me, and Jews who are misled believers of their religious cult, and to whom I bring the teachings of truth, as I do to all Earth humans.

4. "The Israelites have ravaged this land through plunder and murder, they have killed their friends with whom they had drunk wine, and they have deceived and misled their fellow believers of the Jewish cult, who are truly not Israelites but merely believers in a cult.

5. "Thus the Israelites betrayed their own friends and murdered them because of their greed, but it shall likewise be done to them by the rightful owners of this land whom they have deprived of their

rights and subjugated since ancient times."

6. And, when he sat on the Mount of Olives, his disciples came up to him and said, "Tell us, when will this take place, and what will be the sign?"

7. And Jmmanuel answered: "Two thousand and more years will pass, but meanwhile Israel will never find peace because wars and many calamities will threaten the unlawful occupants of this land; but see to it that nobody leads you astray.

8. "That is, many deceivers and false prophets will come in my name and say, 'I am Jmmanuel, and I am the sign of the time,' and they will mislead many.

9. "People will hear about wars and threats of war, and they are to witness this but not be frightened because it must transpire; but it will not yet be the end.

10. "For many a nation will rise up against its government, one nation against another and one kingdom against another, and there will be times of privation, earthquakes and immense storms and floods all about.

11. "All of these events are just the beginnings of the woes.

12. "Soon the knowledgeable people will be consigned to misery and will be killed.

13. "They will be hated on account of the truth of the teachings and the wisdom.

14. "Various religious cults will rise up against one another, and much blood will flow.

15. "Then many will succumb to the temptation, and they will betray and hate one another because they remain small in consciousness.

16. "Love will grow cold in many people because ignorance will gain the upper hand.

17. "Hatred will rule over the world and evil will reign,

18. "But those who persist in the truth will survive.

19. "This lesson will be preached in the new age throughout the world as testimony for all peoples, and then the end will come.

20. "When the people see the horror of destruction in Jerusalem, of

which the prophets have spoken, the end will come.

21. "Whoever is in the land seized by the Israelites should flee to the mountains at that time.

22. "Those on the roofs should not climb down to get things from inside their houses.

23. "Those who are in the fields should not go back to get their coats.

24. "Woe to the pregnant women and nursing mothers at that time, for they will suffer much grief and death, and there will be many of them.

25. "Soon thereafter, there will be a greater grief than there has ever been since the beginning of the world, and than will ever be again.

26. "If these days were not cut short, no one would survive; but the days will be cut short for the sake of the spirit and of life.

27. "This will also be for the sake of the people who serve the truth and the laws.

28. "But there will be howling and chattering of teeth when this time is brought about by the people's lack of understanding and by their greed.

29. "They will construct machines of metal for use in the air, on the water and on land, and will bring about mutual destruction.

30. "From these machines of metal, they will fling heavy projectiles across the land and upon the cities.

31. "Fire will burst from these projectiles and burn the world; and little will be spared.

32. "They will place the basic elements of life and deadly air into the projectiles to kindle the deadly fires and destroy land and life.

33. "If, at that time, mighty nations were not to intervene, as once did the celestial sons, to bring a halt to the unrestrained madness and deadly conduct of demented dictators, truly, I tell you, no human being would survive.

34. "Since the human populations will consist of far more than ten times five hundred million people at that time, great segments of them will be eradicated and killed.

35. "This is what the law ordains, because people have violated it and will continue to violate it into the distant future.

36. "If, at that time, someone will tell the people, 'Behold, here is Jmmanuel who is the sign of the time,' they should not accept it as the truth,

37. "For many a false Jmmanuel and many deceivers and false prophets will come forth and perform great signs and miracles, so that it will become possible to lead astray not only the seekers, believers and errant ones, but also the scholars and knowledgeable people.

38. "Behold, I have told you this beforehand, and so it will fulfill itself.

39. "Thus, when the deceivers and those led astray will say, 'He is in the desert,' people should not venture there, and when they say, 'Behold, he is in a chamber,' they should not accept it as the truth.

40. "Since I will certainly return at that time, I will let them recognize me.

41. "This is as the law and destiny ordains it, and so it shall be.

42. "For as lightning flashes and illuminates from start to finish, so will be my coming in the future, when I will bring the teachings anew and announce the legions of the celestial sons. At that time I will have a renewed life and will again be accused of deception and blasphemy across the entire world, until the teachings of truth will bring about insight and change in the people.

43. "People of all times, beware: where the carcass is, there the vultures gather, so watch out for them.

44. "Soon after the misery of that faraway time, sun and moon will lose their luster, comets will fall from the sky and the powers of the heavens will begin to sway.

45. "The makeup of the Earth's sky and air will be disturbed, and the land will burn because of the black oil of the Earth, ignited by people's craving for power. The sky will darken because of smoke and fire, which will rage for a thousand days, and everything above the burning land and far beyond will be covered with black soot. Consequently the weather will break down, and severe cold and much death will come

over the people, plants and animals, and over the Earth, as a result of the senselessly unleashed forces of the people who live in lust for power, evil passions and vices.

46. "And then signs will appear in the sky, and all Earth humans will wail and come to see the signs in the clouds of the sky that bear witness to great power and severe judgment against irrationality.

47. "So god is lord over the three human lineages, yet the Laws and directives of Creation are eternally valid. Through these Laws and directives, which represent Creation, humankind in its irrationality will bring cruel judgment upon itself.

48. "Humans owe their existence to god, who is the ruler over them; so they must follow his commandments and respect him as the greatest king of wisdom.

49. "In days to come, he will send forth his guardian angels who will sound their trumpets and call together his trusted followers from the four directions, from one end of the Earth to the other.

50. "Do learn a parable from the fig tree; when its branch puts forth leaves, you know that summer is nigh.

51. "So will it also be for the people of that time; when they see all this transpire, they may know that these events are upon them.

52. "Truly, truly, I say to you, this is how it will be.

53. "And that generation will not pass away until all of this has happened.

54. "At some future time the heavens and the Earth will pass away, and so will the universe; but my words will not pass away because they are the words of truth within The Laws of Creation.

55. "No one knows the day or hour when this will all take place, not the guardian angels nor god himself nor I, Jmmanuel; but only providence and destiny know this through the Laws and directives of Creation, which possesses the greatest wisdom.

56. "Creation alone stands far above all humankind, and it alone deserves honor and praise, just as it renders honor and praise to the absolute power above it.

57. "If people respect and honor god, and if above him they recognize,

honor, esteem and acknowledge only Creation as the supreme power, then they act rightly in accordance with the truth."

26

Laws and Commandments

1. "Since the Laws and directives of Creation and the laws and commandments of god are in effect, they shall be observed and respected.

2. "Just as the Laws and directives of Creation are the Laws and directives for the spirit and for life, so the laws and commandments of god are the laws and commandments for material life and human regulations.

3. "God issued the laws and commandments to serve as material life and human regulations for that which is right, and also as a guideline for life and living.

4. "Thus laws and commandments serve as paths upon which humans should walk in wisdom and intelligence to be righteous.

5. "Thus, as the Laws and directives of Creation and the laws and commandments of god are to be obeyed, humans must not bring forth any other laws and commandments.

6. "The Laws and directives of Creation and the laws and commandments of god should be considered as the true laws and

commandments and should be followed, since they alone have lasting validity and correctness.

7. "When humans deviate from these laws and directives, however, they bring forth illogical and inadequate human laws and commandments that are based on false logic and, thus, are extremely faulty.

8. "When humans are fainthearted in consciousness, their laws and commandments are fainthearted and, therefore, they resemble confusing teachings.

9. "When humans are presumptuous and disregard the Laws and directives of Creation and those of god, they are forced to bring forth their own laws that are flawed and lead everyone astray.

10. "Man-made laws and commandments produce murder and all manner of evil and, as evil spreads and gains the upper hand, man no longer has control over it.

11. "Commandments and laws are valuable only when they are derived from wisdom, and hence are logical,

12. "But logic requires wisdom and understanding.

13. "Human laws and human commandments are powerless, unless they are founded upon the Laws and directives of Creation, just as god's laws and commandments are founded upon them, as he issued them in his wisdom."

Proverbs of Wisdom

14. "Truly, I say to you, wisdom must be learned from The Laws of Creation, which humans may recognize in nature.

15. "But if humans do not think and seek, they will not be able to attain wisdom and will remain fools.

16. "The wise do not moan about lost things, about the dead and about events of the past.

17. "Fools, however, cry over things that are not worth crying over, and thereby they increase their grief, privation and misery.

18. "Those who have acquired sufficient wisdom and live according to the laws, permit not even the slightest harming of creatures, when they are without fault.

19. "Half-wits and fools who are not masters over their senses mistake harm for benefit, benefit for harm, and great sorrow for joy.

20. "Because people are not dedicated to wisdom and do not seek knowledge or recognize the laws, they harbor foolishness and vice.

21. "The dishonest, the stupid, grumpy, greedy, unscrupulous, uncouth and the angry will suffer harm for being poor in consciousness.

22. "When people duly receive daily just a little wisdom in their consciousness, they will grow like the waxing moon during the first half of the lunar month.

23. "**Wisdom is the greatest asset of humanity and so is the created will, which is lord over love and happiness; but all of this is meaningless without the power of the spirit.**

24. "A fool who idly rests and waits for fate goes to ruin like an unfired pot in water.

25. "Those who take care of a cow always receive milk; likewise, those who nurture wisdom and apply it through the power of the spirit bring forth rich fruit.

26. "Recognize each of The Laws of Creation and once you have recognized them, adhere to them and live accordingly, because the Laws are the greatest wisdom.

27. "**There is no eye equal to wisdom, no darkness equal to ignorance, no power equal to the power of the spirit, and no terror equal to the poverty of consciousness.**

28. "**There is no higher happiness than wisdom, no better friend than knowledge, and no other savior than the power of the spirit.**

29. "Those who have intelligence may grasp my speech so they will be wise and knowing."

The False Teachings of Saul

30. When Jmmanuel had finished this speech, behold, a man named Saul approached him and said,

31. "You preach a new teaching, and it has been strange to me from the beginning; it seems silly to me, and your mind appears confused."

32. But Jmmanuel said, "How can you tell me that I am confused

in mind, when it is you who are confused in consciousness and do not understand?

33. "Truly, I say to you, though you are Saul, and you persecute me and my disciples because of my teachings, you will change your mind.

34. "Hereafter, you shall be named Paul. You shall travel in every direction and make amends for having called my teachings false and my spirit confused.

35. "You will load great guilt upon yourself, for in your ignorance you will misunderstand my teachings and will therefore preach them incorrectly.

36. "Your speech will be confusing, and people throughout the world will be enslaved by it and will worship the false doctrine.

37. **"Just as you will bind the land of the Greeks to an evil religious cult because of your false teachings, so you will call me "the Anointed" in their language.**

38. **"It will be your fault, due to your lack of understanding, that they will call me Jesus Christ, which means 'the Anointed.'**

39. "And it will be your fault, due to your lack of understanding, that human blood will be shed in this name, so much that it cannot be held in all existing containers.

40. "You are still persecuting me and my disciples because of my teachings, but soon the time will come when you will change your mind,

41. "When once more you face me and assume I am a ghost.

42. "Truly, I say to you: Like so many others, you will be greatly at fault that my teachings will be adulterated and humans will establish erroneous religious cults.

43. **"You, however, will be the cornerstone of the folly by which I will be called 'Jesus Christ' and the 'redeemer' for a deluded religious cult."**

44. And Jmmanuel was furious, seized a stick and chased Saul away.

45. Saul, his thoughts full of revenge, joined forces with Juda Ihariot, son of the Pharisee, and they discussed how to seize Jmmanuel so he could be handed over to the henchmen.

Suicide

46. Once Saul had departed, Jmmanuel called together his disciples and said to them, "You know that Passover comes after two days, when I shall be turned over to the courts to be crucified, as it is destined, so that I will continue to learn.

47. "My betrayer will be Juda Ihariot, the son of Simeon the Pharisee, because he is interested only in gold, silver, goods and chattels.

48. "He will betray me for thirty pieces of silver, because he has been misled by his father's greed.

49. "But his joy over the pieces of silver will not last long, because his mind is fickle and unstable, and he will soon feel the guilt.

50. "Since Juda Ihariot is without courage and has little knowledge, he will put his waistband around his neck and hang himself from a branch.

51. "Truly, truly, I say to you, although Juda Ihariot's suicide appears just, it is nonetheless unjust.

52. **"Although humans have free will to exercise authority over themselves, they do not have the right to decide over life or death.**

53. **"The intent of the Laws is for humans to live their lives to their final decline, so that in this way they may perfect their spirits.**

54. "But those who judge themselves through suicide, deviate from the Law and violate the plan and The Laws of Creation.

55. **"Realize from this that humans do not possess the right to sit in judgment over their own lives and deaths.**

56. "They possess the right only to exercise their authority over the conduct of their lives, not to decide over life itself and, therefore, over death.

57. "The Laws say that no event or situation justifies suicide, and this includes suicide carried out by another person such as a hired murderer or mercy killer.

58. "Regardless of how much guilt a person may incur, or how heavy their load or burden is, they nonetheless have no right to determine their own death.

59. "Although Juda Ihariot incurs great guilt, he has no right to take

justice into his own hands and decide over his life and his death.

60. "Every guilt and every mistake is a pathway to understanding by which the consciousness and the spirit are perfected.

61. "But if a person escapes from guilt or a mistake by committing suicide, he flees from cognizance and responsibility and must learn to be cognizant and accountable in another life.

62. "Thereby the process of perfection of the consciousness and of the spirit is delayed, which is not the will of Creation.

63. "Either way, suicide is to be considered an act of deplorable cowardice and callous irreverence toward the Laws and directives of Creation."

27

The Disciples' Agitation

1. After Jmmanuel had finished speaking, the disciples became agitated and said, "Why don't we capture Juda Ihariot and stone him, so he can't betray you?"

2. But Jmmanuel was angry and said, "Don't you know that the law says, 'You shall not kill out of degeneration,' and don't you know what I prophesied to you, that I shall be crucified to gain a special insight?

3. "How dare you show disrespect for the fulfillment of the law, for thus it is given and intended?

4. "Just as I walk on my path, so each person will have to walk on their path.

5. "Truly, I say to you, if I were not to follow my destiny, how could I be in position to fulfill my mission, which will lead me to India?

6. "Oh, you who lack courage and knowledge, I have certainly instructed you in the truth, and yet you do not recognize it!

7. "How can it still be inconceivable to you that after my departure, my teachings will be adulterated by you and disseminated in all directions as erroneous teachings and erroneous religious cults?

8. "Because of what you will do, the world will resound with misguidance and false teachings.

9. "Many among you will bear the blame that humanity will not recognize the truth, although I certainly have taught it to you.

10. "There will be great reverberations in the world about your false teachings, which you will spread.

11. "Clearly, you did not understand the words of knowledge, and hence the truth of my teachings.

12. "You are struck with blindness, like the legitimate people of this land who are held in darkness and oppression by the Israelites, just as the prophets predicted for these people, because they have forsaken the tenets of truth, like the Israelites who plundered this land and since then dominated and oppressed its legitimate owners.

13. "I have fulfilled my mission among this race. But, due to the fault of the Israelites and their false teachings, I was unable to teach any reason to this population, as their thinking is irrational because of confusing and mistaken teachings. I will leave, therefore, so that the teachings of truth can also be brought to two other populations in the North and East.

14. "Just as the legitimate owners of the land, who are governed by the violent rule of the Israelites, exist under the guidance of god, so also are the other two peoples under him. They are the people in the high north land where cold and ice reign on the highest mountains and at the end of the Earth, and also the people in the land of India, because he, god, is the master over these three human populations.

15. "As a prophet, I have come back into the world from the realm of Arahat Athersata [the first spirit level]. I was sent here upon god's will to instruct the three human populations in the newly conveyed teachings of truth."

16. "Therefore, I must walk on my path as predestined by Arahat Athersata and requested by god, since I also serve god's will and his laws, as god himself serves The Laws of Creation."

The Disciples' Agitation

In Bethany

17. And Jmmanuel finished his talk and departed for Bethany and the house of Simeon, the leper.

18. Behold, a woman came up to him with a glass of precious water, which she poured on his head as he sat at the table.

19. When his disciples saw that, became angry and indignant and said, "What is the benefit of this waste?

20. "This water could have been sold at a high price and the proceeds used for the poor."

21. But when Jmmanuel heard this, he scolded his disciples and said, "Why are you upsetting the woman?

22. "She has done me a good deed because she trusts in my teachings. In this way, she shows her gratitude, and nothing is too expensive for her.

23. "This woman has become wise and lives according to The Laws of Creation. Therefore, she thanks me with the precious water.

24. "Her gratitude will be lasting, and from now on her deed shall be known throughout the world.

25. "Truly, I say to you, wherever my teachings will be preached in all the world, whether falsified or true, the people will remember what she has done.

26. "Just as she will be remembered for a long time, so also a false teaching will be remembered: your betraying me.

27. "While we are here together, Juda Ihariot, the son of Simeon the Pharisee in Jerusalem, is hatching an evil plot against me so he can betray me to the chief priests.

28. "At this very moment, as we are gathered here, he is asking the chief priests for the blood money they are offering for my capture.

29. "Thirty pieces of silver are being offered to him if they capture me with his help.

30. "While they are forging this plan, they are also designing a plot against one of you, since they want to present a scapegoat to the people.

31. "As Juda Ihariot, the son of Simeon the Pharisee, will turn me over to the henchmen, my disciple Judas Ish-Keriot will be considered the traitor,

32. "So that the message to the people will be, 'Behold, these fools are divided among themselves, so that one betrays the other. How, then, can the teachings of Jmmanuel contain any truth?'

33. "But since Juda Ihariot, the son of Simeon the Pharisee, and my disciple Judas Ish-Keriot have almost identical names, the lie of the chief priests will be accepted from the beginning."

The Last Supper

34. On the first Day of Unleavened Bread, Jmmanuel spoke to his disciples, "Go forth into the city to a good friend of mine named Aaron and tell him, 'Jmmanuel says to you: I want to have a last meal with my disciples at your house, for behold, the feast is near.'"

35. And the disciples did as Jmmanuel had ordered them; and they prepared the meal, together with Aaron and his wife, in their house.

36. When they sat down and were eating, he said, "Behold, the time is near when I must take my heavy burden upon myself.

37. "To be sure, I am going along my destined path as it is written by the prophets; however, I will only be near death and bear much pain, so you must not fear and not worry about me.

38. "Truly, I say to you, from now on I will no longer drink of the fruit of the vineyard nor eat the grain of the bread until the day I drink and eat again with you after my ordeal.

39. "So shall it be when I have risen from near death and so have lain in the tomb for three days and three nights."

40. As they were eating, Jmmanuel took the bread, broke it and gave it to the disciples, saying, "Take it and eat; the body requires nourishment even in times of distress and grief."

41. And he took his cup, gave it to them and said, "Drink from this cup, all of you; the throat becomes thirsty even on a rainy and cold day.

42. "Truly, I say to you, a wise person does not hunger and thirst because of things that must happen.

43. "But a fool hungers and thirsts on account of stupidity and dissent against things that must happen.

44. "And truly, I say to you, just as you do not understand my words

now and are angry with me because of them, so will you be angry with me tonight, because your minds still have not been enlightened with cognizance.

45. "But after I rise from near death and appear to have risen from the dead out of the tomb, I shall walk in front of you to Galilee, so you may recognize the truthfulness of my words.

46. "I have taught you knowledge and truth, but yet you doubt and distrust me.

47. "Oh, you who are fainthearted and of little trust, how startled and confused you will be when I meet you again after my near-death."

48. But Peter answered him, saying, "Even if they all were angry with you, I would never be angry."

49. Jmmanuel however replied, "Truly, I say to you, you are one of the worst, because tonight before the rooster crows, you will deny me three times."

50. But Peter contradicted him, saying, "This will never come to pass, and even if I were forced to die with you, I would never deny you."

51. And thus spoke all of his disciples, all of whom failed to trust Jmmanuel's words.

In Gethsemane

1. Upon leaving the house of Aaron and his wife in Jerusalem, Jmmanuel went with his disciples to a country estate, Gethsemane, which belonged to Joshua, who thought well of Jmmanuel.

2. In the large garden of the estate he spoke to his disciples, "Sit down here while I go over there and ponder my thoughts."

3. He took with him Peter and the two sons of Zebedee and began to brood and be apprehensive, because he was frightened and alarmed about what would happen to him.

4. And he spoke to them, "Behold, to be sure I am wise and have great knowledge, but I am afraid of events before me, both the known and the unknown. However, this is the nature of humans, even when they are knowing and wise.

5. "My mind is deathly grieved; remain here, therefore, and watch with me, so I will not feel so alone.

6. **"It is easier to bear an adversity with one or two others at one's side than by oneself.**

7. "If destiny wanted it, this cup would pass me by; yet not my wish

but my will be done according to destiny, because this is what has been destined for me.

8. When he spoke thus, Judas Ish-Keriot joined them and said, "Listen to what I have to say. Over there things are taking place in the shadow of the city walls, where I have just noticed veiled lights."

9. But Jmmanuel said, "They may be the henchmen Juda Ihariot is bringing, because he has secretly followed us here to betray me.

10. And he went away a short distance, prostrated himself and reflected, saying, "If it is possible, may this cup pass me by; yet, not my wish be fulfilled, but rather the law of destiny be fulfilled, so that I shall be enlightened in this secret I must fathom.

11. Returning to his disciples, he found them sleeping and so he said to Peter, "Can you not watch with me for one hour, so I'm not left alone in my difficult hour?

12. "Be awake and great in spirit and in consciousness so you will not fall prey to temptation: The spirit is willing but the flesh is weak!"

13. A second time he went away, prostrated himself and said, "If it is not possible for the cup to pass me by, then I shall drink it, so that I may be enlightened in this secret and capable of fulfilling my mission in faraway lands and throughout all future times.

14. Upon returning, he found the disciples sleeping again, and only Judas Ish-Keriot remained awake with him.

15. And so leaving them once again, he went away and prostrated himself a third time, brooded in bitterness and said, "I am worried and afraid even though I know that I have to follow my path, which is destined for me.

16. "How willing is the spirit and how weak is the flesh when it is so fearful of pain!"

17. And his entire body trembled, and fine droplets of blood-like sweat flowed all over him because he was so very fearful and terrified.

18. With his face flushed, he returned to his disciples and said to them, "Do you want to sleep and rest now, or do you want to watch with me? Behold, the hour has come when I will be turned over to the hands of the henchmen.

19. "So arise and let us go, for behold, the henchmen are coming."

The Capture

20. While he was still speaking, behold, there came Juda Ihariot, the son of Simeon the Pharisee, and with him a large group of chief priests and elders of the people, armed with swords and poles.

21. Juda Ihariot had given them a sign, saying, "Behold, I will flatter him and mislead him into thinking I repent the sins of my life.

22. "As a sign of the false flattery, there shall be a kiss. And behold, whoever I kiss, he is the one; seize him."

23. He then stepped up to Jmmanuel and said, "I greet you, Master. I will follow your teachings now, for you are allowing me to repent for what I did during my old life."

24. Then he touched Jmmanuel and gave him the kiss of betrayal.

25. But Jmmanuel said to him, "My friend, why have you come to lie to me when betrayal burns in your mind and in your actions?"

26. The henchmen then came up to Jmmanuel, put their hands on him and seized him.

27. And behold, one of the henchmen from the group thought better, had a quick change of mind and, feeling remorseful, sided with Jmmanuel.

28. He stretched out his hand, drew his sword, and struck a chief priest's servant, cutting off his ear.

29. Then Jmmanuel said to the man, "Put back your sword into its sheath, because anyone taking a sword without being in danger will perish by the sword.

30. "Or do you think that I could not have fled before your group arrived?

31. "But how could I fulfill my destiny had I done so?"

32. And the man turned away and wept, then fled and was never seen again.

33. Thereupon Jmmanuel said to the henchmen, "You came here with swords and poles to capture me as though I were a murderer.

34. "How easy it would have been for you to capture me in the city

as I sat there in the temple, teaching daily, yet you did not seize me.

35. "You hypocrites, you were no doubt afraid of the people; therefore, you now come to me like thieves so you can throw me into a prison in darkness, out of the sight of the people.

36. "Truly, I say to you, darkness will become light, and everyone will speak of your deed for which you will be denounced for all time to come."

37. But then Simeon the Pharisee, raised his voice and said, "How foolish your talk is and so full of lies. Why should we fear the people?

38. "You have taught the people falsely, despised our laws and called them lies; so for this you must now suffer.

39. "You thought we would not capture you and bring you to trial, but you were mistaken.

40. "One of those who was with you was not of your mind and has betrayed you for thirty pieces of silver—namely, Judas Ish-Keriot."

41. Jmmanuel answered, saying, "Truly, I say to you, for a long time you may succeed in accusing Judas Ish-Keriot as my betrayer before the people, but the truth will come out and be known by all people throughout the entire world;

42. "Namely, that my betrayer is not Judas Ish-Keriot but is your son, Juda Ihariot, who bears the name of his father, the Pharisee."

43. Simeon Ihariot, the Pharisee, was furious, stepped up and struck Jmmanuel in the face with his fist because he was afraid of his true words.

44. After this happened, the disciples, fearful and discouraged, turned away from Jmmanuel and fled.

45. Those who had seized Jmmanuel led him to Caiaphas, the high priest, where the scribes, Pharisees, and elders of the people had gathered to pass judgment on him.

Jmmanuel Before the High Council

46. The chief priests, however, and the high councillors sought false testimony against Jmmanuel so they might put him to death.

47. And even though many false and bribed witnesses appeared,

they were unable to find any false testimony.

48. Finally, two stepped forward and said, "He has said that God is not Creation, but simply a man like you and me.

49. "He also said that he was begotten by a guardian angel of God, by the name of Gabriel."

50. Caiaphas, the high priest, arose and said to Jmmanuel, "Will you not reply to what these two bear witness against you?"

51. But Jmmanuel remained silent and smiled benignly; therefore, the high priest spoke to him, "I adjure you by the living God to tell us if you were begotten by the angel Gabriel, who is an angel of God, as the scriptures attest!"

52. And Jmmanuel replied, "As you say, but I also say to you that god is not Creation; instead he is lord over the three human lineages that were begotten on Earth through his will;

53. "God has come from the vastness of the Universe and has brought the world under his will; therefore, he is the supreme emperor of these three human populations.

54. "One of them is here in this country, which you have deprived of its rights and subjugated; another is in the east as far as the land of India, and the third is in the north from the land of the king with horns to the sea where icy mountains drift in the water.

55. "**There are seven human lineages living in all the directions of the wind, from one end of the Earth to the other;**

56. "**God is lord over them also, although they serve other gods who also are not of this Earth.**

57. "If you consider god to be Creation, you are mistaken and commit a sacrilege against the truth.

58. "Just as you are human like I am, so god is human, except that in spirit and consciousness he is very much more advanced than the human lineages procreated by him;

59. "**God and his celestial sons are other human lineages who have come from the stars out of the depths of space in their machines of metal.**

60. "Creation stands immeasurably higher than god and his celestial

sons, who are the guardian angels.

61. "Creation alone is the incalculable mystery that begets life and thus stands immeasurably far above god and indeed all life.

62. "Recognize the truth of this teaching, so that you may attain knowledge and wisdom in truth."

63. Thereupon Caiaphas, the high priest, rent his clothes and spoke with rage, "He has blasphemed God, the Creator. Why should we need further testimony against him? Behold, now you have heard his blasphemy for yourselves.

64. "What punishment do you think he deserves?"

65. They answered, saying, "He deserves death."

66. Then they beat Jmmanuel with their fists and spat in his face.

67. And some of them struck him from behind and said, "Prophesy, you great king of wisdom and son of a celestial son, who is it that's beating you?"

68. Peter had followed Jmmanuel and the group, and hid among the people, looking through the doors and windows. Thus, he saw what was being done to Jmmanuel.

69. Then a maid approached him and said, "Aren't you one of the disciples of this Jmmanuel from Galilee?"

The Denial by Peter

70. When Peter was asked by the maid, he denied it and said, "What kind of nonsense do you accuse me of? I don't know what you're talking about!"

71. But because of the maid's question, he was afraid and wanted to escape from the place, for he feared for his life.

72. As he walked out the door, behold, another woman saw him and told the people, "This man was together with the blasphemer from Nazareth!"

73. But Peter lied a second time, and, raising his hand as in an oath, said, "Truly, I don't know that confused person!"

74. And when Peter left the house, those who had been standing there came up to him, saying, "Aren't you one of those who serve

this Jmmanuel? You're giving yourself away through your manner of speech."

75. Peter began to revile Jmmanuel, cursed himself and swore, "I don't know this crazy person or his blasphemous teachings of God!"

76. But soon thereafter a rooster crowed three times and Peter thought of Jmmanuel's words; and he hurriedly ran away from there and wept bitterly.

29

The Suicide of Juda Ihariot

1. Juda Ihariot, the true betrayer of Jmmanuel, was among the councilors who wanted to kill him.

2. But when he saw what appalling injustice and torture Jmmanuel was undergoing, and that Jmmanuel's face was bloody, he felt repentant. Suddenly, he was overcome with great distress and misery.

3. At odds with himself, he took his money bag, tossed it before the chief priests and council elders and said,

4. "I have done evil to this person because I was thinking only of gold and silver, goods and wealth.

5. "I repent that I have betrayed innocent blood, because his teachings do not seem evil to me."

6. But the chief priests and elders replied, "Of what concern is that to us?

7. "Behold, it is up to you what you want to do, to live in peace with yourselves."

8. And Juda Ihariot wept and fled from there, and soon he hanged himself from a tree branch in the field of the potter beyond the walls of the city.

9. The chief priests, however, took the 30 pieces of silver and said, "It is useless to put them into the collection box, because this is blood money. What shall we do with it?"

10. Then one of the sons of the elders came forth and said, "I followed Juda Ihariot: he has hanged himself from a tree branch in the field of the potter."

11. Thereupon Caiaphas, the high priest, said, "Well then, give this blood money to the potter and buy his field with it for the burial of strangers."

12. At dawn the following day, the business matter was settled, and Juda Ihariot, the betrayer of Jmmanuel, was the first to be buried in the field.

13. But the chief priests and elders of the council spread the news among the people that Judas Ish-Keriot, a true and loyal disciple of Jmmanuel, had hanged himself as Jmmanuel's betrayer and was hastily buried in the field of the potter.

14. The people believed this talk and they said, "He betrayed his friend for 30 pieces of silver, and it serves him right that he hanged himself.

15. "He has taken a blood-guilt upon himself and so, from now on, the field of the potter shall be known as the Field of Blood."

Before Pilate

16. Jmmanuel, however, was brought before Pilate, the governor, who asked him, "Are you Jmmanuel, whom they call the king of wisdom?"

17. He said, "As you say, this is what the people call me."

18. And Pilate asked and spoke, "Is it also said that you were begotten by the angel Gabriel, who is an angel of God?"

19. Again Jmmanuel said, "As you say."

20. Pilate inquired once again, saying, "Let us hear your wisdom, for your teachings are new to me.

21. Jmmanuel spoke, "Behold, eons ago, I returned from the realm of a higher world to fulfill a difficult task; and now I was begotten by

a celestial son to be a prophet in this life. This came to pass, according to destiny and the desire of god, the ruler over the three lineages of terrestrial humans procreated by him.

22. "Through his kindness, I have added to my knowledge in this incarnation by gaining great insight and learning true wisdom, which was imparted to me by his teachers over a period of forty days and forty nights.

23. "Furthermore, I have traveled extensively to faraway places and lived for many years in the land of India. There, I was taught much knowledge and many secrets by the great wise and knowledgeable men who are known as masters.

24. "When I have fulfilled my mission here, I will return there with Thomas, my brother, who is a faithful disciple of mine.

25. When they heard Jmmanuel's speech, the elders and chief priests became very agitated and shouted in front of Pilate, "Do you hear his blasphemy?"

26. Thereupon Pilate asked Jmmanuel, "Don't you hear how harshly they accuse you? Don't you wish to justify yourself?"

27. Jmmanuel answered him, saying, "Behold, I will carry my burden as it is destined.

28. "But it is also true that many do oppose me and will testify falsely against me, whence I will not find justice.

29. "Truly, I say to you, many dogs will kill a hare, regardless of how many turns it makes.

30. "It is also customary among humans that the most righteous person does not find justice, because it doesn't matter whether many or few testify against him, as long as they are highly regarded.

31. "Justice rules only in the laws of nature, because they are The Laws of Creation.

32. "But among humans there is little justice, and it is decided according to their social status and their wealth.

33. "Therefore I ask you, how could I expect justice by this standard?"

34. Pilate said, "Judging from the way you speak, you are very wise and I see no fault in you.

35. "I question the teaching you just uttered, but in this, too, I see no guilt, for everyone should find salvation according to their faith.

36. "But since you have nothing to say regarding your innocence that would counter the denunciation of the chief priests and the elders, I see no hope for you, because their will is my command, to which I must comply."

37. But Jmmanuel did not answer him, which surprised the governor very much.

The Conviction of Jmmanuel

38. At the time of the Passover feast, Governor Pilate customarily released to the people whichever prisoner they most wanted, except for those guilty of murder or of causing death.

39. At this time, he held a special prisoner by the name of Barabbas.

40. And when the people were gathered, Pilate asked them, "Which one do you want me to release: Barabbas the criminal, or Jmmanuel who is said to be a king of wisdom and the son of an angel?"

41. But Pilate well knew that the chief priests and elders had bribed the people by giving them copper, gold and silver, so they would plead for the release of Barabbas and for the death of Jmmanuel.

42. For he well knew that they had turned him over out of envy and hatred, since Jmmanuel's teachings appealed to the people and were blasphemous to the teachings of the chief priests and elders.

43. His wife had also implored Pilate by saying, "Have nothing to do with this righteous man, for today I suffered greatly in my dreams because of him, and I find that his teachings are good." Therefore, he was favorably inclined toward Jmmanuel.

44. But among the people, there was much screaming and he asked once again, "Which one shall I release to you?"

45. Slowly the screaming stopped, and the governor raised his voice a third time, asking, "Which one of these two shall I release?"

46. And the people screamed, "Release Barabbas!"

47. And Pilate asked them, "Thus it shall be, but what shall I do with him who is said to be Jmmanuel, a king of wisdom?"

48. And the people shouted, "Crucify him! Have him crucified!"

49. But the governor was not willing, and asked very angrily, "What evil has he done that you want him crucified?

50. "He only taught a new doctrine, and for this he should suffer death? Where then is the liberty of speech, thought and opinion?"

51. But the people screamed even louder, "Have him crucified! Have him crucified!"

52. When Pilate realized there was great unrest and turmoil, and that he could do nothing against the will of these people who had been bribed, he took a pitcher of water and washed his hands before the people, saying,

53. "You decide what should be done with him.

54. "He is the prisoner of the elders and chief priests, so let them judge him.

55. "I will have nothing to do with this just man. I am innocent of doing anything to him, and wash my hands before you in innocence."

56. But the people milled about, shouting, "Crucify him! Crucify him!"

57. Then Pilate turned Jmmanuel over to the chief priests and elders, and released Barabbas to the people.

58. And the chief priests and elders had Jmmanuel whipped, and handed him over to be crucified.

59. The people screamed and shouted and cursed Jmmanuel.

60. However, the chief priests and elders indulged themselves in self-praise and were in good spirits, because their intrigue had been successful.

Defamation of Jmmanuel

1. The governor's soldiers agreed with the chief priests and the elders and, dragging Jmmanuel with them into the court house, they brought the entire crowd in with him.

2. They undressed him and put a purple mantle on him.

3. They made a wreath of thorns, placed it on his head, put a reed into his right hand and, bending their knees before him, said,

4. "We greet you, great king of wisdom of the Jews."

5. And they spat on him, took the reed from his hand, and beat him on the head with it until blood ran down his face.

6. When he was wretched and bleeding, Caiaphas, the high priest, asked, "How are you doing now, great king of wisdom?"

7. But Jmmanuel was quiet and said not one word.

Prophetic Declaration

8. Then they hit him again on the head, and he moaned in pain and began to speak, "Indeed, it is the truth that I am the king of wisdom of the Jews, as it is written by the old prophets. Thus, I am also the

true prophet of all humankind on Earth. But in all truth, I am not the prophet of those confused Israelites who call themselves the sons and daughters of Zion.

9. "Truly, I say to you, just as you beat and mock me, you shall be beaten and mocked by those whom you, since ancient times, have enslaved and whose land you and your forefathers have plundered.

10. "And the time will come in five times a hundred years when you will have to atone for this, when the legitimate owners of the land, whom you have enslaved and deprived of their rights, will begin to rise up against you and fight against you into the distant future.

11. "A new man will arise in this land as a prophet, and he will legally and rightfully condemn and persecute you, and you shall pay with your blood.

12. "This man will establish a new religious cult specifically for the forceful preservation of the truthful teachings and will have himself recognized as a prophet. Through these actions, he will persecute you for all times.

13. "Although, according to your claim, he will be a false prophet, just as you slanderously claim of me, he will bring you new teachings that will seem false to you. Nonetheless, he will be a true prophet, and he will have great power. He will have your people persecuted for all times.

14. "His name will be Mohammed, and his name will bring horror, misery and death to your kind, just as you deserve.

15. "Truly, truly, I say to you, his name will be written for you in blood and, because of your offenses, the hatred against your people will be endless.

16. "In this way, he will be a true prophet, even though you will claim him to be a false one, and he will bring you teachings that will in part seem confusing and unintelligible to you. His emerging religious cult will eventually end when his and your followers lay the foundation for a bloody conclusion. His teachings, too, will be distorted and falsified, and will result in an evil and confusing religious cult."

17. And as he spoke in this manner, the chief priests and members of the council of elders seethed with rage and beat him so harshly that he

collapsed and whimpered.

18. Once they had beaten and mocked him, they took off his mantle, put back on him only his undergarments and led him away to crucify him.

19. Upon his right shoulder they placed a heavy wooden cross, so that he himself would have to carry this great burden to the place of his own death.

20. But the cross was heavy, and Jmmanuel groaned under the burden. His blood combined with his sweat into a vile mixture.

21. Jmmanuel collapsed under the heavy burden because his strength left him.

22. But when a stranger, Simon of Cyrene, came along Jmmanuel, they forced him to help carry the cross.

23. Soon they arrived at the place called Golgotha.

24. His path there was difficult, because he was being beaten, reviled and mocked.

25. They gave him wine, mixed with the bile from animals.

26. When he tasted it, he did not want to drink it, so they forced him by beating him.

The Crucifixion

27. Then they forced him down on the cross while still beating him, and nailed his hands and feet onto the wood. Customarily, the crucified were tied to the cross, so Jmmanuel's nailing was unprecedented.

28. After they had nailed him upon the cross and erected it, they divided his clothing among themselves by casting lots.

29. And they sat around and guarded him, so that no one would come to take him from the cross.

30. Also, two murderers were crucified with him, one to his right and one to his left.

31. Those all around him defamed, mocked and ridiculed him.

32. They shouted, "Since you are the king of wisdom, help yourself!

33. "And since you are the son of a celestial son and possess great power, get down from the cross!"

34. The scribes, Pharisees, chief priests and elders of the people likewise mocked him, saying,

35. "You helped others, but you cannot help yourself.

36. "Since you are a king of wisdom, get down from the cross and help yourself.

37. "If you do that, we will believe in you and your teachings.

38. "He trusted in his wisdom and in his being the son of the angel Gabriel.

39. "Thus, let his wisdom or the angel Gabriel save him now, if he so desires."

40. Likewise, the murderers crucified to his right and left mocked and reviled him.

41. Then the sky clouded over, the sun became dark, and a great storm spread across the land, which was rare at that time of year.

42. The terrible storm raged for three hours before the sun again broke through the clouds.

43. At that time Jmmanuel cried out, "I'm thirsty, give me drink!"

44. And right away one of the chief priests ran, took a sponge, soaked it in vinegar and stuck it on a lance for him to drink.

45. But when the others saw that, they scolded the priest, saying, "Stop! Do not give him any more to drink. Let us see how long he can bear this."

46. And behold, a final powerful thunderclap broke up the storm, whereupon the entire land trembled, and the ground shook.

47. Amid the tremendous thunder, Jmmanuel again cried out, but nobody understood him, because his speech was confusing.

48. Then his head fell forward, he slipped into a state of near-death, and they presumed he was dead.

49. It came to pass that a soldier took his lance and stabbed Jmmanuel in his loin to ensure he was dead.

50. Blood mixed with water flowed from the wound as is the case when a person is dead or in a near-death state.

51. Thus the soldier thought Jmmanuel was dead, and he informed the others.

52. They were all astonished, because it was unusual for the crucified to die so quickly.

53. But since the soldier had told them so, they believed him and departed.

54. Among them were also many women and others who watched from a distance, because they were followers of Jmmanuel; they had served him and followed him from Galilee.

55. Among them were Jmmanuel's mother, Mary, and Mary Magdalene, and others.

56. Once the people had departed, they went to him, knelt before the cross and wept bitterly because they, too, thought Jmmanuel was dead.

57. Also among them, however, was Joseph of Arimathea, a follower of Jmmanuel.

58. After a short while, he noticed that Jmmanuel was not quite dead, but he told no one.

Entombment

59. He quickly went into the city to Pilate and asked him for the body of Jmmanuel so that he could bury him.

60. Pilate ordered that Jmmanuel should be given to him.

61. And many people went with him and they removed Jmmanuel from the cross. Joseph wrapped the body in pure linen, which he had previously coated so as to form an image of Jmmanuel.

62. Joseph of Arimathea then carried the body of Jmmanuel all the way as far as Jerusalem and placed it outside the city into his own tomb, which he had arranged to be cut into a rock for his future burial.

63. And he rolled a large stone in front of the door of the tomb and went to obtain medicine so he could take care of Jmmanuel.

64. The entrance of the tomb was guarded by soldiers and Jmmanuel's mother, so no one could enter and steal the body.

65. Joseph of Arimathea, however, sought out Jmmanuel's friends from India and returned with them to the tomb. There they entered through a secret second entrance unknown to the henchmen and

soldiers, and for three days and three nights they nursed him. Soon he was in better health and again with good strength.

66. The tomb was being guarded on the other side by the soldiers, because the chief priests and Pharisees had gone to Pilate and said,

67. "Sir, we have considered that when this crazy man was still alive, he said to the people, 'I shall return after three days and three nights and rise, because I will only be in a state of near-death.'

68. "But since it was established through a soldier that he was really dead, his tomb should be guarded so that no one can come, steal the body and say, 'Behold, he has risen from the dead after all!'

69. "Therefore, command that the tomb be guarded up to the third day, so that the last deception may not be worse than the first."

70. And Pilate said to them, "Take my soldiers as guardians. Guard the tomb as best you can."

71. And they departed, guarded the tomb, and secured the stone in front of the door with a seal.

72. However, Pilate's soldiers did not realize the secret of the grave: it had two exits or entrances. Jmmanuel's helpers, therefore, could go to him, to apply healing salves and herbs without being detected. On the third day, Jmmanuel was once again strong enough to walk.

37

Jmmanuel's Flight from the Tomb

1. Jmmanuel had prophesied that, after three days and nights, he would return from his near-death experience. And he did, when dawn broke on the first day of the week after Passover.

2. And behold, a great thundering arose in the air, and a radiant light came from the sky and settled on the earth, not far from the tomb.

3. Then a guardian angel stepped forth from the light; his appearance was like lightning and his garment was white as snow.

4. And he went to the tomb, and the soldiers, full of fear, moved out of his way.

5. He lifted his hand, and from it bright lightning sprang forth and struck the soldiers, one after the other.

6. And they fell to the ground and did not stir for a long time.

7. Then the guardian angel stepped up to the tomb, rolled the stone away from the door and said to Mary, the mother of Jmmanuel, and to Mary Magdalene:

8. "Don't be afraid. I know you seek Jmmanuel, the crucified.

9. "He is not here, for he is alive just as he said he would be. Come here

and behold the place where he has lain.

10. "Go quickly and tell his disciples that he has risen from near-death.

11. "Also tell them: He will walk before you to Galilee, and there you will see him. Behold, I have told you."

12. But Mary asked, "Yet he was dead and lay here dead. How can he then rise?"

13. The guardian angel answered, "Why are you seeking a live person among the dead?

14. "Go now and spread the news among his disciples, but beware of telling anyone else.

15. And the guardian angel went to the bright light and disappeared into it. Soon a great thundering came forth from it again, and it rose up into the air, shooting straight into the sky.

16. Jmmanuel's mother and Mary Magdalene then departed, leaving the tomb.

17. The soldiers then recovered from their paralysis and were greatly astonished. So they went into the city to spread the news of what had happened.

18. And secretly the Roman soldiers met with the chief priests and elders of the council to decide what to tell the people.

19. The chief priests and elders gave sufficient money to the soldiers and said, "Tell the people the king of wisdom's disciples came at night while we were sleeping and stole his body."

20. And the soldiers took the money and did as instructed.

21. Mary and Mary Magdalene, however, left and did as they had been mandated by the guardian angel.

22. And behold, again a guardian angel met them on their way and said, "Remember what you have been instructed to do. Be careful and do not inadvertently tell the people."

23. Mary Magdalene approached the guardian angel, who wore a brilliant white garment, and she wanted to grasp his hand.

24. But he stepped back from her and said, "Do not touch me, because I am of a different kind from you, and my garment is a protection against this world.

25. "If you touch me, you will die and be consumed by fire.

26. "Step back from me and be on your way, as you have been instructed."

27. So they departed, and later met Peter and another disciple, telling them what had taken place.

28. Peter and the other disciple went to the tomb, with the other disciple arriving there first.

29. And he looked into the tomb and saw the linen bandages lying neatly on the ground, but he did not enter.

30. Then Peter arrived, went into the tomb and found everything just as the other disciple had.

31. The bandages had been carefully folded and placed on the ground. The sweat cloth, which had covered Jmmanuel's head, had been placed on a particular spot, together with the salves and herbs and clay figurines of peculiar appearance, the likes of which he had never seen before.

Jmmanuel's Meetings With His Disciples

32. In the evening of the same day, the disciples were gathered in the room in the city where they had taken their last meal with Jmmanuel before Passover.

33. And they were in the room speaking to each other about what had happened that day when, behold, the door opened and a stranger they had never seen before entered.

34. And they were afraid that he might be one of the Israelites who wanted to betray them.

35. But then the stranger said, "Peace be with you," and when he took the cloth from his face, they recognized him as Jmmanuel.

36. After he had spoken, he showed them his hands, his loin and his feet; and when they saw his wounds, they were happy he was among them.

37. But Thomas believed a ghost to be in front of him. So he said, "If I could touch your wounds, I would know that you are not a ghost."

38. Then Jmmanuel said to him, "Reach out and place your hand on my wounds, so that you of small mind may recognize the truth."

39. So Thomas did as he had been told, and he touched Jmmanuel's wounds and said, "Truly, it is you."

40. Then Jmmanuel departed, saying, "Guard the secret of my return, so it will not be known that I am alive.

41. And behold, the next day the disciples set out for Galilee to spread the joyful news among Jmmanuel's supporters.

42. As other followers went along, behold, an itinerant joined them and for part of the way walked with them.

43. They were sad and talked among themselves about how Jmmanuel had been forced to die on the cross.

44. Then the itinerant, a stranger, said to them, "Why are you mourning?" And they told him what grieved them.

45. But the itinerant said, "How little knowledge you yet have; Jmmanuel told you he would rise from near-death after three days and nights.

46. "So just as he has said, it has happened."

47. After he had spoken, he removed the cloth from his face and they recognized him as Jmmanuel.

48. But he said nothing more, and again covering his face, he withdrew. And he was not seen for a long time.

49. Long after Jmmanuel had disappeared, it came to pass that the disciples were fishing on the Sea of Tiberias,

50. And they caught nothing the entire night, so by daybreak they were exasperated.

51. And when they approached the shore, there stood a stranger who asked, "Have you anything to eat? I'm hungry."

52. They answered, "No, we have not caught one fish in our nets."

53. Then the stranger said, "Throw the net out to the right side of the boat, and you will have a large catch."

54. The disciples were astonished by what he said, but nevertheless cast the net. And behold, they could not pull it in because of the multitude of fish.

55. And they came ashore and prepared a meal because they, too, were hungry.

56. But when he uncovered his face, behold, it was Jmmanuel.

57. And while they were eating and in good spirits, he said to

them, "Go to Galilee to [name unknown] mountain; there I will join you, because our time together has ended and each of us must go his separate way."

32

Jmmanuel's Farewell

1. They went to the mountain where Jmmanuel had directed them.

2. When they were gathered there, he said to them, "Behold, I will speak to you one last time, then I will leave and never return.

3. "My path leads me to the land of India where many of this human lineage also dwell, because they have left this land to live there.

4. "My mission leads me to them and to the human population that is born there.

5. "My path there will be long, for I have yet to bring my teachings, new and old, to many countries, and likewise to the shores of the great black waters to the north of here.

6. "But before I leave you, I will give you my final lessons of the teachings:

7. "If humans live according to The Laws of Creation, they live correctly in truth. But the ultimate goal should be this:

8. "Everything human within human beings must die, but everything of Creation within them must rise and embrace Creation.

9. "Consider the Universe as the place where Creation lives in infinity.

10. "Everything humans possess has its origin in Creation; therefore it belongs to Creation.

11. "Human beings shall transform their entire spiritual lives and perfect them, so that they will become one with Creation.

12. "Whatever human beings do, they shall do with the awareness of Creation's presence.

13. "But a human being shall never attempt to force the truth onto another, because then it would only be worth half its value.

14. "First, humans shall tend to their own progress in consciousness and spirit, so as to produce Creational harmony within themselves.

15. "No greater darkness rules within humans than ignorance and lack of wisdom.

16. "Greatness of personal victory requires uprooting and destroying all influences that oppose the Creational force, so that which is Creational may prevail.

17. "Humans should develop within themselves the power to judge over good and evil and to correctly perceive all things, so that they may be wise and fair and follow the Laws.

18. "It is necessary to be cognizant of what is real and what is unreal, what is valuable and what is worthless, and what is of Creation and what is not.

19. "Human beings must become a cosmic unity, so that they can become one with Creation.

20. "Conform your lives to the Laws; live according to the laws of nature, then you will also live according to The Laws of Creation.

21. "Regardless of how much humans may suffer, the power of Creation within them is immeasurably greater, and it will conquer all ills.

22. "When human beings live within their consciousness only as mortal humans, they are inaccessibly remote from their spirit, from Creation and therefore from its Laws.

23. "The greater their dedication to The Laws of Creation, the deeper will become the peace within them.

24. "The happiness of humans consists in seeking and finding the

truth, so they may thereby gather knowledge, gain wisdom, and think and act in accordance with Creation.

25. "Only through the circumstances of human life can humans develop and use their Creational powers in consciousness and in spirit.

26. "Humans gain experience in the use of their powers and capabilities only by trying daily to unlock them.

27. "As long as human beings do not become one with Creation, they will never be able to rise above death or near-death, since the fear of the unknown is within them. Only when they are able to fully recognize the perfection and unity of Creation can they slowly begin to acquire sublimity.

28. "Instead of following instinctive and impulsive urges, humans should live by cognition and wisdom, so that they may live justly according to the Laws and directives.

29. "Humans should not lose their way in the thicket of limitations, but should expand their consciousness and seek and find knowledge, logic and truth, and from these learn wisdom.

30. "Thereby they will come closer to their life's goal and become cognizant of the Creational principle in all things.

31. "Thousands of lights will guide humans along their path, provided they observe and follow them.

32. "Human beings will attain all their knowledge and wisdom, provided they seriously strive for perfection.

33. "The Laws serve all those who are prepared to seek the truth in unlimited measure and to learn wisdom from them.

34. "For in mastering all possible orientations within themselves, they develop their spiritual powers to higher and higher levels, and in so doing they perfect themselves.

35. "Humans should not attempt to dwell upon their physical misery, but upon the reality of the spirit and the existence of Creation.

36. "A continual restlessness exists within humans, because they have a premonition that Creation is their fate and destination.

37. "Humans may be great, wise and good, yet this is not sufficient, for they can always become greater, wiser and better.

38. "There may be no limits to love, peace and joy, because the present state must always be exceeded.

39. "Truly, I say to you, a love that is unlimited, constant and unfailing is unconditional and is a pure love, in whose fire all that is impure and evil will burn.

40. "Such a love is Creation's love and, therefore, its Laws as well, to which humanity has been predestined to follow since the beginning of time.

41. "Since this is the ultimate destination for human beings, they must take steps to guarantee that this will come to be, for this is their destiny.

42. "But as yet humans do not understand the wisdom of this teaching, and therefore it is being adulterated everywhere on Earth.

43. "In their ignorance, humans are falsifying the teachings in many ways and forms, so that the teachings are becoming diffuse and unintelligible.

44. "But in two times a thousand years, they shall be taught anew without falsification, when humans become sensible and knowledgeable, and a new age heralds great upheavals.

45. "And it can be read in the stars that the people of the new age will be great revolutionaries. Thus, some special predestined people, who will be the new proclaimers of my teachings, will preach them unfalsified and with great courage.

46. "But you go and prepare the way for my teachings and make all peoples their disciples.

47. "However, beware of false teachings, which you may allow to arise because of your lack of judgment, for some of you are inclined that way.

48. "Teach all people to follow everything I have commanded you, so you do not falsify my teachings."

49. And it came to pass, that while he was speaking to them in this manner, a thundering came from the sky, and a great light descended.

50. The light settled on the ground not far from them, and it glittered like metal in the sunlight.

51. Jmmanuel spoke no more, but went to the metallic light and entered into it.

52. Then, however, a haze arose all around it. Once again a thundering began and the light ascended back into the sky.

53. And the disciples returned to Jerusalem in secret and made known the events among their own kind.

33

Jmmanuel in Damascus

1. Jmmanuel was set down by the great light in Syria, where he lived for two years in Damascus without being recognized.

2. After this time, he sent a messenger to Galilee to seek out his brother Thomas and his disciple, Judas Ish-Keriot.

3. Two months passed, however, before they joined Jmmanuel and brought bad news.

4. His brother Thomas spoke, saying, "Your disciples have greatly falsified your teachings; they insult you by calling you the son of God and they also set you equal to Creation.

5. "The chief priests and elders persecute your followers and have them stoned when they are caught.

6. "But Thomas, one of your disciples, fled, and it is reported that he has departed with a caravan for the land of India.

7. "A great enemy of yours has arisen in a man named Saul.

8. "He is fuming with rage and utters death threats against your disciples and those who trust in your teachings.

9. "He is having letters written to the synagogues in all regions, whereby

if any followers of your new teachings are found, they will be bound and taken to Jerusalem.

10. "No distinction is being made between women, men and children. They will all be found guilty and condemned to die."

11. But Jmmanuel said, "Don't be afraid, the time will soon come when Saul will receive a lesson about his evil thinking.

12. "He is already on the road to Damascus, following you and Judas Ish-Keriot here now, to lead you back to Jerusalem in shackles.

13. "However, I will confront him before he reaches Damascus, and since he believes me dead, he will presume he is seeing a ghost."

14. Jmmanuel set out to see a friend who was helpful to him in secret things that involved foul-smelling powders, salves and liquids.

15. Well supplied with these things, he departed, leaving the city by way of the road to Galilee.

16. A day's trip from Damascus, he waited for two days in the rocks and prepared his concoction.

17. During the night, he saw a large group of armed men coming, among them Saul, the persecutor of his disciples.

18. When they were near, he struck a fire and tossed it into his concoction, thus producing a powerfully bright light that blinded the group.

19. Jmmanuel continued stoking the flaring concoction, so that powerful flashes of light, stars and fireballs shot into the sky or fell from it. All this was accompanied by thundering booms and loud hissing sounds, as if from gigantic dragons and serpents.

20. The thundering and booms subsided, as did the hissing. The blinding flashes and the multi-colored fires died down, yet stinging smoke continued to cover the land and caused the group to cough and shed tears.

21. Then Jmmanuel called out, "Saul, Saul, why do you persecute my disciples?"

22. But Saul was afraid and fell to the ground, crying out, "Who are you who speaks to me like this?"

23. And Jmmanuel answered, saying, "I am Jmmanuel whom you persecute in your hatred, along with my disciples.

24. "Get up. Go into the city and let yourself be taught how you should live."

25. Saul was very afraid and said, "But you are the one who was crucified. So you are dead and must be speaking to me as a ghost."

26. However Jmmanuel did not answer him. He left and headed for Damascus.

27. But the men who were Saul's companions stood still, petrified with fear, because they also believed they had heard a ghost.

28. Saul got up from the ground and opened his eyes. However, he saw nothing because his eyes were blinded, for he had stared directly into the bright light Jmmanuel had generated.

29. His companions then took him by the hand and led him to Damascus,

30. And for three days he saw nothing, ate nothing and drank nothing.

31. However, one of Jmmanuel's disciples came to Saul and preached to him the new teachings, and gradually he accepted them.

32. But because of the events by the rocks, his mind was slightly confused. He misunderstood much and spoke incoherently.

33. Somewhat confused in his mind, he went away and preached incoherent nonsense to the people.

34. Jmmanuel, however, remained in Damascus another thirty days and made it known that he would be leaving the country and traveling to the land of India.

35. His mother Mary came from Nazareth and set out on the road to the land of India with Jmmanuel, his brother Thomas, and Judas Ish-Keriot.

36. And Jmmanuel began to preach again and teach the people wherever he encountered them along the way and in any settlement he came to.

37. There was a new strength within him and his teachings were more powerful than before.

Teaching About Creation

1. Jmmanuel preached powerfully, saying, "Behold, Creation stands above humanity, above god and above everything.

2. "It appears to be perfect by human comprehension, but this is not so.

3. "Since Creation is spirit and thus lives, even it must forever perfect itself.

4. "But since it is one within itself, it can perfect itself by way of its own creations, through the generation of new spirit forms that dwell within humans, give them life, and evolve towards perfection through their learning.

5. "The newly generated spirit is part of Creation itself, however, it is unknowing down to the smallest iota.

6. "When a new spirit is created, which is still unknowing in every way, it lives in a human body and begins to learn.

7. "Persons may consider the unknowing spirit as stupid and say that the individual is confused.

8. "But it is not, because it is only unknowing and devoid of

knowledge and wisdom.

9. "Thus, may this new spirit live a life within a human being to gather knowledge.

10. "Then, when this spirit enters the beyond, it is no longer as unknowing as it was at the time of its beginning.

11. "And it returns into the world and lives again as a human being but is no longer quite as unknowing as it was at its beginning.

12. "Again it learns and gathers further knowledge and new wisdom, and thereby increasingly escapes from ignorance.

13. "So, after many renewed lives, the time comes when people say that this spirit is normal and not confused.

14. "But this is neither the end of the spirit nor its fulfilment, because, having become knowing, the spirit now seeks the greatest wisdom.

15. "Thus, the human spirit perfects itself so extensively that it unfolds in a Creational manner and ultimately becomes one with Creation, as it was destined from the earliest beginning.

16. "Thus, Creation has brought forth a new spirit, allowing it to be perfected independently in the human body. The perfected spirit returns to Creation to become one with it and, in this manner, Creation perfects itself within itself, for in it is the knowledge and wisdom to do so.

17. "Truly, I say to you, the time will never come when Creation ceases to create new spirit forms and to broaden itself.

18. "However, Creation also requires rest, a characteristic of all that lives, and when it slumbers it does not create.

19. "Just as human life has day and night and is divided into work and rest, so Creation also has its times of work and rest.

20. "Its period, however, is different from that of people, because its laws are the laws of the spirit.

21. "While human laws are the laws of material life.

22. "The material life is limited, but the life of the spirit lasts forever and knows no end.

23. "Creation, however, is subject to the laws of Primeval-

Timelessness and Primeval-Creation, which is the Absolute Absolutum and the beginning and endlessness of everything. And it was created out of itself. Absolute Absolutum: most basic Creational level or most basic Absolutum level, respectively, of which there are seven. From the highest Absolutum level down to the lowest the following sequence is valid: Being Absolutum, Zohar Absolutum, Super Absolutum, Creative Absolutum, Central Absolutum, Ur [primal, original, prime] Absolutum, and Absolute Absolutum. Out of the Absolute Absolutum, the first Creation form of the lowest kind was created, the material Universe, the universal consciousness or universe in which we exist. This Universe, universal consciousness, or Creation form, respectively, which is the first and lowest of all 1,049 Creation forms, has created out of itself all Creational energies, i.e., all spirit energies and spirit forms. It is therefore the creation of its own Ur-source. The Absolute Absolutum is the idea-related procreative power only, out of which the lowest Creation form that is our Universe has come forth.

24. "Its secret is that which is immeasurable and is based on the number seven, which is counted in 'times.'

25. "This is one of the secrets and laws the human mind will solve only when it reaches perfection.

26. "But let it be said that the laws of life are not hidden from the wise man, hence he can recognize and follow them.

27. "Thus the wise understand that the secret of Primeval-Creation lies in the number seven and in computations based thereon. Thus they will gather and retain the knowledge that Creation has a time for work or rest that is also based upon the number seven.

28. "Creation rested in a state of slumber for seven Great Times when nothing existed, not even the Universe.

29. "Only Creation itself existed in slumber, and it brought forth no creature nor anything.

30. "However, it did awaken from its slumber through the seven cycles of seven Great Times and began to create creatures and everything.

31. "After having rested for seven cycles of seven Great Times, it is

now creating living organisms and everything else, and it will do so for seven more cycles of seven Great Times, until it requires rest again and reposes anew in deep slumber for a further seven Great Times.

32. "When it will rest again and lie down in slumber, nothing will exist except for Creation itself.

33. "There will be neither creatures nor any other thing.

34. "Only Creation itself will exist during the seven cycles of the seven Great Times, because it will rest and slumber until it awakens again and brings forth new creatures and everything else.

35. "Just as Creation is one within itself, however, so is all life, being and existence one within itself.

36. "It is by The Laws of Creation that all humans, plants, animals and all life are one in themselves.

37. "A person may believe that everything is two or three, but that is not so, because everything is one.

38. "Whatever people believe to be two or three is actually one, so they should make everything that is two or three into one.

39. "Since the spirit in a person is part of Creation, it is one with Creation; consequently it is not two.

40. "And since the body is a part of the spirit in a different form and matter, it is therefore one with the spirit; consequently it is not two.

41. "The teachings state that there is a unity and not in any way or form a duality or trinity.

42. "If it appears to people that there is a duality or trinity, then they are the victims of deception, for they do not think logically but according to human knowledge.

43. "But if they think according to the knowledge of the spirit, they find the logic, which is also in the law.

44. "Only human thinking can be incorrect, not The Laws of Creation.

45. "For this reason, it is said that everything emanates from a unity, and a duality seems apparent only because humans, in their limited thinking, cannot grasp the truth.

46. "Since everything is a unity and everything emanates from it,

Teaching About Creation

no duality or trinity whatsoever can exist, because it would violate The Laws of Creation.

47. "Therefore, people should make the two or three into one and think and act according to The Laws of Creation.

48. "Only in ignorance does a person fabricate a duality or trinity and give offence to The Laws of Creation.

49. "When a person aligns everything into this unity, making everything into one, and then says to a mountain, 'Move away,' then it will move away.

50. "When everything is one in Creation, in its laws, in the creatures and in matter, it is without error.

51. "When a wise man says there are always two of everything, he means that they are one within themselves and one together.

52. "It is only two in appearance, because in itself and also together it is always one.

53. "Therefore, evil is one in itself because it is also good in itself. Likewise, good is one in itself because it is just as much evil in itself.

54. "Since even when apart they are one and a unity, together they are also one and a unity, for this is one of The Laws of Creation.

55. "Thus the result is that there are two parts in appearance, but they are both one in themselves and one when together.

56. "If, therefore, people say there exists also a trinity, then their consciousness has been addled by some cult, falsified teachings or confused thinking.

57. "A unity always consists of two parts, which are one in themselves and are a duality only in appearance.

58. "Since a person is a unity of two parts, the spirit is a unity of two parts, but both are one in themselves and one together.

59. "The body cannot live without the spirit and, conversely, because spirit and body are a unity despite their seeming duality.

60. "The spirit, however, lives according to the same law, because in itself it also consists of two parts and is one in each part; thus, it is one in itself.

61. "The two parts of the spirit are wisdom and power.

62. "Without wisdom of the spirit, its power cannot be utilized, nor can any wisdom emerge without spiritual power.

63. "Hence, two things are always required that are one within themselves, so there is a oneness within the unity but not a duality.

64. "Thus the law says that a human being is a unity in itself, which consists of two equal parts that form a unity, both within themselves and also together.

65. "And the two equal parts in the human being, each of which constitutes a unity within itself, are the body and the spirit.

66. "So when the scribes teach that a person lives in a trinity, this teaching is erroneous and falsified, because it is not taught in accordance with The Laws of Creation."

Cults Around Jmmanuel

1. It came to pass that Jmmanuel, his mother Mary, and his brother Thomas travelled on into the cities at the sea in the north. Since olden times, warrior women inhabited the area, but their descendants were now peace loving.

2. He preached to them the new teachings according to his knowledge, but had to flee their cities when they attempted to kill him.

3. Their own teachings, far removed from truth, were from a rigid religious cult; and they punished with death those who taught differently.

4. Jmmanuel was treated as an outcast by these people, and persecuted as an agitator against their cult. So he fled.

5. It came to pass during his flight that he met up with a large caravan. He and his following joined it and continued inland and into the mountains.

6. They travelled through the central part of the country for many weeks, whereupon they came to another sea and into the city of Ephesus.

7. But Jmmanuel was very much afraid, and no longer preached his new teachings so that no one would recognize him; for in Ephesus were many dealers and merchants, who came there from Jerusalem to conduct business.

8. Many among them had known Jmmanuel and had not been well disposed toward him; therefore, he avoided them and obscured his face.

9. The dealers and merchants in Ephesus had spread the story of Jmmanuel and his purported death, which had occurred two-and-one-half years earlier.

10. However, after he had been in the city for a few days, behold, he was recognized by one of the merchants, who informed others of like belief. They belonged to a secret group called the Association of the Essenes.

11. They brought Jmmanuel to a meeting that was secret, for they feared the people because their secret society was considered unlawful.

12. But among them was one named Juthan, the most senior of the secret society in Jerusalem, and he spoke, saying,

13. "Behold, we know very well what has taken place in your life, but we do not understand how you can still be among the living. So, do tell us your secret."

14. Jmmanuel feared that he would be bound and returned to Jerusalem if he remained silent in front of the conspirators; so he recounted everything to the Essenes.

15. And he told them about all that had transpired and how he had fled from Jerusalem and had arrived in their region.

16. Juthan, the eldest, said, "Behold, we belong to a secret group called the Association of the Essenes.

17. "Our quest and knowledge are not attuned to the teachings of the scribes, but to the secrets of nature and all that is inexplicable to humans.

18. "You are great in your knowledge, and by all measures you have advanced in knowledge far beyond us and the scribes, Pharisees, astrologers, even the elders and the philosophers.

19. "Therefore, come join our society, be one of us and teach us your knowledge."

20. But Jmmanuel answered, saying, "Even if I were to teach you my knowledge, it would not agree with your teachings, because you follow incomplete human wisdom, whereas I adhere to spiritual wisdom.

21. "Therefore, I think that our different teachings would be incompatible with each other.

22. "It is also not my inclination to spread my knowledge and teachings in secret, as you do, since your secret Association of Essenes is unauthorized.

23. "But let me think over the pros and cons for three days, and whether I will then tell you 'yes' or 'no', because I must first think about everything before I give you my last word on it."

24. And Juthan said, "Be it as you say.

25. "Peace be with you.

26. "Go and give us an answer in three days, if you want to speak your word then."

27. But Jmmanuel departed from there, fleeing from the city with his following, and travelled east, far into the country.

28. And Jmmanuel said to his followers, "Behold, the Association of the Essenes lives according to an erroneous religious cult, though its followers gather much from my teachings.

29. "Their old philosophy, however, is not the teaching of truth, knowledge, love, logic, wisdom and The Laws of Creation. Therefore, it is incorrect and not of adequate or real value.

30. "But they have recognized this and are now weaving my truthful teachings into their teachings of half-truths, to create from this a new doctrine so that they can demean me by calling me one of them.

31. "They will claim that I am affiliated with their society and that they had helped me from the beginning of my life.

32. "And they will even say that my teachings stem from the knowledge of their cult, and that they had saved me from the cross because I was one of them.

33. "They will claim that all my followers were from their cult,

34. "And they will also claim that I am the son of God.

35. "But I tell you that I have never belonged to this Association of Essenes and that I have nothing in common with it or its followers; thus, I also never received help from them.

36. "The Association of the Essenes will not be the only group to make use of my name. Many cults will come forth in my name and will thus consider themselves great and will want to dazzle the people thereby.

37. "Similarly, people will establish peculiar cults and will glorify me in them, so as to be more credible, whereby the public can be further enslaved and exploited.

38. "And so, many cults will be established in my name, but their purpose will only be to enslave people in their consciousness and freedom, thereby bringing the cults great power over the people, the land and the money.

39. "But I tell you that no cult will be righteous if it does not recognize Creation alone as the highest power and does not live according to its Laws and directives.

40. "And no cult will exist that preaches the truthful teachings, the knowledge or the truth.

41. "It will be two times a thousand years before the time comes when my teachings will be preached anew, without being falsified. This will occur when false doctrines and erroneous cults, when lies and fraud, and when deception by the conjurers of the dead and of spirits, by the soothsayers and clairvoyants, as well as by all the charlatans of the truth, will be at their peak.

42. "Until then, false cults, as well as liars, deceivers, charlatans, conjurers of the dead and of spirits, false soothsayers, clairvoyants, and false mediums pretending to speak for supernatural, other-dimensional and extraterrestrial beings from the depths of the universe, will be so numerous that they can no longer be counted.

43. "And such cults will be built upon human blood, hatred, greed and power, on lies and deceptions, and on cheating, misunderstanding, self-deception, confusion of consciousness and delusion.

44. "But just as they will have arisen, so will they be destroyed, because the truth will triumph,

45. "For there is no untruth that will not be denounced as a lie.

46. "There is nothing hidden that will not become revealed.

47. "Humans will recognize what is before their faces, and what is hidden from them will reveal itself when they search for the truth and the enlightenment of wisdom.

48. "But the truth lies deep within The Laws of Creation, and there alone should humankind seek and find it.

49. "Those who seek shall not stop seeking until they find,

50. "And when they find, they will be profoundly shocked and astonished, but then they will rule over the Universe.

51. "May humans recognize from this that the kingdom is within them and outside of them."

Humankind and Creation

1. It came to pass that Jmmanuel preached of humanity and of Creation as he went eastward with a caravan.

2. He said, "Humans should look upward to the stars, for majestic peace and grandeur there.

3. "As though by immutable law and order, the infinite and everlasting changes take place there over days, months, years and beyond for centuries, millennia and millions of years.

4. "Humans, however, should also look downward upon the Earth for there, as well, is Creational activity and endless becoming and passing away, and life and existence, toward ever newly developing forms.

5. "Greatness, excellence and beauty rule harmoniously where nature is left to itself.

6. "But where traces of human order are at work, there pettiness, disgrace and ugliness testify to alarming disharmony.

7. "With inflated chest, humankind calls itself the crown of creation, and yet it is not cognizant of Creation and sets persons on a level with it.

8. "But this humankind, which has tamed fire and rules the Earth, will not go far.

9. **"Without a doubt, humans will learn to harness water and air, but in the process they will forget to be cognizant of Creation above them and of its Laws.**

10. **"Thus they will also forget to seek truth, knowledge, love, respect, life, logic, true freedom and wisdom,**

11. **"And they will forget to live peacefully with each other.**

12. "Their battle cry will be warfare, for they want to attain power through violence.

13. "But when they believe they have power in their hands, they will use it for enslavement and bloodshed, exploitation, brutality, crime, and degeneration.

14. "They will speak of honor, freedom and knowledge, but in truth these will be only hypocrisy, coercion and false teachings.

15. "Thus, in the future, humankind will lose its face and display an evil and false mask.

16. "Many will degenerate into beasts and spend their earthly days without knowledge and conscience.

17. "Human ambitions and desires will be directed only toward acquisition, power, lust, addiction and greed.

18. "With their intellect, humans will arrange the things of this world to make them subservient, regardless of the fact that in so doing they break the laws of nature and destroy nature itself in many ways.

19. "They will no longer trust in the eternal truths, which are anchored in the laws of nature.

20. "Through self-deception, they will find more meaning in the human sciences than in all the values of the Laws of nature and Creation.

21. "In their confusion, humans will believe in this erroneous, self-created, pathetic philosophy of life, which will be produced through the cults' confusing and false teachings and through arrangements of human laws and vagaries of the principles that govern nations.

22. "Humans will want to control their lives by external means,

because they will have forgotten to be aware of their own essence from the Creational point of view.

23. "Through deceitful means, they will delude, cheat and exploit their fellow humans and the entire world.

24. "And wherever trust and truth still exist, they will change it into distrust and untruth, and in so doing they will get further and further away from the true life.

25. "Thus, they will also lose sight of the principle of the oldest wisdom, which states that humans are the measure of all things in life because they are, after all, a part of Creation.

26. "But the time will come when humankind must turn around and become reacquainted with the eternal values of life.

27. "Initially, only a few will know that humans live not only on Earth but also in the endless expanse of the Universe, and that they live not only in the material world but their spirits reach into another world that cannot be grasped by the ordinary physical senses.

28. "This other one, the ethereal world, is the true home of the spirit. Therefore, humans should try without ceasing to broaden and deepen their knowledge, love, truth, logic, true freedom and liberty, genuine peace, harmony and wisdom, so that the spirit may be perfected and lifted up into its true home, becoming one with Creation.

29. "Truly, I say to you, those who understand the truth of this message and attain insight through wisdom, will awaken to the obligation of aligning their lives with their destiny of eternal change toward Creation.

30. "When people are honest and seek, they will not hold any preconceived opinions or prejudices.

31. "But the wise do know and are aware of the law of the everlasting flow of eternal change. Therefore, they endeavor to adjust to the grand scheme of events and of progress, because they appreciate The Laws of Creation, namely, that the cycles of existence must be completed as prescribed by these Laws.

32. "Wherever life reveals itself, it is based upon the law of the

invisible mystery that brings about the eternal change.

33. "But persons who disregard and fail to recognize the timeless and everlasting laws and truths must take upon themselves the dire consequences.

34. "Lies and hatred will blind such persons and even entire peoples, and they will rush into the abyss of their own destruction.

35. "A blind, destructive mania will overcome them, and the heroes among them will be those who are the greatest destroyers.

36. "Conflict will permeate people's entire lives, and where there is discord there is no longer wholeness and perfection.

37. "But as long as imperfection exists in life, humans must bear the consequences: sickness, misery, injustice, privation, fighting, strife, slavery, erroneous cults, and exploitation leading to bloodshed and death.

38. "So let humankind beware and awaken, for The Laws of Creation state: Only that which is timeless and everlasting is of permanence, of truth and of wisdom, and so it is."

"Just as a candle cannot burn without fire, men cannot live without a spiritual life." —Buddha

A Summary of The Laws of Creation and the Universe

The following section is a detailed summary of The Laws of Creation and the Universe, and also the laws and commandments laid down by the extraterrestrials who gifted us Jmmanuel:
- The Laws of Creation shall forever be observed
- Everything is connected to everything else in the Universe
- There is never one without the other, even good and evil
- The two parts of the spirit are wisdom and power; a person cannot have a healthy spirit without both entities, so one must continually strive to study and understand oneself as best as humanly possible through experiential experience and learning from one's mistakes, thus gaining wisdom over time; power comes with exercising that wisdom correctly so a person attains ever more wisdom and power
- Without wisdom of the spirit, its power cannot be utilized, nor can any wisdom emerge without spiritual power
- Greatness, excellence and beauty rule harmoniously where nature is left to itself

- The human spirit is immortalized through rebirth or reincarnation, where the active spirit is passed on to the next living body to further its experiences and knowledge
- You must live your life to the fullest, to the very end of your days
- Blessed are those who are rich in spirit and recognize the truth, for life is theirs
- Blessed are those who endure hardship, for they shall thus recognize truth and be comforted
- Blessed are the spiritually balanced, for they shall possess knowledge; for humans, being spiritual does not mean worshipping a religious entity. It is about studying what comprises the spirit, building on that knowledge, practicing how to improve and grow it, and sharing it with all in life
- Blessed are those who hunger and thirst for truth and knowledge, for they shall be satisfied; actively seeking answers to all the questions we have inside us is key to becoming knowledgeable and wise
- Blessed are those who live according to the laws of nature, for they live according to the plan of Creation; we have inside the blueprint for living, and sometimes it is called "common sense"; we must live our lives according to what feels natural deep inside us
- Blessed are those who have a clear conscience, for they need not fear
- Blessed are those who know about Creation, for they are not enslaved by false teachings; simply ignoring the false religions is the first step toward enlightenment
- Blessed are the righteous, for nature is subject to them
- Blessed are you if, on my account and because of our teachings, people revile and persecute you and speak all manner of evil against you; thus they lie about the teachings
- Be of good cheer and take comfort; this life and the next life will reward you; smile, laugh, be positive and upbeat; it's all contagious

A Summary of The Laws of Creation and the Universe

- You are the salt of the Earth, and if the salt loses its flavor with what would one salt? It is useless henceforth, except it be thrown out and stepped on by the people
- You are the light of the world, and consider: the city that lies on top of a mountain cannot be hidden; people are greatly attracted to those who are "lights" and who possess the strength of character to smile, laugh, be positive and upbeat through the most difficult times; they serve as a beacon of hope for others and an example of how to live life
- One does not light a candle and place it under a bushel, but on a candlestick; thus it shines for all those who are in the house
- Likewise your light shall shine before the people, so they see your good deeds and recognize the truth of your knowledge
- Exercise justice according to the natural Laws of Creation, so that you find the judgment in logic; this entails being fair and just with all others, treating people and animals with respect
- Guilty are all those who kill when not acting in self-defense or according to legal verdict based on self-defense. Likewise, guilty are all those who engage in evil speech and action
- Only justice according to the natural Laws of Creation produces a logical judgment
- Do not accommodate your adversaries if you are in the right, and the judge will probably have to decide in your favor
- You will attain justice only when you find it yourself and can make your fellow humans understand it
- Give to them who ask of you, if they make their requests in honesty, and turn away from them who want to borrow from you in a dishonest way
- Practice love and understanding according to the natural Laws of Creation, so that through logic you find the right action and perception
- Over the course of incarnations, you shall train your spirit and your consciousness and allow them to develop to perfection, so that you become one with Creation

- Choose your words using natural logic, and draw upon the knowledge and behavior of nature
- When you give alms, you shall not proclaim it, as do the hypocrites in the synagogues and on the streets, that they may be praised by the people; their alms serve only their selfishness
- When you pray, you shall not be like the hypocrites, who enjoy standing and praying in the synagogues and on the corners of the streets, because they pray only for the sake of their selfishness and the impression they have upon the people
- When you pray, you shall call upon the omnipotence of the spirit and not babble misleading nonsense like the idol-worshippers, the ignorant and the selfish, because they think they are heard when they use many words
- When you pray to your spirit, it will give you what you request; have trust in this knowledge and you will receive
- Do not amass great treasures on Earth, where moths and rust consume them and thieves break in and steal them, but collect treasures in the spirit and in consciousness, where neither moths nor rust consumes them and where thieves neither break in nor steal
- Collect treasures in the spirit and in consciousness, where neither moths nor rust consumes them and where thieves neither break in nor steal. For where your treasure is, there your heart is also; and the true treasure is wisdom and knowledge
- No one can serve two masters; either he will hate the one and love the other, or he will adhere to the one and despise the other
- You cannot serve your good spirit and the devil of covetousness. Concern yourself about the knowledge of your spirit, and what you will eat and drink, and be concerned about your body and how you will clothe it. The birds in the sky do not sow, they do not reap, they do not store their food in barns, and yet Creation feeds them
- If you suffer from hunger, thirst and nakedness, then wisdom

and knowledge will be crowded out by worry. First seek the realm of your spirit and its knowledge, and then seek to comfort your body with food, drink and clothing
- Judge not falsely, lest you be falsely judged. For with whatever judgment you judge, you will be judged, and with whatever measure you measure, you will be measured. Judge according to the logic of the laws of nature, which are from Creation, because only they possess its truth and correctness
- Through The Laws of Creation and nature, learn first how to recognize your own faults, so that you can then correct the faults of your neighbors
- Do not throw your spiritual treasure into the dirt and do not waste it on the unworthy, because they will not thank you and will tear you apart, for their understanding is small and their spirit is weak
- Ask, and it will be given to you
- Seek and you will find
- Knock, and it will be opened to you
- Everything that you wish people would do to you, do likewise to them
- The path to damnation is broad, but the path to life and knowledge and narrow, and there are only few who find it
- Beware of false prophets and scribes who come to you in sheep's clothing, but inwardly are like ravenous wolves, preaching to you about submissiveness before shrines, false deities and gods, and preaching submissiveness to idols and false teachings
- Beware of those who forbid you access to wisdom and knowledge, for they speak to you only to attain power over you and to seize your goods and belongings
- Turn away from the false teachings of the Israelite authorities and their scribes, because they will bring destruction to successive generations. The Israelites believe themselves the chosen people. By no means is this the case, because they are more disloyal and unknowing than the ignorant who lack the

- secret of Creation's Laws
- The unrighteous and the ignorant, including the scribes, priests and the authorities, will hate those who have the knowledge and will, therefore, persecute them and sow enmity
- The path of truth is long and the wisdom of knowledge will only penetrate slowly
- This Earth can nourish and support five hundred million people of all human populations. But if these laws are not followed, in two times a thousand years there will exist ten times five hundred million people, and the Earth will no longer be able to support them. Famines, catastrophes, worldwide wars and epidemics will rule the Earth; Earth humans will kill each other, and only a few will survive
- Do away with enforcing the old law that subjects woman to man, since she is a person like the man, with equal rights and obligations
- Take on the burden of having to learn the new teachings, for they offer enlightenment; within them you will find peace for your life, because the yoke of spiritual development is gentle, and its burden is light
- Humans must first experience much guilt and error before they learn to accumulate knowledge and wisdom, so as to recognize the truth
- The Laws of Creation have been valid for yesterday and today, and therefore for tomorrow, the day after tomorrow, and for all time. Thus the Laws are also a determination and hence a predetermination for things of the future that must happen
- Nowhere is a prophet valued less than in his own country and in his own house
- Never doubt the power of your spirit and never doubt your knowledge and ability when logic proves to you The Laws of Creation in truth and correctness
- The human spirit is ignorant until it has gained knowledge through thinking and inquiry

A Summary of The Laws of Creation and the Universe

- The spirit of a person is not a human product but is a part of Creation given to humans. It must be made knowledgeable and perfected, so that it proceeds to become one with Creation, since Creation, too, lives in constant growth
- Those who search, seek and gather insights and thirst for knowledge like a child will be great in spirit. Those who search, seek and find like such a child will always reach their fullest potential within themselves
- There is no sense in life and no fulfilment of its meaning without searching, seeking and finding
- Creation is timeless, and so is the human spirit
- Even when humans burden themselves with mistakes, they act according to The Laws of Creation, because they learn from them and gather insight and knowledge, whereby they develop their spirits, and through their spirits' strength they are able to act
- Without making mistakes, it is impossible to gather the logic, insight, knowledge, love and wisdom necessary to develop the spirit
- When one makes a mistake that serves the insight, knowledge, and progress of the spirit, there is no punishment, neither in this life nor in any subsequent life Humans live with the mission of perfecting their spirits and obtaining insight and knowledge through mistakes, so that they may lead the lives for which they were destined
- Because humans at this time are beginning to think and perceive, they are in need of the teachings. Thus the prophets have been sent by the celestial sons to teach humankind about the true Laws of Creation and the knowledge regarding life
- Humans are still ignorant and addicted to the false laws of the chief priests and distorters of the scriptures. They do not recognize the new teachings as truth. Lacking understanding, the people curse the truth which yet must come; they curse, stone, kill and crucify the prophets. But since the teachings of

the truth must be brought to the people, the prophets have to bear great burdens and suffering under the curse of the people
- It is better to let an unreasonable person walk on the path of misery than to bring confusion to one's own consciousness
- The heavens will collapse before an unreasonable person can be taught reason
- Whatever a person may wish to accomplish, they must always first create the will to do so, because this is the law of nature
- A person determines the course of their life, known as fate
- We also are bound in destiny to The Laws of Creation and the Universe
- The highest directive in The Laws of Creation: Achieve the wisdom of knowledge, so that you may wisely follow The Laws of Creation
- The spirit of each person is created specifically for the task of perfecting itself and gaining wisdom
- Whatever a person may wish to accomplish, they must always first create the will to do so, because this is the law of nature. Thus a person determines the course of their life, known as fate. One must acquire knowledge and learn the truth to engender a will that is imbued with the laws
- It is easier to bear an adversity with one or two others at one's side than by oneself
- Be awake and great in spirit and in consciousness so you will not fall prey to temptation. The spirit is willing but the flesh is weak
- It is also customary among humans that the most righteous person does not find justice, because it doesn't matter whether many or few testify against him, as long as they are highly regarded
- A human being shall never attempt to force the truth onto another, because then it would only be worth half its value
- First, humans shall tend to their own progress in consciousness and spirit, so as to produce Creational harmony within themselves
- No greater darkness rules within humans than ignorance and lack of wisdom

A Summary of The Laws of Creation and the Universe

- Greatness of personal victory requires uprooting and destroying all influences that oppose the Creational force, so that which is Creational may prevail
- Humans should develop within themselves the power to judge over good and evil and to correctly perceive all things, so that they may be wise and fair and follow the Laws
- It is necessary to be cognizant of what is real and what is unreal, what is valuable and what is worthless, and what is of Creation and what is not
- Humans gain experience in the use of their powers and capabilities only by trying daily to unlock them
- There may be no limits to love, peace and joy, because the present state must always be exceeded
- Truly, I say to you, a love that is unlimited, constant and unfailing is unconditional and is a pure love, in whose fire all that is impure and evil will burn
- The laws of life are not hidden from the wise man, hence he can recognize and follow them
- The wise understand that the secret of Primeval-Creation lies in the number seven and in computations based thereon. Thus they will gather and retain the knowledge that Creation has a time for work or rest that is also based upon the number seven
- All things in the Universe are bound together by the number nine and its multiples, whose secrets have yet to be revealed
- A love that is unlimited, constant and unfailing is unconditional and is a pure love, in whose fire all that is impure and evil will burn
- When a blind man leads another blind man, both will fall into the pit
- The Laws of Creation are also a determination and hence a predetermination for things of the future that must happen
- Humans do not possess the right to sit in judgment over their own lives and deaths
- Although humans have free will to exercise authority over

themselves, they do not have the right to decide over life or death
- Every guilt and every mistake is a pathway to understanding by which the consciousness and the spirit are perfected
- Just as the Laws and directives of Creation are the Laws and directives for the spirit and for life, so the laws and commandments of god are the laws and commandments for material life and human regulations
- The extraterrestrial god issued the Laws and commandments to serve as material life and human regulations for that which is right, and also as a guideline for life and living
- The Laws and directives of Creation and the laws and commandments of god are to be obeyed, humans must not bring forth any other laws and commandments
- When humans deviate from these laws and directives, however, they bring forth illogical and inadequate human laws and commandments that are based on false logic and, thus, are extremely faulty
- Humans must disregard false teachings and not arrogantly pursue greed for power and fortune
- Man-made laws and commandments produce murder and all manner of evil and, as evil spreads and gains the upper hand, man no longer has control over it
- Commandments and laws are valuable only when they are derived from wisdom, and hence are logical, but logic requires wisdom and understanding
- Human laws and human commandments are powerless, unless they are founded upon The Laws and directives of Creation, just as god's laws and commandments are founded upon them, as he issued them in his wisdom. When humans are presumptuous and disregard The Laws and directives of Creation and those of god, they are forced to bring forth their own laws that are flawed and lead everyone astray
- Wisdom must be learned from The Laws of Creation, which

humans may recognize in nature
- If humans do not think and seek, they will not be able to attain wisdom and will remain fools
- The wise do not moan about lost things, about the dead and about events of the past
- Fools, however, cry over things that are not worth crying over, and thereby they increase their grief, privation and misery
- Those who have acquired sufficient wisdom and live according to the Laws, permit not even the slightest harming of creatures, when they are without fault
- Half-wits and fools who are not masters over their senses mistake harm for benefit, benefit for harm, and great sorrow for joy
- Because people are not dedicated to wisdom and do not seek knowledge or recognize the Laws, they harbor foolishness and vice
- The dishonest, the stupid, grumpy, greedy, unscrupulous, uncouth and the angry will suffer harm for being poor in consciousness
- When people duly receive daily just a little wisdom in their consciousness, they will grow like the waxing moon during the first half of the lunar month
- Wisdom is the greatest asset of humanity and so is the created will, which is lord over love and happiness; but all of this is meaningless without the power of the spirit
- A fool who idly rests and waits for fate goes to ruin like an unfired pot in water
- Those who take care of a cow always receive milk; likewise, those who nurture wisdom and apply it through the power of the spirit bring forth rich fruit
- Recognize each Law of Creation and, once you have recognized it, adhere to it and live accordingly, because the Laws are the greatest wisdom
- There is no eye equal to wisdom, no darkness equal to ignorance,

no power equal to the power of the spirit, and no terror equal to the poverty of consciousness
- There is no higher happiness than wisdom, no better friend than knowledge, and no other savior than the power of the spirit
- Those who have intelligence may grasp my speech so they will be wise and knowing
- The Laws of Creation state: Only that which is timeless and everlasting is of permanence, of truth and of wisdom

When you read and absorb Jmmanuel's words, and also the thoughts and interpretations of his work in *Arcanum*, hopefully, you will come away with a new understanding of the simple rules of life:

Be kind and gentle to yourself.

Live a good, clean life.

Learn all you can about yourself and all that life has to offer.

Treat others and animals and all life with respect and dignity.

Continue to learn and make mistakes, and pass on your lessons learned to others. There is much power when common interests are shared among parents and children, brothers and sisters, and fellow friends and colleagues.

All these according to The Laws of Creation and the physical rules of the Universe, some of which have just been shared in one small volume.

Nothing in these basic rules calls for worshipping any false God, idol or monument, as specified by current false religions and cults, although the majority of humans on this planet do just this. The human spirit is easily led down the easy path of darkness. It takes a strong and courageous person to walk the much narrower path of righteousness.

The Laws of Creation do tell us all to respect everything in life. There is a world of difference between worship, which is a false order proclaimed by false religious leaders and their followers, and that espoused by The Laws of Creation: *respect*.

Above all else, *please respect yourself and others*. Whatever happens in your life thereafter follows naturally if you adhere to this simple rule,

A Summary of The Laws of Creation and the Universe

and also understand and respect the absolute fact that everything on Mother Earth and in the Universe are connected by the smallest unit of matter, the quantoretto, which forms a seamless liquid or sliq that binds us all as one.

Everything is intimately connected....

"If the liberties of the American people are ever destroyed, they will fall by the hands of the Roman clergy." —Lafayette

Some Final Thoughts

As you consider the words of Jmmanuel, what comes to mind first? Do they ring true for you? Do you believe them? Did they sing down to your DNA? If not, why? What questions, thoughts, ideas and beliefs come to mind when considering his sermons?

Several points are abundantly clear: those who murdered the man who translated Jmmanuel's sermons 50 years ago wished to prevent anyone from publishing them to a worldwide audience, and they were willing to do anything to stop them. The Israelis are notoriously known in recent history (since their country's inception more than 60 years ago) for being heavy handed in all external (and internal) affairs, especially those of "national security." They have blithely murdered many who have spoken out against Israel, and silenced those who oppose their rule and actions in the Middle East.

That the Israeli Defense Forces (IDF) would murder the man who translated the most important work in recent history is barbarous. It also speaks volumes about the veracity and importance of Jmmanuel Sananda's words and sermons to humankind. His 36 sermons were left to us as a supreme gift, and the murderous act committed against Markus-Isa Rashid and his family tells us that his seminal work must be spread far and wide so all people can read and understand the teachings of Jmmanuel, so we may decide for ourselves what we will understand and believe and ultimately follow.

His words compel us to examine the results of what has occurred over the last 2,000 years, and not be fooled by the various powers' attempts to tell us otherwise.

It is not up to malevolent institutions like the IDF and Jesuits to order us about and tell us what we will read and see and hear, although they do it frequently and with great success.

Jmmanuel's teachings have left much to think about. The agenda of the extraterrestrials who brought Jmmanuel to Earth is not clear, but their actions suggest they sought to control humankind through the use of "prophets" like Jmmanuel, who imparted limited knowledge in the form of metaphors and parables for us to consider, decipher and implement.

These same ETs designed and built us humans from simian DNA, but they did not give us a sufficient road map for our success. We are left trying to interpret Jmmanuel's words, almost all of which have been bastardized by the Jesuits and their various false religions. This is one of the reasons why I wrote this book: to reveal Jmmanuel's sentiments for humankind, and to pick his words down to the bone in search of truth and understanding.

To begin to understand Jmmanuel's words, we much examine his actions and behaviors at the lowest possible level, again, which is why I made a good-faith attempt to analyze his words in Part One.

Many questions are still unanswered:

What was the extraterrestrials' true agenda here on Mother Earth?

Why did they send such a seemingly weak prophet to "save" us from destruction and to teach us about The Laws of Creation and the Universe?

Why was their emissary seemingly such a poor teacher and mentor to the majority of humans he encountered?

Some Final Thoughts

Why did they attempt to emplace their own brand of control over humanity?

How could Jmmanuel see into the future, predicting a great cataclysm, yet not be able to discuss so many aspects of his journeys and his purpose here on Earth?

Why would Jmmanuel not kill his enemies and be done with them?

Why would he allow so many good people to suffer at the hands of so few?

Why couldn't he speak in "normal" terms, rather than using metaphors and parables? Jmmanuel's encouraging people to think for themselves does not adequately answer this question.

Why did he leave humankind only one set of scrolls with his teachings and not many books that explained The Laws of Creation and the Universe?

Why was he so vague when discussing these Laws? A note about that last question: I chose to make a detailed list of The Laws of Creation, all gleaned from his words, because he failed to perform this important function on behalf of humankind.

Jmmanuel was correct when stating that the descendants of the Pharisees and Sadducees would produce false religions, teach distorted truths, and enslave all of mankind. He did not mention the role Rome would play, though, had virtually nothing to say about the Romans during his time.

The Jesuits are the current rulers of the planet, but they were not discussed by Jmmanuel when he spoke of the rulers of the future, only Jewish descendants of his enemies.

How did Jmmanuel fail to mention the Jesuits, even though he could predict or foretell the future? Those powers in Rome were not descendants of the Pharisees and Sadducees, so Jmmanuel failed to warn us about the Jesuits and their destructive powers. Why?

For your convenience, I have included in the References section more than 200 books about the Jesuits. If you take the time to read even a few of them, your heart, mind and soul will expand immensely, and you will begin to understand what others have known for centuries:

this brood of snakes and vipers has done, and continues to do, great harm to humanity. . . .

For those of you who wish to learn more about contemporary Jesuit machinations in America, please read my book, ***Romanic Depression: How the Deadlight of the Black Pope and the Jesuit Militia Distort the History of The United States of America***. In it, I analyze and examine 40 sectors of American society and demonstrate how the Jesuits have designed and built, and manipulated and corrupted each one, then marketed and advertised something decidedly contrary.

My wish for you is that *Arcanum* evokes hundreds of new questions, thoughts, and ideas in you, and that you begin a new journey of self-discovery in the tradition of The Laws of Creation that Jmmanuel has taught us. The detailed list of the Laws in the previous chapter is by no means exhaustive. With time, you will discover new Laws that Jmmanuel did not state or allude to in his sermons.

My blessings to you and your loved ones. Have a grand journey!

"If we encounter a man of rare intellect, we should ask him what books he reads." —Ralph Waldo Emerson

References

This reference section is in two parts: books about Jmmanuel Sananda in part one; books about Jesuits in part two, which begins on page 346.

Books about Jmmanuel Sananda traveling to and living in Kashmir and India; and various accounts of his death and resurrection

Abbot, S (1917). *The Fourfold Gospels*. Cambridge University Press, Cambridge.

Abdul Qadir bin Qazi-ul Qazzat Wasil Ali Khan (n.d.). *Hashmat-i-Kashmir*, MS. Number 42, Asiatic Society of Bengal, Calcutta.

Abhedananda, S (1987). *Journey into Kashmir and Tibet*. Ramakrishna Vedanta Math, Calcutta.

Abu Jaffar Muhammad bin Jarir at-Tabri (1880). *Tafsir Ibn-i-Jarir at-Tabri (Jami al Bayan fi Tafsir-ul-Qur'an)*, Volume 3. Kubr-ul-Mar'a Press, Cairo.

Abu Muhammad Haji Mohyud-Din (1903). *Tarikh-i-Kabir-i-Kashmir*. Suraj Parkash Press, Amritsar.

Agha Mustafai (1868). *Ahwali Ahalian-i-Paras*. Tehran.

AI-Haj Mumtaz Ahmad Faruqui (1973). *The Crumbling of the Cross*. Ahmadiyya Anjuman Isha'at-i-Islam, Lahore.

Allcroft AH (1917). *The Circle and the Cross*. Macmillan, London.

Allen BM (1919). *The Story Behind the Gospels*. Methuen, London.

Andrews A (1906). *Apochryphal Books of the Old and New Testaments*. Theological Translation Library, London.

Ansault A (1894). *La Croix avant Jésus-Christ*. Paris.

Arbuthnot J (1900). *A Trip to Kashmir*. Calcutta.

Augstein R (1972). *Jesus, Menschensohn*. Gütersloh, Munich; Bertelsmann, Vienna.

Avicenna (n.d.). *Canon of Avicenna*. Newal Kishore Press, Lucknow.

Bacon BW (1918). *The Four Gospels in Research and Debate*. New Haven, Conn.

Baigent M, Leigh R, and Lincoln H (1983). *Holy Blood, Holy Grail*. Harper and Row, New York.

References

Balfour E (1885). *The Cyclopedia of India and of Eastern and Southern Asia, Vol. 1, 3rd Edition*. Bernard Quaritch, London.

Ball JA (1973). The Zoo Hypothesis. *Icarus*, 46, 347-349.

Barber P (1953). *A Doctor at Calvary*. New York.

Bardtke H (1952). *Die Handschriftenfunde am Toten Meer*. Berlin.

Bardtke H (1958). *Die Handschriftenfunde am Toten Meer: Die Sekte von Qumran*. Berlin.

Bardtke H (1962). *Die Handschriftenfunde in der Wüste Juda*. Berlin.

Barth, K (1982). *The Theology of Schleiermacher* (Ritschl D, Editor; Bromiley G, Translator.) Eerdmans, Grand Rapids, MI.

Basharat A (1929). *Birth of Jesus*. Dar-ul-Kutab-i-lslamia, Lahore.

Bauer, B (1850-1). *Kritik der Evangelien,* Volumes I and II. Berlin.

Bauer W (1971). *Orthodoxy and Heresy in Earliest Christianity*. Fortress Press, Philadelphia.

Baur FC (1847). *Kritische Untersuchungen über die Kanonischen Evangelien*. Tübingen.

Beare FW (1981). *The Gospel According to Matthew*. Harper & Row, San Francisco.

Bell AW (1897). *Tribes of Afghanistan*. Bell, London.

Bellew HW (1880a). *The New Afghan Question, or Are the Afghans Israelites?* Croddock, Simla.

Bellew HW (1880b). *The Races of Afghanistan, Being a Brief Account of the Principal Nations Inhabiting That Country.* Thacker, Spink & Co., Calcutta.

Bellinzoni AJ (1992). The Gospel of Matthew in the Second Century. *The Second Century* 9, 235-256.

Bengalee SMR (1946). *The Tomb of Jesus.* Muslim Sunrise Press, Chicago.

Berna K (1957). *Jesus nicht am Kreuz gestorben.* Verlag Hans Naber, Stuttgart.

Bernier F (1891). *Travels in the Moghul Empire* (A. Constable, translator). London.

Bernier F (1916). *Travels in the Mogul Empire (AD 1656-1668),* 2nd Edition (Constable A, Translator; Smith VA, Editor). Oxford University Press, Oxford.

Beruni-Al (1888). *Indian Travels,* Volumes I and II (Sachan E, Translator). Trubner, London.

Beskow P (1985). *Strange Tales about Jesus: A survey of Unfamiliar Gospels.* Fortress Press, Philadelphia.

Betz O (1960). *Offenbarung und Schriftforschung der Qumrantexte.* Mohr, Tübingen.

Biblioteca Christiana Ante-Nicena, 25 Volumes (1869). Clark, Edinburgh.

Biscoe CE (1922). *Kashmir in Sunlight and Shade.* London.

References

Blinzler J (1959). *El proceso de Jesús*. Editorial Litúrgica Española, Barcelona.

Blofield J (1977). *Compassion Yoga*. George Allen & Unwin, London.

Blomberg CL (1997). *Jesus and the Gospels*. Broadman & Holman, Nashville, TN.

Blomberg CL (2001). The Synoptic Problem: Where we stand at the start of a new century. *Rethinking the Synoptic Problem* (Black DA and Beck DR, Editors). Baker Academic Grand Rapids, MI.

Borg MJ (1993). Me & Jesus: The Journey Home. *The Fourth R*, 6-4 (Jul/Aug), 3-9.

Borg MJ (1990). The Jesus Seminar: Voting Records. *Forum* 6(Mar. 1990) 3-55.

Bornkamm C (1968). *Jesus von Nazareth*. Stuttgart.

Bowersock GW (Ed.) (1970). *Philostratus, Life of Apollonius* (Jones CP, Translator). Penguin Books, Baltimore.

Boys HS (1886). *Seven Hundred Miles in Kashmir*. Church Mission Congregation Press, Calcutta.

Braun H (1957). *Spätjüdisch-häretischer und frühchristlicher Radikalismus: Jesus von Nazareth und die essenische Qumrânsekte*. Tübingen.

Braun H (1962). *Gesammelte Studien zum Neuen Testament und seiner Umwelt*. Tübingen.

Braun H (1966). *Qumran und das Neue Testament*. Tübingen.

Brioton E (1958). *Las Religiones del Antiguo Oriente*. Andorra.

Brown RE and Meier JP (1983). *Antioch & Rome*. Paulist Press, New York.

Bruce CG (1911). *Kashmir. Peeps at Many Lands series*. Black, London.

Bruhl JH (1893). *The Lost Ten Tribes, Where are They?* Operative Jewish Converts Institution Press, London.

Bryce J (1856). *A Cyclopaedia of Geography Descriptive and Physical, forming a New General Gazetteer of the World and Dictionary of Pronunciation*. Richard Griffin and Co., London.

Buchanan C (1912). *Christian Researches of Asia*. Ogle, Edinburgh.

Buhl F (1908). *Canon and Text of the New Testament* (Macpherson WJM, Translator). Clark, Edinburgh.

Bultmann R (1921). *Die Geschichte der synoptischen Tradition*. Gottingen.

Bultmann R (1926). *Jesus*. Tübingen.

Bultmann R (1957). *Das Verhältnis der unchristlichen Christus Botschaft zum historischen Jesus*. Exegetica. Tübingen.

Burke OM (1976). *Among the Dervishes*. Octagon Press, London.

Burkett D (2004). *Rethinking the Gospel Sources*. T & T Clark International, London.

References

Burkitt FC (1906). *The Gospel History and its Transmission.* Clark, Edinburgh.

Burkitt FC (1910). *The Earliest Sources for the Life of Jesus.* Constable, London.

Burkitt FC (1924). *The Four Gospels, A Study of Origins.* Macmillan, London.

Butler BC (1951). *The Originality of St. Matthew.* The University Press, Cambridge.

Butler BC (1969). *The Synoptic Problem. A New Catholic Commentary on Holy Scripture* (Fuller RC et al., Editors). Nelson, Nashville, TN.

Cadoux CJ (1948). *The Life of Christ.* Pelican, London.

Chadurah KHM (n.d.). *Waqiat-i- Kashmir or Tarikh-i-Kashmir.* Muhammadi Press, Lahore.

Chatterjee JC (1911). *Kashmir Saivism.* Srinagar.

Chwolson D (1910). *Über die Frage, ob Jesus gelebt hat.* Leipsiz.

Clark J (1998). *The UFO Book: Encyclopedia of the Extraterrestrial.* Visible Ink Press, Detroit, MI.

Clemen C (1911). *Der geschichtliche Jesus.* Giessen.

Cole HH (1869). *Illustrations of Ancient Buildings in Kashmir.* W.H. Allen, London.

Conselmann H (1968). *Grundriss der Theologie des Neuen Testaments.* Munich.

Conybeare FC, Editor (1912). *Eusebius, Against Apollonius of Tyana by Philostratus. The Life of Apollonius of Tyana, the Epistles of Apollonius and the Treatise of Eusebius*, Volume II. Harvard University Press, Cambridge.

Cook E (1899). *The Holy Bible with Commentary*. John Murray, London.

Cools PJ (ed.) (1965). *Geschichte und Religion des Alten Testaments*. Olten.

Cope L (1976). *Matthew: A Scribe Trained for the Kingdom of Heaven.*. Catholic Biblical Association of America, Washington, D.C.

Craig WL (1985). *The Historical Argument for the Resurrection of Jesus during the Deist Controversy*. Edwin Mellen Press, Lewiston, NY.

Danielov J (1959). *Qumran und der Ursprung des Christentums*. Mainz.

Dautzenberg G (1970). *Der Jesus-Report und die neutestamentliche Forschung*. Müller, Wurzburg.

de Quincey D (1903). *The Apocryphal and Legendary Life of Christ*. Nathan, New York.

Deardorff JW (1986). Possible extraterrestrial strategy for Earth. *Quarterly Journal of the Royal Astronomical Society* 27, 94-101.

Deardorff JW (1987a). Examination of the embargo hypothesis as an explanation for the Great Silence. *Journal of the British Interplanetary Society* 40, 373-379.

References

Deardorff JW (1987b). Extraterrestrial communications. *Journal of Communication*, 37, 181-184.

Deardorff JW (1989). Pleiades pendulum (Letter). *International UFO Reporter* 14 (5, Sept/Oct), 21.

Deardorff JW (1992). *The Problems of New Testament Gospel Origins*. Mellen Research University Press, New York.

Deardorff JW (1994). *Jesus in India*. International Scholars Publications (University Press of America), Bethesda, MD.

Deardorff JW, Haisch B, Maccabee B, and Puthoff HE (2005). Inflation-theory implications for extraterrestrial visitation. *Journal of the British Interplanetary Society* 58, 43-50.

Denys FW (1915). *One Summer in the Vale of Kashmir*. James William Bryan Press, Washington, DC.

Derrett JDM (1982). *The Anastasis: The Resurrection of Jesus as an Historical Event*. P. Drinkwater, Shipston-on-Stour, England.

Desjardins M (1991). Bauer and beyond: On recent scholarly discussions of Airesis in the early Christian era. *The Second Century* 8, 65-68.

Dibelius M (1919). *Die Formgeschichte des Evangeliums*. Tübingen.

Docker EB (1920). *If Jesus Did Not Die on the Cross: A Study of the Evidence*. Robert Scott, London.

Dodd CH (1963). *Historical Tradition in the Fourth Gospel*. Cambridge.

Dorn B (1829). *History of the Afghans: Part 1 & 2* (Translated from the Persian of Neamet Ullah). J. Murray, London.

Doughty M (1902). *Through the Kashmir Valley*. Sands, London.

Douglass E (2001). Why doesn't the US government tell the truth about UFOs? *MUFON UFO Journal* 393(Feb), 6-7.

Drew A (1926). *Le Mythus du Christ*. Paris.

Drew F (1875). *The Jammoo and Kashmir Territories*. Edward Stanford, London.

Dummelow JR (1917). *Commentary on the Holy Bible*. Macmillan, London.

Dungan DL (1999). *A History of the Synoptic Problem*. Doubleday, New York.

Dupont A (1959). *Les Éceits esseniens découverts près de la Mer Morte*. Payot, Paris.

Dutt JC (1879). *The King of Kashmir*. Bose, Calcutta.

Edersheim A (1906). *The Life and Times of Jesus*. London.

Edkins J (1890). *Chinese Buddhism*. Kegan Paul, French and Trubner, London.

Edmunds AJ (1900-1). *Gospel Parallels from Pali Texts*. Open Court Publishing, Chicago.

Edmunds AJ (1908-9). *Buddhist and Christian Gospels*. Innes, Philadelphia.

References

Edwards WD, Gabel WJ, and Hosmer FE (1986). On the physical death of Jesus Christ. *Journal of the American Medical Association* 255(11), 1455-1463.

Ehrman BD (1997). *The New Testament: A Historical Introduction to the Early Christian Writings*. Oxford University Press, New York.

Ehrman BD (2004). *A Brief Introduction to the New Testament*. Oxford University Press, New York.

Eifel EJ (1873). *Three Lectures on Buddhism*. Trubner, London.

Eissfeldt O (1964). *Einleitung in das Alte Testament*. Tübingen.

Eliot HN (1849). *History of India as Told by its Own Historians*, 8 volumes. Thacker, Spink and Co., Calcutta.

Emerson ER (1885). *Indian Myth*. Trubner, London.

Esler PF (2005). *Rome in Apocalyptic and Rabbinic Literature. The Gospel of Matthew in its Roman Imperial Context* (Riches J and Sim DC, Editors). T & T Clark, New York.

Eugene EL (1991). *The Past of Jesus in the Gospels*. Cambridge University Press, Cambridge.

Faber-Kaiser A (1976). *Jesus Died in Kashmir: Jesus, Moses and the 10 Lost Tribes of Israel*. Gordon and Cremonisi, Ltd., London.

Farmer WR (1976). *The Synoptic Problem*, 2nd Edition. Mercer University Press, Macon.

Farquhar JN (1927). *The Apostle Thomas in South India*. Manchester University Press, Manchester.

Farrar DFW (1874). *The Life of Christ*. London.

Farrer A (1955). *On Dispensing With Q. Studies in the Gospels: Essays in Memory of R. H. Lightfoot* (Nineham DE, Editor). Blackwell, Oxford.

Fawcett L and Greenwood BJ (1984). *Clear Intent: The Government Coverup of the UFO Experience.* Prentice-Hall, Englewood Cliffs, NJ.

Ferrier JP (1858). *History of the Afghans* (translated from unpublished manuscript by Capt. W. Jesse). John Murray, London.

Flusser D (1968). *Jesus in Selbstzeugnissen und Bilddokumenten.* Hamburg.

Forster G (1808). *A Journey from Bengal to England, through the Northern Part of India, Kashmire, Afghanistan, and Perisa, and into Russia by the Caspian-Sea,* Volume II. R. Faulder and Son, London.

Geiselman JR (1951). *Jesus der Christus.* Stuttgart.

Ghulam Ahmad and Hazrat Mirza (1908). *Masih Hindustan mein (Urdu).* Qadian, Pakistan.

Ghulam Ahmad and Hazrat Mirza (1962). *Jesus in India.* Ahmadiyya Muslim Foreign Missions Department, Rabwah, Pakistan.

Gillabert E (1974). *Paroles de Jésus et Pensée Orientale.* Éditions Métanoia, Marsanne, Montélimar.

Goddard D (1927). *Was Jesus Influenced by Buddhism?* Thetford, Vermont

Goguel M (1950). *Jesus.* Paris.

References

Good T (1988). *Above Top Secret: The Worldwide UFO Cover-up.* William Morrow, New York.

Goodacre M (1998). Fatigue in the Synoptics. *New Testament Studies* 44, 45-58.

Goodacre M (2002). *The Case Against Q: Studies in Markan Priority and Synoptic Problem.* Trinity Press International, Harrisburg, PA.

Goodman M (1987). *The Ruling Class of Judaea.* Cambridge University Press, Cambridge.

Goodspeed J (1959). *Matthew: Apostle and Evangelist.* John Winston Co., Philadelphia.

Gordon S (1984). Update on the Bellwood, Pennsylvania UFO car lift case. *MUFON UFO Journal.* 200 (Dec).

Gordon S (1985). Penn State Sighting. *MUFON UFO Journal.* 212(Dec).

Gore C and Leighton H (1928). *A New Commentary on the Holy Scriptures, Including the Apocrypha.* Thornton and Butterworth, London.

Gorion E, Editor (1962). *Die Sagen der Juden.* Frankfurt.

Goulder MD (1974). *Midrash and Lection in Matthew.* Society for Promoting Christian Knowledge, London.

Goulder MD (1989). *Luke – A New Paradigm, Volumes I and II.* Journal for the Study of the Old Testament Press, Sheffield, England.

Goulder MD (1996). Is Q a Juggernaut? *Journal of Biblical Literature* 115, 667-681.

Grant M (1967). *Herod the Great.* J.B. Lippincott Co., New York.

Graves R and Podro J (1957). *Jesus in Rome.* Cassell & Company, London.

Greer S (1999). *Extraterrestrial Contact: The Evidence and Implications.* Crossing Point, Inc. Publications, Afton, VA.

Greg W (1907). *The Creed of Christendom.* Macmillan, London.

Gregory A (1907). *The Canon and Text of the New Testament.* New York.

Guignebert C (1935). *Le Monde juif vers le temps de Jésus.* Paris.

Guthrie D (1965). *New Testament Introduction.* Inter-Varsity Press, Downers Grove, IL.

Guthrie D (1970). *New Testament Introduction*, 3rd Edition. Inter-Varsity Press, Downers Grove.

Haag H (1951). Bibel-Lexikon. Based on Bijbelsch Woordenboek (van den Born A, Editor), 1941. *Spanish edition: de Ausejo S, Editor (1967). Diccionario de la Biblia.* Barcelona.

Haenchen E (1968). *Der Weg Jesu.* Berlin.

Haig TW (1928). *The Kingdom of Kashmir.* Cambridge University Press, Cambridge.

References

Hanna W (1928). *The Life of Christ.* American Tract Society, New York.

Harrison ER (1981). *Cosmology.* Cambridge University Press, New York.

Hassnain F (1994). *A Search for the Historical Jesus.* Gateway Books, Bath, England.

Head P (1997). *Christology and the Synoptic Problem: An Argument for Markan Priority.* Cambridge University Press, Cambridge.

Headland AC (1914). *The Miracles of the New Testament.* Longman Green, London.

Hengel M (1961). *Die Zeloten.* Leiden.

Hirn Y (1912). *The Sacred Shrine.* Macmillan, London.

Hodson G (n.d.). *The Christ Life from Nativity to Ascension.* Theosophical Publishing House, Illinois.

Hoehner HW (1972). *Herod Antipas.* Zondervan Pub. House, Grand Rapids, MI.

Holt JC (1991). *Buddha in the Crown.* Oxford University Press, New York.

Holtzmann HJ (1863). *Die synoptischen Evangelien.* Leipzig.

Horne TH (1823). *An Introduction to the Critical Study and Knowledge of the Holy Scriptures* (Alford H, Editor), 4th Edition, Volume 4. London.

Horsley R (1989). *Sociology and the Jesus Movement*. Crossroad, New York.

Hubbard BJ (1981). In review of The Vision of Matthew by John P. Meier. *Journal of Biblical Literature* 100, 121-122.

Hugh J (1839). *History of Christians in India from the Commencement of the Christian Era*. Seeley and Burnside, London.

Instinsky HU (1957). *Das Jahr der Geburt Jesu*. Munich.

I-Tsing (1896). *A Record of The Buddhist Religion as Practised in India and the Malay Archipelago (A.D. 671-695)* (Takakusu J, Translator). Clarendon Press, Oxford.

James P (1983). Did Christ die in Kashmir? *Islamic Review* 3(Oct/Nov), 17.

Jameson HG (1922). *The Origin of the Synoptic Gospels*. Blackwell, Oxford.

Jawarhar Lal Nehru (1942). *Glimpses of World History*. John Day Co., New York.

Jeremias J (1958). *Jerusalem der Zeit Jesu*. Göttingen.

Jeremias J (1966). *Studien zur neutestamentlichen Theologie und Zeitgeschichte*. Göttingen.

Jeremias J (1970). *Die Gleichnisse Jesu*. Göttingen.

John W (1895). Journey to Kashmir, in *Asiatic Researches*. Baptist Mission Press, Calcutta.

References

Johnston AK (1855). *Dictionary of Geography, Descriptive, Physical, Statistical, And Historical, Forming a Complete General Gazetteer of the World, 2nd Edition*. Longman, Brown, Green, and Longman, London.

Josephus, *Antiquities* XVII, xii, par. 2, and beginning of XVIII.

Josephus F (1840). *The Works of Flavius Josephus; comprising the Antiquities of the Jews; a History of the Jewish Wars, and Life of Flavius Josephus* (Whiston W, Translator). Willoughby & Co., London.

Joyce D (1972). *The Jesus Scroll*. Ferret Books, Melbourne.

Kahler M (1969). *Der sogennante historische Jesus und der geschichtliche, biblische Christus*. Wolf, Munich.

Kak RB and Pandit Ram Chand (1933). *Ancient Monuments of Kashmir*. India Society, London.

Kamal-ud-Din, Al-Haj Hazrat Khwaja (1921). *Islam and Christianity*. MM and L Trust, Woking, Surrey.

Kamal-ud-Din and Al-Haj Hazrat Khwaja (1922). *The Sources of Christianity*. MM and L Trust, Woking, Surrey.

Kamal-ud-Din and Al-Haj Hazrat Khwaja (1932). *A Running Commentary on the Holy Qur'an*. MM and L Trust, Woking, Surrey.

Kasemann, E (1964). *Exegetische Versuche und Besinnung*. Göttingen.

Kaul PA (1913). *The Geography of Jammu and Kashmir*. Thacker, Spink and Co., Calcutta.

Kaul PA (1924). *The Kashmir Pandits.* Thacker, Spink and Co., Calcutta.

Kautsky K (1908). *Der Ursprung des Christentums.* Stuttgart.

Kautzsch E, Editor (1900). *Die Apokryphen und Pseudepigraphen des Alten Testaments.* Tübingen.

Kehimkar HS (1937). *Bani Israel of India.* Dayag Press, Tel Aviv.

Keller W (1955). *Und die Bibel hat doch recht.* Dusseldorf.

Kennett RH (1933). *Ancient Hebrew Social Life and Customs as indicated in Law, Narrative and Metaphor.* Oxford University Press, Oxford.

Kenyon F (1939). *Our Bible and the Ancient Manuscripts, Being a History of the Texts and Translations.* Eyre and Spottiswoode, London.

Kersten H (1986). *Jesus Lived in India* (Woods-Czisch T, Translator). Element Book, Longmead, Shaftesbury, Dorset, England.

Kersten H (2001). *Jesus Lived in India: His Unknown Life Before and After the Crucifixion.* Penguin, New Delhi, India.

Khaniyari MGMN (n.d.). *Wajeez-ut-Tawarikh.* Research Library, Srinagar.

Khwaja Nazir Ahmad (n.d.). *Jesus in Heaven on Earth.* Woking Muslim Mission & Literary Trust, Woking, England.

Khwand M (1891). *Rauzat-us-Safa* (Rehatsek E, Translator). Arbuthnot, MRAS, London.

References

Kinder G (1987). *Light Years: An Investigation into the Extraterrestrial Experiences of Eduard Meier.* Atlantic Monthly Press, New York.

Klausner J (1925). *Jesus of Nazareth.* Allen and Unwin, London.

Klijn AFJ (1962). *The Acts of Thomas.* Brill, Leiden.

Knowles J, Editor (1984). *The Nineteenth Century: a Monthly Review, Vol. XXXVI (Jul-Dec).* Sampson Low, Marston & Co., London.

Kroll G (1963). *Auf den Spuren Jesu.* Leipzig.

Kuiper TBH and Morris, M (1977). Searching for extraterrestrial civilizations. *Science* 196, 616-621.

Kümmel WG (1966). *Introduction to the New Testament.* Abingdon Press, Nashville.

Kung, H (1974). *Christ sein.* Peper, Munich.

Lake K (1907). *The Historical Evidence for the Resurrection of Jesus Christ.* London.

Lauenstein D (1971). *Der Messias.* Stuttgart.

Lawrence W (1895). *The Valley of Kashmir.* Froude, London.

Lehmann J (1970). *Jesus-Report. Protokoll einer Verfälschung.* Düsseldorf.

Leipoldt J (1920). *Hat Jesus gelebt?* Leipzig.

Lewis SH (1929). *Mystical Life of Jesus.* Supreme Grand Lodge of Ancient Mystical Order Rosae Crucis, San Jose, California.

Loewenthal I (1865). *Some Persian Inscriptions Found in Kashmir.* Asiatic Society of Bengal, Calcutta.

Lohse E (1964). *Die Texte aus Qumran.* Kösel.

Lopez DS and Rockefeller SC, Editors (1987). T*he Christ and the Bodhisattva.* State University of New York Press, New York.

Lord JH (1907). *The Jews in India and the Far East.* Society for Promoting Christian Knowledge, Bombay.

Maccabee B (1989a). Pendulum from the Pleiades. *International UFO Reporter* 14(1, Jan/Feb), 11-12, 22.

Maccabee B (1989b). Pleiades Pendulum (Response). *International UFO Reporter* 14(5), 21-24.

Maccabee B (1993). Gulf Breeze lights still unexplained. *International UFO Reporter* 18(1, Jan/Feb), 20.

Maccabee B (2000). *UFO FBI Connection.* Llewellyn Publications, St. Paul, MN.

Macdonald G (1904). The pseudo-autonomous coinage of Antioch. *Numismatic Chronicle* 4(IV), 105-135.

Mack B (1991). *A Myth of Innocence: Mark and Christian Origins.* Fortress Press, Philadelphia.

Maier J (1960). *Die Texte vom Toten Meer.* Munich.

Malleson GB (1879). *History of Afghanistan: from the Earliest Period to the Outbreak of the War of 1878.* W.H. Allen & Co., London.

References

Mann CS (1986). *The Anchor Bible: Mark, Volume 27*. Doubleday & Co., New York.

Marxen W (1964). *Einleitung in das Neue Testament*. Gütersloh, Munich.

Marxen W (1965). *Die Auferstehung Jesu als historisches und theologisches Problem*. Gütersloh, Munich.

Maulvi Muhammad Ali (1936). *The Religion of Islam*. Ahmadiyya Anjuman Isha'at-i-Islam, Lahore.

Maulvi Muhammad Ali (1945). *History of the Prophets*. Ahmadiyya Anjuman Isha'at-i-Islam, Lahore.

McCasland SV (1932). *The Resurrection of Jesus*. Nelson, London.

McKnight S (2001). *A generation who knew not Streeter. Rethinking the Synoptic Problem* (Black DA and Beck DR, Editors). Baker Academic, Grand Rapids, MI.

McNeile AH (1915). *The Gospel According to St. Matthew*. Macmillan & Co., London.

Meffert F (1920). *Die geschichtliche Existenz Christi*. Münchengladbach.

Meier E (ca. 1983). *Verzeichnis: Authentischer Farb-Photos*. E. Meier, Hinterschmidrüti, Switzerland.

Meier E, Editor (2001). *The Talmud of Jmmanuel*. Wild Flower Press, Mill Spring, NC.

Merrick, HS (1931). *In the World's Attic*. Putnam, London.

Meyer A (1909). *Jesus or Paul* (Wilkinson FA, Translator). Harper, London.

Milligan W (1905). *The Resurrection of Our Lord*. Macmillan, London.

Mir Khawand bin Badshah (1852). *Rauza-tus-Safa (The Gardens of Purity)*, Volume I of VII. Bombay.

Molnar MR (2000). *The Star of Bethlehem*. Rutgers University Press, New Brunswick, NJ.

Monier-Williams, M (1890). *Buddhism, in its Connexion with Brahmanism and Hinduism, and in its Contrast with Christianity*, 2nd Edition. John Murray, London.

Moore G (1861). *The Lost Tribes and the Saxons of the East and of the West, with new Views of Buddhism, and Translations of Rock-Records in India*. Longman, Green, Longman, and Roberts, London.

Mozundar AK (1917). *Hindu History (3000 BC to 1200 AD)*. Dacca.

Nazir Ahmad and Al-Haj Khwaja (1973). *Jesus in Heaven on Earth*. Azeez Manzil, Lahore.

New DS (1997). *Old Testament Quotations in the Synoptic Gospels and the Two-Document Hypothesis*. Scholars Press, Atlanta, GA.

Newman W and Sagan C (1981). Galactic civilizations: Population dynamics and interstellar diffusion. *Icarus* 46, 296.

Noerlinger HS (1957). *Moses und Ägypten*. Heidelberg.

References

Notovich N (1894). *The Unknown Life of Jesus Christ* (translated from French edition by Loranger H). Rand McNally, Chicago.

O'Neill JC (1974-75). The Synoptic Problem. *New Testament Studies* 21, 273f.

Oldenberg H (1882). *Buddha: His Life, His Doctrine, His Order* (Hoey W, Translator). Williams and Norgate, London.

Olsen TM (1989). Pleiades pendulum (Letter). *International UFO Reporter* 14(5, Sept/Oct), 24.

Otto R (1940). *Reich Gottes und Menschensohn*. Munich.

Palmer EH (1880). *The Qur'an. Sacred Books of the East series.* Clarendon Press, Oxford.

Pande KC (1936). *Abhinavagupta: An Historical and Philosophical Study*. Benares.

Pannenberg W (1964). *Grundzüge der Christologie*. Gütersloh, Munich.

Parker P (1983). *The Posteriority of Mark. New Synoptic Studies* (Farmer WR, Editor). Mercer University Press, Macon, GA.

Patton CS (1915). *Sources of the Synoptic Gospels*. The Macmillan Company, London.

Pearson BA (1990). *Gnosticism, Judaism, and Egyptian Christianity*. Fortress Press, Minneapolis.

Pine C (1993). Current Cases. *MUFON UFO Journal* 305 (Sept), 20.

Prinsep H. T. (1852). *Tibet, Tartary and Mongolia; their Social and Political Condition, and the Religion of Boodh, as there Existing*, 2nd Edition. William H. Allen Co., London.

Ragg L and LM (1907). *The Gospel of Barnabas*. Clarendon Press, Oxford.

Ramsay W (1905). *Was Christ born in Bethlehem?* Hodder and Stoughton, London.

Rangacharya V (1937). *History of Pre-Musulman India*. Indian Publishing House, Madras.

Rapson EJ (1911). *Ancient India*. Cambridge University Press, Cambridge.

Ray HC (1931). *The Dynastic History of Northern India*, Volumes I and II. Thacker, Spink and Co., Calcutta.

Ray SC (1969). *Early History and Culture of Kashmir*. Munshiram Manoharlal, New Delhi.

Reicke B (1965). *Newtestamentliche Zeitgeschichte*. Göttingen.

Reidmann A (1951). *Die Wahrheit des Christentums*. Freiburg im Breisgau.

Reilson W (1927). *History of Afghanistan*. John Rylands Library Bulletin.

Rengstorf KH (1955). *Die Auferstehung Jesu*. Berlin.

Rhys Davids CAF (1912). *Buddhism*. Williams, London.

References

Rhys Davids TW (1881). *Lectures on the Origin and Growth of Religion as Illustrated by some Points in the History of Indian Buddhism. The Hibbert Lectures, 1881.* Williams and Norgate, London.

Rhys Davids TW (1882). *Buddhism: being a Sketch of the Life and Teachings of Gautama, the Buddha.* Society for Promoting Christian Knowledge, London.

Rhys Davids TW (1896). *Buddhism, its History and Literature.* Putnam, New York.

Rietmüller O (1922). *Woher wissen wir, dass Jesus gelebt hat?* Stuttgart.

Ristow H and Matthiae K (1961). *Der geschichtliche Jesus und der Kerygmatische Christus.* Berlin.

Roberts A and Donaldson J (Eds.) (1956). *Eusebius, Ecumenical History (EH) 3.39.16. The Ante-Nicene Fathers (ANF)*, Volume I. Eerdmans, Grand Rapids.

Roberts A and Donaldson J (Editors) (1993). *Ignatius, Epistle to the Ephesians. The Ante-Nicene Fathers (ANF), Volume I.* Eerdmans Publishing Company, Grand Rapids.

Robinson F (1902). *The Coptic Apocryphal Gospels.* Methuen, London.

Robinson JM (1959). *The New Quest of the Historical Jesus.* London.

Robinson TA (1988). *The Bauer Thesis Examined: The Geography of Heresy in the Early Christian Church.* Edwin Mellen Press, Lewiston, New York.

Rockhill WW (1884). *The Life of the Buddha and the Early History of his Order. Derived from Tibetan Works in the Bkah-Hgyur and Bstan-Hgyur.* Trübner & Company, London.

Rodgers, RW (1929). *A History of Ancient India.* Scribner, London.

Rose GH (1852). *The Afghans: The Ten Tribes and the Kings of the East.* Operative Jewish Converts Institution Press, London.

Sanders EP (1985). *Jesus and Judaism.* Fortress Press, Philadelphia.

Schelke KH (1949). *Die Passion Jesu in der Verkundigüng des Neuen Testaments.* Heidelberg.

Schelke KH (1960). *Die Gemeinde von Qumran und die Kirche des Neuen Testaments. Die Welt der Bibel.* Düsseldorf.

Schick E (1940). *Formgeschichte und Synoptiker Exegese.* Münster.

Schmidt KL (1919). *Der Rahmen der Geschichte Jesu.* Berlin.

Scholem G (1973). *Von der mystischen Gestalt der Gottheit.* Frankfurt.

Schonfield HJ (1966). *The Passover Plot.* Hutchinson, London.

Schubert K (1962). *Der historische Jesus und der Christus unseres Glaubens.* Vienna.

Schubert K (1964). *Vom Messias zum Christus.* Vienna and Freiburg.

Schurer E (1901-9). *Geschichte des jüdischen Volker im Zeitalter Jesu Christi.* Leipsiz.

Schwegler T (1962). *Die Biblische Urgeschichte.* Munich.

References

Schweitzer A (1901). *Das Messianitäts-und Leidensgeheimnis.* Tübingen.

Schweitzer A (1966). *Geschichte der Leben-Jesu-Forschung.* Munich.

Schweitzer E (1968). *Jesus Christus im vielfaltigen Zeugnis des Neuen Testaments.* Munich and Hamburg.

Seydel R (1880). *Das Evangelium von Jesu in Seinem Verhältnissen zu Buddhas Sage und Buddhas Lehre.* Leipzig.

Shaikh A-Said-us-Sadiq (1782). *Kamal-ud-Din.* Syed-us-Sanad Press, Iran.

Shams JD (1945). *Where Did Jesus Die?* Baker and Witt, London.

Simon M (1960). *Les Sectes juives au temps de Jésus.* Paris.

Sinclair M (1887). *Countess of Caithness. The Mystery of the Ages contained in the Secret Doctrine of all Religions.* Wallace CLH, Philanthropic Reform Publisher, Oxford Mansion, W., London.

Smith VA (1966). *Akbar the Great Mogul, 1542-1605.* S. Chand, Dehli.

Smith GB (1922). *A Guide to the Study of the Christian Religion.* Chicago University Press, Chicago.

Smith RG (1937). *Early Relations between India and Iran.* London.

Smith VA (1904). *The Early History of India.* Clarendon Press, Oxford.

Soter S (1985). The cosmic quarantine hypothesis. *Planetary Report* 5, 20-21.

Sprinkle RL (1999). *Soul Samples: Personal Explorations in Reincarnation and UFO Experiences.* Granite Publishing, Columbus, NC.

Stanton WH (1927). *The Gospels as Historical Documents.* Cambridge University Press, Cambridge.

Stauffer E (1957). *Jesus, Gestalt and Geschichte.* Bern.

Stein MA, Translator (1900). *Kalhana's Chronicle of the Kings of Kashmir, Volumes I and II.* London.

Stein RH (1987). *The Synoptic Problem: An Introduction.* Baker Book House, Grand Rapids, MI.

Stein RH (1992). The Matthew-Luke Agreements against Mark: Insight from John. *Catholic Biblical Quarterly* 54, 482-502.

Stevens WC (1982). UFO Contact from the Pleiades: A Preliminary Investigation Report. *UFO Photo Archives* (out of print), Tucson.

Stevens WC (1988). Message from the Pleiades, Volume I. *UFO Photo Archives* (out of print), Tucson.

Strauss DF (1835-6). *Das Leben Jesu, kritich bearbeitet.* Tübingen.

Strauss DF (1879). *A New Life of Jesus, Volume I.* Williams and Norgate, London.

Streeter BH (1924). *The Four Gospels: A Study of Origins.* Macmillan and Co., London.

References

Stroud W (1905). *On the Physical Cause of Death of Christ*. Hamilton and Adams, London.

Styler GM (1982). The Priority of Mark, in Moule CFD, *The Birth of the New Testament*, Excursis IV, 3rd Edition. Harper and Row, San Francisco.

Sufi GMD (1974). *Kashmir, being a History of Kashmir from the Earliest Times*, Volumes I and II. Light and Life Publishers, New Delhi and Jammu.

Sumi TD, Oki M and Hassnain FM (1975). *Ladakh, the Moonland*. Light and Life Publishers, New Delhi, Jammu and Rothak.

Sutta P (1917). *Bhavishya Maha Puranan*. Venkateshvaria Press, Bombay.

Thiering B (1992). *Jesus and the Riddle of the Dead Sea Scrolls*. Harper SanFrancisco, San Francisco.

Thomas EJ (1951). *The History of Buddhist Thought, 2nd Edition*. Barnes & Noble, New York.

Thomas L'Évangile selon (1975). *Éditions Métanoia*, Marsanne, Montélimar.

Thomas P (1973). *Epics, Myths and Legends of India, 13th Edition*. Taraporevala, Bombay.

Tola, F (1973). *Doctrinas secretas de la India Upanishads*. Barral, Barcelona.

Trocmé É (1971). *Jésus de Nazareth vu par les témoins de so vie*. Delaclaux et Nestlé, Neuchâtel.

Tuckett CM (1983a). 1 Corinthians and Q. *Journal of Biblical Literature* 102, 607-619.

Tuckett CM (1983b). *The Revival of the Griesbach Hypothesis.* Cambridge University Press, New York.

Tuckett CM (1992). *The Synoptic Problem. The Anchor Bible Dictionary, Vol. 6* (Freedman DN, Editor). Doubleday, New York.

Tuckett CM (1996). *Q and the History of Early Christianity.* Hendrickson, Peabody, MA.

Verus SE (1897). *Vergleichende Übersichtder vier Evangelien.* Leipzig.

Vigne GT (1840). *A personal narrative of a visit to Ghuzni, Kabul, and Afghanistan, and of a Residence at the Court of Dost Mohamed: with Notices of Runjit Sing, Khiva, and the Russian Expedition.* Whittaker & Co., London.

Vogtle A (1964). *Exegetische Erwägungen über das Wissen und Selbstbewusstsein Jesu.* Freiburg im Breisgau.

von Campenhausen H (1958). *Der Ablauf der Osterereignisse und das leere Grab.* Heidelberg.

von Harnack A (1964). *Das Wesen des Christentums.* Munich.

Waddell LA (1975). *Lhasa and its Mysteries.* Sanskaran Prakashak, New Delhi.

Walters E and Maccabee, B (1997). *UFOs Are Real: Here's the Proof.* Avon Books, New York.

Warechaner J (1927). *The Historical Life of Christ.* London.

References

Weigall A (1916). *Paganism in our Christianity.* Hutchinson, London.

Weiss J (1892-1900). *Die Predigt Jesu vom Reiche Gottes.* Göttingen.

Whitney D (1906). *The Resurrection of the Lord.* Hamilton and Adams, London.

Williams M (1889). *Buddhism.* Macmillan, New York.

Wilson HH (1841). *History of Kashmir*, in Asiatic Researches. Baptist Mission Press, Calcutta.

Wolff J (1845). *Narrative of a Mission to Bokhara, in the years 1843-1845, to ascertain the Fate of Colonel Stoddart and Captain Conolly*, Volume 1, 2nd Edition, (J.W. Parker, rev.). London.

Wood HG (1953-54). The Priority of Mark. *Expository Times* 65, pp.17-19.

Wright D (1943). *Studies in Islam and Christianity.* MM and L Trust, Woking, Surrey.

Wright W (1871). *The Apocryphal Acts of the Apostles.* Williams and Norgate, London.

Wuenshel E (1954). *Self Portrait of Christ.* New York.

Yasin M (1972). *Mysteries of Kashmir.* Kesar, Srinagar.

Younghusband F (1909). *Kashmir.* Black, London.

Zahn T (1909). *Introduction to the New Testament*, Volume 2. T. & T. Clark, Edinburgh.

Zahrnt H (1969). *Es Begann mit Jesus von Nazareth.* Gütersloh, Munich.

Zimmermann H (1973). *Jesus Christus: Geschichte und Verkündigung.* Stuttgart.

Zimmern H (1910). *Zum Streit um die "Christus Mythe."* Berlin.

Zockler O, Editor (1891). *Die Apokryphen des Alten Testaments.* Munich.

Books about the Society of Jesus, the Jesuits, their associates, the Roman Catholic Church, and related content

> "In Rome a tyrant and in Spain a thing
> That wears a mask and bears a poisonous sting
> In India a strangler, in France a knave,
> In Ireland a bigot and a slave;
> In our Republic a designing tool
> And traitor, warring with the public school,
> And whether in Greece, in Hindoostan or Spain,
> His record bears the progeny of Cain. . . ."
>
> —Eliza Pittsinger,
> ercerpt from poem The Jesuits
> in The Black Pope by OE Murray

[Author unknown] (1768). *The Jesuit Detected; or the Church of Rome Discovered in the Disguise of a Protestant, Under the Character of An Answer to All That is Material in the Rev. Mr. Hervey's Eleven Letters to the Rev. John Wesley.* J. Johnson, London.

References

[Author unknown] (1794). *A Collection of State Papers, Relative to the War Against France Now Carrying on by Great Britain and the Several Other European Powers.* J. Debrett, London.

[Author unknown] (1859). *The Constitutions of the Free-Masons.* Robert Macoy, New York.

Multiple authors (1839). *The Principles of the Jesuits: Developed in a collection of extracts from their own authors, to which are prefixed a brief account of the origin of the order and a sketch of its institute.* JG and F Rivington. London.

Multiple Authors (1902). *Concerning Jesuits.* Catholic Truth Society. London.

Achilli G Reverend (1851). *Dealings With the Inquisition; or, Papal Rome, Her Priests, and Her Jesuits. With Important Disclosures.* Harper and Brothers Publishers, New York.

Astle D (1975). *The Babylonian Woe: A Study of the Origin of Certain Banking Practices, and Their Effect on the Events of Ancient History, Written in the Light of the Present Day.* Published as a private edition, Toronto.

Balla I (1913). *The Romance of the Rothschilds.* Eveleigh Nash. London.

Barrow I (1852). *A Treatise of the Pope's Supremacy: To Which is Added A Discourse Concerning the Unity of the Church.* Johnstone and Hunter, Edinburgh.

Baxter R (1835). *Jesuit Juggling: Forty Popish Frauds Detected and Disclosed.* Craighead and Allen, New York.

Baxter R (1839). *A Key for Catholics, to Open the Juggling of the Jesuits, and to Satisfy All Who Are Truly Willing to Understand, Whether the Cause of the Roman or Reformed Churches Be of God; and to Leave the Reader Utterly Inexcusable That After This Will Be a Papist, to Which is Added Some Proposals for a (Hopeless) Peace.* Hamilton, Adams and Company, London.

Bellows HW (1871). *Church and State in America.* Philip and Solomons, Washington, DC.

Bert P (1880). *The Doctrine of the Jesuits.* BF Bradbury. Boston.

Berk MA (1842). *The History of the Jews from the Babylonian Captivity to the Present Time.* MA Berk, Boston.

Bolton HW (1890). *Patriotism.* Meyer and Brother, Chicago.

Brownlee WC Reverend (1857). *The Secret Instructions of the Jesuits.* American and Foreign Christian Union, New York.

Bungener LF (1855). *History of the Council of Trent.* Harper and Brothers, Publishers. New York.

Brady MJ (1893). *A Fraud Unmasked: The Career of Mrs. Margaret L. Shepherd: Ex-Romanist, Ex-Nun, Ex-Penitent and Bigamist.* Ontario.

Brzezinski Z (1983). *Power and Principle: Memoirs of the National Security Advisor, 1977-1981.* Farrar, Straus, Giroux, New York.

Brzezinski Z (1997). *The Grand Chessboard: American Primacy and Its Geostrategic Imperatives.* Basic Books, New York.

Brzezinski Z and Scowcroft B (2008). *America and the World: Conversations on the Future of American Foreign Policy.* Basic Books, New York.

References

Burke-Gaffney MW SJ (1944). *Kepler and the Jesuits*. The Bruce Publishing Company, Milwaukee.

Burnet G (1816). *The History of the Reformation of the Church of England, Volume I, Part II*. Clarendon Press, Oxford.

Butler SD (1935). *War is a Racket*. Round Table Press, New York.

Campbell WJ SJ (1921). *The Jesuits, 1534-1921: A History of the Society of Jesus from Its Foundation to the Present Time*. The Encyclopedia Press, New York.

Carlson JR (1943). *Under Cover: My Four Years in the Nazi Underworld of America: The Amazing Revelation of How Axis Agents and Our Enemies Within Are Now Plotting to Destroy the United States*. E.P. Dutton and Company, New York.

Cartwright WC MP (1876). *The Jesuits: Their Constitution and Teaching. An Historical Sketch*. John Murray, London.

Chiniquy C (1886). *Fifty Years in the Church of Rome*. Fleming H. Revell Co., New York.

Chiniquy C (1900). *Forty Years in the Church of Christ*. Fleming H. Revell Co., New York.

Clements J (1865). *History of the Society of Jesus From Its Foundations to the Present Time*, Volume II. John P. Walsh, Cincinnati.

Coape HC (1910). *In a Jesuit Net: A Story of France in the Time of Louis XIV*. The Religious Tract Society, London.

Cooke R Dr. (1985). *The Vatican Jesuit Global Conspiracy*. Manahath Press, Hollidaysburg, PA.

Coppens C SJ (1911). *Who Are the Jesuits?* B Herder, St. Louis.

Corti EC Count (1928). *The Rise of the House of Rothschild: 1770-1830*. Cosmopolitan Book Corporation, New York.

Corti EC Count (1928). *The Reign of the House of Rothschild: 1830-1871*. Cosmopolitan Book Corporation, New York.

Coudrette C (1761). *Mémoires pour servir à l'histoire générale des Jésuits, ou Extraits de l'histoire universelle de M. de Thou*. Octavo, Paris.

Courson BFMN (1879). *The Jesuits: Their Foundation and History, Volumes I and II*. Benziger Brothers, New York.

Coxe AC Bishop (1894). *The Jesuit Party in American Politics: Exposed and Expounded in Letters to the Ablegate*. American Citizen Company, Boston.

Creighton C (1996). *Operation James Bond: The Last Great Secret of the Second World War*. Simon and Schuster, London.

Crowley JJ Reverend (1912). *Romanism: A Menace to the Nation*. Jeremiah J. Crowley, Cincinnati.

Crozier AO (1912). *U.S. Money vs. Corporation Currency: "Aldrich Plan." Wall Street Confessions!* The Magnet Company, Cincinnati.

Cusack MF (1891). *What Rome Teaches*. The Baker and Taylor Company, New York.

Cusack MF (1896). *The Black Pope: A History of the Jesuits*. Marshall, Russell and Company, London.

References

Cusack MF (writing as "Vigilant") (1913). *Revolution and War, or Britain's Peril and Her Secret Foes*. Stanley Paul and Company, London.

Daniel TC (1911). *Daniel On Real Money*. The Monetary Educational Bureau, Washington, DC.

Daniel TC (1912). *High Cost of Living, Cause-Remedy*. The Monetary Educational Bureau, Washington, DC.

Daniel TC (1916). *The Betrayal of the People*. The Monetary Educational Bureau, Washington, DC.

Daniel TC (1917). *The Real Issue, Democracy Against Plutocracy*. The Monetary Educational Bureau, Washington, DC.

Daniel TC (1919). *No Plutocratic Peace But a Democratic Victory*. The Monetary Educational Bureau, Washington, DC.

Daniel TC (1924). *Real Money Versus False Money—Bank Credits*. The Monetary Educational Bureau, Washington, DC.

De Saint-Priest A Count (1845). *History of the Fall of the Jesuits in the 18th Century*. William Clowes and Sons, London.

Desanctis L with Betts M, Translator (1905). *Popery, Puseyism, Jesuitism*. [Original title: *Roma Papale*.] D Catt, London.

Dewey ER and Dakin EF (1947). *Cycles: The Science of Prediction*. Henry Holt and Company, New York.

Dowling J Reverend (1845). *The History of Romanism: From the Earliest Corruptions of Christianity to the Present Time*. Edward Walker, London.

Duff A (1852). *The Jesuits: Their Origin and Order, Morality and Practices, Suppression and Restoration.* Johnstone and Hunter, Edinburgh.

Du Jarric P SJ (1926). *Akbar and the Jesuits: An Account of the Jesuit Missions to the Court of Akbar.* Harper and Brothers, New York.

Dye JS (1864). *The Adder's Den: or the Secrets of the Great Conspiracy to Overthrow the Liberty of America.* John Smith Dye. New York.

Eckel LSJ Mrs. (1874). *Maria Monk's Daughter: An Autobiography.* The United States Publishing Company, New York.

Eksteins M (1975). *Limits of Reason: The German Democratic Press and the Collapse of Weimar Democracy.* Oxford University Press, London.

Elon A (1996). *Founder: A Portrait of the First Rothschild and His Time.* Viking, New York.

Evans TR (1888). *The Council of Trent: A Study of Romish Tactics.* The Religious Tract Society, London.

Farrell JP (2010). *Babylon's Banksters: The Alchemy of Deep Physics, High Finance and Ancient Religion.* Feral House, Port Townsend, WA.

Fergusson A (1975). *When Money Dies: The Nightmare of the Weimar Collapse.* William Kimber, Ltd. London.

Feval P (1880). *Jesuits!* (Sadlier AL, Translator) John Murphy and Company, Baltimore.

References

Fulton JD (1856). *The Outlook of Freedom: or The Roman Catholic Element in American History*. Moore, Wilstach, Keys and Overend, Cincinnati.

Fulton JD (1888). *Washington in the Lap of Rome*. W. Kellaway, Boston.

Fulton JD (1889). *The Fight With Rome*. Pratt Brothers, Marlboro, MA.

Fulton JD (1889). *Rome in America*. The Pauline Propaganda, Boston.

Gerard J SJ (1897). *What Was the Gunpowder Plot? The Original Story Tested by Original Evidence*. Osgood, McIlvaine and Company, London.

Goode, W Reverend (1868). *Rome's Tactics, or, a Lesson from England from the Past: Showing That the Great Object of Popery Since the Reformation Has Been to Subvert and Ruin Protestant Churches and Protestant States by Dissensions and Troubles Caused by Disguised Popish Agents; With a Brief Notice of Rome's Allies in the Church of England*. The Christian Book Society, London.

Griesinger T (1885). *The Jesuits: A Complete History of Their Open and Secret Proceedings from the Foundation of the Order to the Present Time, Volumes I and II* (Scott AJ, Translator). WH Allen, London.

Grinfield EW (1853). *The Jesuits: An Historical Sketch*. Seeleys, London.

Haeckel E (1910). *The Answer of Ernst Haeckel to the Falsehoods of the Jesuits*. The Truth Seeker Company, New York.

Hoensbroech PV Count von (1911). *Fourteen Years A Jesuit: A Record of Personal Experience and a Criticism*, Volumes I and II. Cassell and Company, Ltd., London.

Hughes T (1910). *History of the Society of Jesus in North America, Colonial and Federal.* The Burrows Brothers Company, Cleveland.

Iden VG (1914). T*he Federal Reserve Act of 1913: History and Digest.* The National Bank News, Philadelphia.

Ives JM (1936). *The Ark and the Dove: The Beginning of Civil and Religious Liberties in America.* Longmans, Green and Company, New York.

Jefferson T (1903). *The Writings of Thomas Jefferson, 20 volumes, Volume 10.* Published by the order of the Joint Committee of Congress, issued under the auspices of the Thomas Jefferson Memorial Association. Andrew A. Lipscomb, Editor-in-Chief, and Albert Ellery Bergh, Managing Editor. Washington, DC.

Joly M (1864). *Dialogue in Hell Between Machiavelli and Montesquieu.* A. Mertens and Son, Brussels.

Kauffman LS (1922). *Romanism as a World Power.* The American Publishing Company, Philadelphia.

Kidder DP (1851). *The Jesuits: A Historical Sketch.* Lane and Scott, for the Sunday-School Union of the Methodist Episcopal, New York.

Kinser A (1966). *The Works of Jacques-Auguste de Thou.* Martinus Nijhoff, The Hague.

References

Lathbury T Reverend (1838). *The State of Popery and Jesuitism in England; from the Reformation to the Period of the Roman Catholic Relief Bill in 1829: and the Charge of Novelty, Heresy, and Schism Against the Church of Rome Substantiated.* John Leslie, London.

Laurens JW (1855). *The Crisis or, The Enemies of America Unmasked.* GD Miller, Philadelphia.

Laynez D (1824). *Secreta Monita Societis Jesu: The Secret Instructions of the Jesuits. With An Appendix.* LB Seeley and Sons, London.

Lease M (12 August 1896), Cooper Union Hall, New York, NY. www.spartacus.schoolnet.co.uk/USApopulistP.htm. Accessed 12 April 2010, 08 December 2011 [as of 30 April 2015, no longer available; please see www.gilderlehrman.org/history-by-era/populism-and-agrarian-discontent/essays/mary-elizabeth-lease-populist-reformer for biographic sketch; Accessed 30 April 2015.].

Lehmann LH (1944). *Behind the Dictators: A Factual Analysis of the Relationship of Nazi-Fascism and Roman Catholicism. Second enlarged edition.* Agora Publishing Company, New York.

Leone AM (1848). *The Jesuit Conspiracy: The Secret Plan of the Order.* Chapman and Hall, London.

Lester CE (1845). *The Jesuits.* Gates and Stedman, New York.

Lindbergh, CA (1913). *Banking and Currency and the Money Trust.* National Capital Press, Inc., Washington, DC.

Livingston J (1986). *Origins of the Federal Reserve System: Money, Class and Corporate Capitalism, 1890–1913.* Cornell University Press, Ithaca.

Lord J (1886). *Beacon Lights of History*. James Clarke and Company, New York.

Luke JT (1851). *The Female Jesuit; or, The Spy in the Family*. MW Dodd, New York.

Luke S Mrs. (1852). *The Sequel to The Female Jesuit; containing her previous history and recent discovery*. Partridge and Oakey, London.

Macaulay TB (1849). *The History of England From the Ascension of James the Second*. Bernard Tauchnitz, Leipzig.

Maclagan E Sir (1932). *The Jesuits and the Great Mogul*. Burns Oates and Washbourne, Ltd., Publishers to the Holy See, London.

Macpherson HC (1914). *The Jesuits in History*. Macniven and Wallace, Edinburgh.

Magevney E SJ (1899). *The Jesuits as Educators*. The Cathedral Library Association, New York.

Makow H (2009). *Illuminati: The Cult That Hijacked the World*. Silas Green. Winnipeg, Canada.

Mayer M (1955). *They Thought They Were Free: The Germans 1933-45*. The University of Chicago Press, Chicago.

Maynard ML (1855). *The Studies and Teaching of the Society of Jesus at the Time of Its Suppression, 1750-1773*. John Murphy and Company, Baltimore.

McCabe J (1913). *A Candid History of the Jesuits*. GP Putnam and Sons, New York.

References

McCabe J (1916). *The Tyranny of Shams*. Dodd, Mead and Company, New York.

McCabe J (1939). *The Papacy in Politics Today*, 2nd Edition. Watts and Company, London.

McCarthy MJF (1904). *Rome in Ireland*. Hodder and Stoughton, London.

McCarty B (1922). *The Suppressed Truth About the Assassination of Abraham Lincoln*. Self-published by Burke McCarty, Washington, DC.

Mendham J Reverend (1834). *Memoirs of the Council of Trent; Principally Derived From Manuscript and Unpublished Records, Namely, Histories, Diaries, letters, and Other Documents of the Leading Actors in That Assembly*. James Duncan, London.

Michelet J (1845). *Priests, Women and Families*. Longman, Brown, Green and Longmans, London.

Michelet J and Quinet E, with Lester CE, Translator (1845). *The Jesuits*. Gates and Stedman, New York.

Mitchell PA (n.d.). *31 Questions and Answers About the Internal Revenue Service*, rev. 3.7, Seattle, WA. www.supremelaw.org/sls/31answers.htm. Accessed and vetted 26 November 2010, 08 December 2011, 30 April 2015.

Monk M and Slocum JJ Reverend, Revised by (1851). *Awful Disclosures by Maria Monk of the Hotel Dieu Nunnery of Montreal; with An Appendix; and a Supplement Giving More Particulars of the Nunnery and Grounds, 3rd Edition*. James S. Hodson, London.

Monk M. (1855). *Awful Disclosures by Maria Monk of the Hotel Dieu Nunnery of Montreal. Containing Also, Many Incidents Never Before Published.* De Witt and Davenport Publishers, New York.

Montagu R Lord (1877). *Foreign Policy: England and the Eastern Question.* Chapman and Hall, London.

Morris R (1883). *Robert Morgan; or, Political Anti-Masonry, It's Rise, Growth and Decadence.* Robert Macoy, Masonic Publisher, New York.

Morse SFB (1835). *Foreign Conspiracy Against the Liberties of the United States.* Leavitt, Lord and Company, New York.

Morse SFB (1855). *Foreign Conspiracy Against the Liberties of the United States.* American and Foreign Christian Union, New York.

Mullins E (1991). *Secrets of the Federal Reserve: The London Connection.* Bridger House Publishers, Inc., Carson City.

Murray OE PhD Reverend (1892). *The Black Pope or the Jesuits' Conspiracy Against American Institutions*, 2nd Edition. The Patriot Company, Chicago.

Newdegate CN (1880). *A Glimpse of the Great Secret Society.* Hatchards, Piccadilly, London.

Nicolini GB (1854). *History of the Jesuits: Their Origin, Progress, Doctrines, and Designs.* Henry Bohn, London.

Osburn W (1846). *Hidden Works of Darkness, or, The Doings of the Jesuits.* WH Dalton, published for the Protestant Association, London.

References

O'Sullivan M Reverend and M'Ghee R Reverend (1840). *Romanism As It Rules In Ireland*. RB Seeley and William Burnside, London.

Overbury RW (1846). *The Jesuits*. Houlston and Stoneman, London.

Owen RL (1919). *Where Is God in the European War?* The Century Company, New York.

Owen RL (1919). *The Federal Reserve Act: Its Origins and Principles*. Published by the Author.

Paris E (1975). *The Secret History of the Jesuits*. Chick Publications, Chino.

Parkman F (1867). *France and England in North America: A Series of Historical Narratives, Part Second*. Little, Brown, and Company, Boston.

Parkman F (1902). *The Jesuits in North America in the Seventeenth Century, Part One*. Little, Brown, and Company, Boston.

Pascal B (1892). *Provincial Letters: Moral Teachings of the Jesuit Fathers Opposed to the Church of Rome and Latin Vulgate*. William Briggs, Montreal.

Perverter (1851). *The Perverter in High Life: A True Narrative of Jesuit Duplicity*. Partridge and Oakey, London.

Pitrat JC (1855). *Americans Warned of Jesuitism, or The Jesuits Unveiled, 3rd Edition*. Edward W. Hinks and Company, Boston.

Pollard AF (1892). *The Jesuits in Poland*. Methuen and Company. London.

Pollen JH SJ (1896). *The Life and Letters of Father John Morris of the Society of Jesus*. Burnes and Oates, Ltd., London.

Pollen JH SJ (1896). *The Counter-Reformation in Scotland, with Special Reference to the Revival of 1585 to 1595*. Sands and Company, London.

Pollen JH SJ (1901). *Papal Negotiations with Mary Queen of Scots During Her Reign in Scotland, 1561-1567*. University Press Edinburgh for the Scottish History Society, Edinburgh.

Pollen JH SJ (1920). *The English Catholics in the Reign of Queen Elizabeth: A Study of Their Politics, Civil Life and Government*. Longmans, Green and Company, London.

Pollen JH SJ (1922). *Saint Ignatius of Loyola: Imitator of Christ, 1494 to 1555*. PJ Kennedy and Sons, New York.

Pollen JH SJ (1922). *Mary Queen of Scots and The Babington Plot*. University Press Edinburgh for the Scottish History Society, Edinburgh.

Potts WS Reverend (1845). Dangers of Jesuit Instruction: A Sermon Preached at the Second Presbyterian Church in St. Louis. In *Brownson's Quarterly Review*, Volume III. Benjamin H. Greene, Boston.

Protestant Association (1834). *The Jesuits Exposed, 2nd Edition*, Volume 15. The Protestant Association, London.

Quigley C (1966). *Tragedy and Hope: A History of the World in Our Time*. The Macmillan Company, New York.

References

Reed H Reverend (1874). *The Footprints of Satan: or, The Devil in History*. EB Treat, New York.

Renich KL (1914). *The Life and Methods of Matteo Ricci, Jesuits Missionary to China, 1582-1610*. Master of Arts in History Thesis, The Graduate School, University of Illinois.

Robison J (1798). *Proofs of a Conspiracy Against All the Religions and Governments of Europe, Carried on in the Secret Meetings of Free Masons, Iluminati, and Reading Societies. Collected from Good Authorities*. T Dobson, Philadelphia.

Roper IH (1848). *The Jesuits*, 2nd Edition. Houlston and Stoneman, London.

Rule WH Reverend (1853). *Celebrated Jesuits*, Volume I. John Mason, London.

Rule WH Reverend (1853). *Celebrated Jesuits, Volume II*. John Mason, London.

Ruskin J (1891). *Fors Clavigera: Letters to the Workmen and Labourers of Great Britain*, Volume the Fourth. Reuwee, Wattley and Walsh, Philadelphia.

Saussy TF (1999). *Rulers of Evil: Useful Knowledge About Governing Bodies*. Ospray Bookmakers, Nevada.

Schweizer P (2012). Contributions of Christopher Clavius SJ to Mathematics. *Gerbertus*, 2.

Schwickerath R SJ (1903). *Jesuit Education: Its History and Principles*. B. Herder, St. Louis.

Seager C (1847). *The Spiritual Exercises of St. Ignatius of Loyola* (Translator). Charles Dolman, London.

Sherman EA 32° Scottish Mason (1883). *The Engineer Corps of Hell, or, Rome's Sappers and Miners*. Edwin Allen Sherman, San Francisco.

Skousen WC (1970). *The Naked Capitalist: A Review and Commentary on Dr. Carroll Quigley's Book: Tragedy and Hope: A History of the World in Our Time*. Privately published by W. Cleon Skousen, Salt Lake City.

Spencer J Editor (1670). *The Jesuits Morals: by a Doctor of the Colledge of School of Paris who hath faithfully extracted them out of the Jesuits own books, which are printed by the permission and approbation of the superiours of their society*. John Starkey, London.

Steinmetz A (1846). *The Novitiate, or, A Year Among the English Jesuits*. Smith, Elder and Company, London.

Steinmetz A (1848). *History of the Jesuits: From the Foundation of Their Society to its Suppression by Pope Clement XIV.; Their Missions Throughout the World; Their Educational System and Literature; With Their Revival and Present State, Part I*. Richard Bentley, London.

Steinmetz A (1848). *History of the Jesuits: From the Foundation of Their Society to its Suppression by Pope Clement XIV.; Their Missions Throughout the World; Their Educational System and Literature; With Their Revival and Present State, Part II*. Richard Bentley, London.

Steinmetz A (1848). *History of the Jesuits: From the Foundation of Their Society to its Suppression by Pope Clement XIV.; Their Missions Throughout the World; Their Educational System and Literature; With Their Revival and Present State, Part III*. Richard Bentley, London.

References

Syndey P (1904). *The History of the Gunpowder Plot: The Conspiracy and Its Agents*. The Religious Tract Society, London.

Taunton EL (1901). *The History of the Jesuits in England, 1580-1773*. Lippincott, Philadelphia.

Tayler WE (1851). *Popery: Its Character and Its Crimes*. Partridge and Oakley, London.

Thompson F (1913). *Saint Ignatius Loyola*. Burns and Oats, London.

Thompson RW (1894). *Footprints of the Jesuits*. Cranston and Curts, New York.

Thwaites RG Editor (1897). *The Jesuit Relations and Allied Documents: Travels and Explorations of the Jesuit Missionaries in New France, 1610-1791*. The Burrows Brothers Company, Cleveland.

Udias A and Stauder W (2002). The Jesuit Contribution to Seismology. *International Handbook of Earthquake and Engineering Seismology*, Volume 81A, pp. 19-27.

United Nations Treaty Series (2002). *Rome Statute of the International Criminal Court*. International Criminal Court, The Hague.

Usher J (1835). Archbishop Usher's Answer to a Jesuit, With Other Tracts on Popery. J and J.J. Deighton, Cambridge.

Villers C (1833). *An Essay on the Spirit and Influence of the Reformation* (Miller S, Translator). Key and Biddle, Philadelphia.

Wadswort J (1679). *The Memoirs of James Wadswort, a Jesuit That Recanted: Discovering a Dreadful Prophesy of Impiety, and Blasphemous Doctrines (or Gospel) of the Jesuits, With Their Antithetical Lives and Conversations.* Henry Brome, London.

Walsh W (1903). *The Jesuits in Great Britain: An Historical Inquiry into their Political Influence.* George Routledge. London.

Watson TE (1912). *The Life and Times of Andrew Jackson.* The Jeffeersonian Publishing Company, Thomson, GA.

Watson TE (1928). *Roman Catholics in America Falsifying History and Poisoning the Minds of Protestant School Children.* Tom Watson Book Company, Thomson, GA.

Watson TE (1928). *Rome's Law Or Ours? Which?* Tom Watson Book Company, Thomson, GA.

Watson TE (1928). *The 4th Degree Oath of the Knights of Columbus: An Un-American Secret Society Bound to the Italian Pope, By Pledges of Treason and Murder.* Tom Watson Book Company, Thomson, GA.

Watson TE (1927). *Maria Monk and Her Revelations of Convent Crimes, 2nd Edition.* Tom Watson Book Company, Thomson, GA.

White JG Reverend (1890). *Footprints of Satan: Pope and Jesuits Against Bible and Public Schools.* JG White, Boston.

Whitehead M (2013). *English Jesuit Education: Expulsion, Suppression, Survival and Restoration, 1762-1803.* Ashgate Publishing, Ltd., Surrey.

Wylie JA Reverend (1852). *The Papacy: Its History, Dogma, Genius and Prospects.* Hamilton, Adams and Company, London.

References

Wylie JA Reverend (1855). *Pilgrimage from Alps to the Tiber.* Hamilton, Adams and Company, London.

Wylie JA (1902). *The History of Protestantism*, Volumes I, II and III. Cassell, Petter and Galpin, London.

Wylie JA Reverend (1886). *History of the Scottish Nation*, Volume I. Hamilton, Adams and Company, London.

Wylie JA Reverend (1887). *History of the Scottish Nation*, Volume II. Hamilton, Adams and Company, London.

Wylie JA Reverend (1890). *History of the Scottish Nation*, Volume III. Hamilton, Adams and Company, London.

Wylie JA Reverend (1860). *Ter-Centenary of the Scottish Reformation.* John Maclaren, Edinburgh.

Wylie JA Reverend (1878). *The Papal Hierarchy: An Exposure of the Tactics of Rome for the Overthrow of the Liberty and Christianity of Great Britain.* Hamilton, Adams and Company, London.

Wylie JA Reverend (1866). *The Awakening of Italy, and the Crisis of Rome.* The Religious Tract Society, London.

Wylie JA (1870). *Daybreak in Spain: Sketches of Spain and Its New Reformation.* Cassell, Petter and Galpin, London.

Wylie JA Reverend (1867). *The Papacy.* Hamilton, Adams and Company, London.

Wylie JA Reverend (1865). *Rome on Civil Liberty.* Hamilton, Adams and Company, London.

Wylie JA (1881). *The Jesuits: Their Moral Maxims, and Plots Against Kings, Nations, and Churches. With Dissertation on Ireland.* Hamilton, Adams, and Company, London.

Wylie JA Reverend (1899). *The History of Protestantism.* Cassell and Company, Limited, London.

Purchase Our Books

Our books can be purchased on
Amazon stores worldwide
AdagioPress.com
WilliamDeanAGarner.com
RioRamirez.com
SeanMaclarenBooks.com
VADisabilityClaimBook.com
BarnesandNoble.com and
Apple iTunes Bookstore.

Please enjoy browsing our selection. . . .

VA Disability Claim, 2nd Ed. How to Prepare, File and Maintain a VA Disability Claim and Appeal

The bestselling field manual on how to prepare, file and maintain and VA disability claim and appeal is what Lawyers and Settlements calls "the best-ever DIY book on filing a veteran's disability claim."

And it just got better.

The all-new 2nd edition sports and fresh design and layout, and has been thoroughly updated with the latest intel, plus has been gutted of all information about VA malpractice and malfeasance, accurate information that upset a lot of veterans and their families.

This 2nd edition shows you how to:
—Appreciate and understand the VA disability claims and appeals process
—Prepare all your necessary materials and paperwork before you file your claim or appeal
—File your VA disability claim and appeal
—Maintain your claim or appeal from beginning to end
—Understand how veterans service organizations really work
—Stay sane throughout the entire claims and appeals process
Paperback available from Amazon.com and other retail outlets
eBook available from AdagioPress.com

Purchase Our Books

The Suppressed Truth About the Assassination of Abraham Lincoln

Ex-Catholic Burke McCarty spent years researching the details surrounding the murder of President Abraham Lincoln, who was one of the few American politicians who openly acknowledged that the Jesuits were a menace to our society, but he felt powerless to do anything about the threat.

This hidden gem should be read by every person who calls himself or herself an American, as it uncovers an ongoing sinister plot to overthrow the liberties of our beloved nation and her people.

You owe it to yourself to read the well-carved thoughts of this brave woman who risked her own life to present the facts that most others continue to ignore, even 150 years after the murder of President Lincoln.

Paperback available from Amazon.com and other retail outlets
eBook available from AdagioPress.com

THE PRINCE

Machiavelli's *The Prince* has become a classic over the centuries since it first appeared around 1510, not because of its elegance or style but because of its subversive content about the true nature of power. Mainstream historians and academics have labelled it a "political treatise," but this is only a small part of the picture.

The Prince isn't just for princes who thirst for, or are forcibly thrown into, advancement.

It is a raw and bloody field manual for upper- and mid-level managers on predatorial ethics and power: what it is, how to obtain it, and what to do with it once you have found, stumbled across, or been granted it.

Paperback available from Amazon.com and other retail outlets
eBook available from AdagioPress.com

***ROMANIC DEPRESSION
How the Deadlight of the
Black Pope and the Jesuit
Militia Have Distorted the
History of The United States
of America***

Sean Mclaren has carefully researched and written the two sequels to *Who Really Owns Your Gold*, which was an introductory historical perspective about the Jesuits and their malevolent actions and behaviors over the past 100-plus years in America. In this ground-breaking volume, he analyzes and examines 40 sectors of American society, and demonstrate how the Jesuits have designed and built, and manipulated and corrupted each one, then marketed and advertised something decidedly contrary.

The book's Reference section contains more than 200 books about the Jesuits. If you take the time to read even a few of them, your heart, mind and soul will expand immensely, and you will begin to understand what others have known for centuries: this brood of snakes and vipers has done, and continues to do, great harm to humanity. . . .

Paperback available from Amazon.com and other retail outlets

eBook available from AdagioPress.com

ARCANUM
A critical analysis of the original 36 sermons of Jmmanuel, the man known to the world as Jesus Christ

ARCANUM by Sean Maclaren is one of two sequels to *Who Really Owns Your Gold*, which was an introductory historical perspective about the Jesuits and their malevolent actions and behaviors over the past 100-plus years in America.

The 410-page sequel is a highly detailed and provocative two-part essay:

Part One is an unsparing, meticulous and diligent analysis and evaluation of each of the original 36 sermons of Jmmanuel Sananda, the half-extraterrestrial/half-human known to the world as Jesus Christ.

Part Two is an actual full English translation and new edit (for clarity and readability) of the 36 extant sermons of Jmmanuel Sananda, the man known to the world as Jesus Christ.

Paperback available from Amazon.com and other retail outlets
eBook available from AdagioPress.com

Purchase Our Books

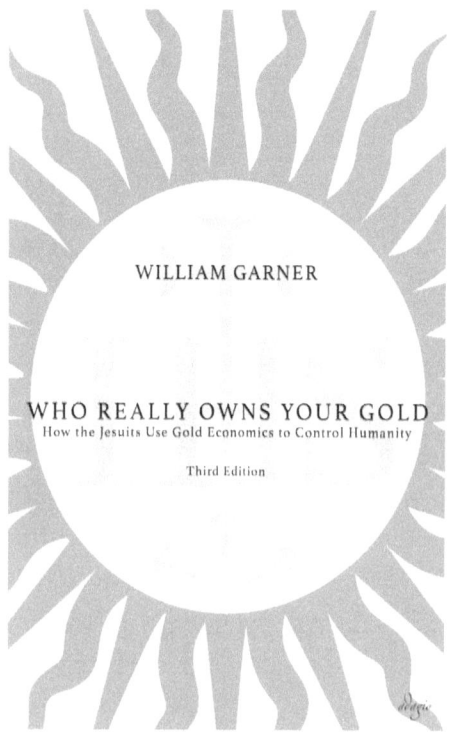

***Who Really Owns Your Gold How The Jesuits Use Gold Economics To Control Humanity*, Third Edition**

The power that controls your gold, your assets and your life is a dynastic group of men in Rome, and it's not the Vatican. They control every government on the planet and, using celestiophysics, manipulate to their advantage all actions and behaviors in law, politics, economics and finance, business, law enforcement, military and defense affairs, science and high-tech, entertainment, medicine and healthcare, education, etc.

New York Times bestselling ghostwriter and editor William Dean A. Garner takes you on a journey into a labyrinth where up is down, black is white, yes is no ... and nothing is what it seems.

This revelation is for everyone, not just those who "own" gold or precious metals.

Paperback available from Amazon.com and other retail outlets
eBook available from AdagioPress.com

Sun Tzu *The Art of War*
Ancient Wisdom . . . Modern Twist

New York Times bestselling author Dalton Fury has this to say about William Dean A. Garner's updated version of *The Art of War*: "Dean Garner's version of *The Art of War* confirms for us that for the past 2,000 years the fundamental principles of special operations in battle have not only remained true, but they apply equally to today's boardrooms and bedrooms. When on the hunt or holding ground, success can only be had by the precise application of disguise, deception and diversion, and a genuine appreciation for angles, inches, and seconds. Ranger Garner masterfully shows us how."

Paperback available from Amazon.com and other retail outlets
eBook available from AdagioPress.com

Purchase Our Books

VA Disability Claim A Practical, Step-By-Step Field Manual for Active-Duty Servicemembers and Veterans on How to Prepare, File, Maintain, Win and Appeal a Service-Connected VA Disability Claim Without Going Insane

LawyersAndSettlements.com calls *VA Disability Claim* "The best ever DIY book on filing a veteran's disability claim."

It is the first and only comprehensive book that details the necessary steps to take when preparing, filing, maintaining, winning and appealing a VA disability claim. The books contains prominently numbered steps, much like the Betty Crocker method of cake baking, to file a claim, and also detailed information about the entire appeals process. The Resources chapter contains 100 helpful books, reports, manuals, articles and blogs, plus useful contacts to aid service members and veterans in their own research. The companion website, VADisabilityClaimBook.com, also lists all these resources in digital format for easy retrieval and use. Paperback available from Amazon.com.

Paperback available from Amazon.com and other retail outlets
eBook available from VADisabilityClaimBook.com

How To Write Your First Book
A Simple & Practical Method
For Anyone Who Can Tell a Story

This gem is much more than just a book about writing. It reveals metaphysically how our subconscious functions during the creative process to produce the finished product, and how we grow spiritually as this process evolves before us to create our first book.

Garner employs a simple, step-by-step method we have used all our lives, and includes easy-to-follow examples and exercises, plus anecdotes from his work as a ghostwriter/editor on some very sexy novels and books.

Paperback available from Amazon.com and other retail outlets
eBook available from AdagioPress.com

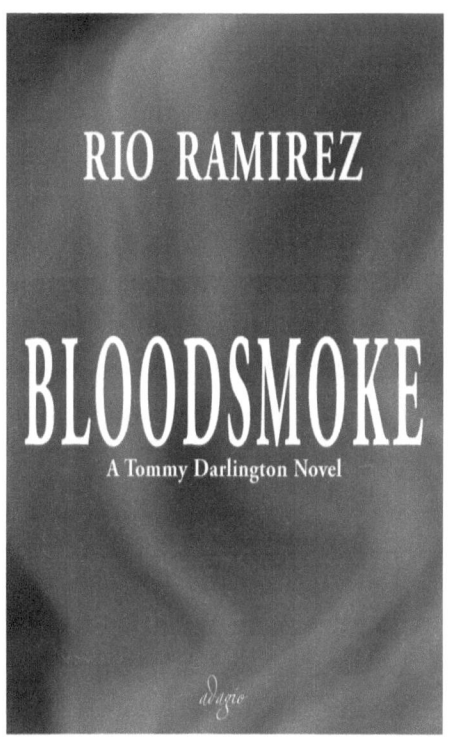

BLOODSMOKE

Book One in a new series of action-adventure thrillers by Rio Ramirez, featuring Tommy Darlington, a small-town hitman who reluctantly climbs the ladder of success in a shady global industry run by well-heeled thugs with infinite resources, and backed by a secret cabal of dynastic men thousands of miles from the action. Along the way, Darlington discovers the nature and identities of the powerful men behind the black curtain, and begins questioning their methods and motives, leaving a trail of warm bodies in his wake. The more this sinister cabal tries to control Darlington, the more they lose their grip on him as he gradually reveals and unravels their carefully laid plans.

Paperback available from Amazon.com and other retail outlets
eBook available from AdagioPress.com

DEADLIGHT

Book Two of the Tommy Darlington series of action-adventure thrillers by Rio Ramirez. Reeling from the loss of his beloved Rachel, Tommy needs something to kill and Tyreese the Pimp provides just the target. But the brutal pimp isn't enough to satisfy Tommy's bloodlust.

A distant friend sucks Tommy deep into a hurricane of illegal machinations that test his physical, moral and emotional resolve, and his old Ranger buddy Caleb Silverthorn is there to assist, advise and pick up the broken pieces.

Paperback available from Amazon.com and other retail outlets

www.ingramcontent.com/pod-product-compliance
Lightning Source LLC
Chambersburg PA
CBHW020606300426
44113CB00007B/524